Nicolai Hartmann's
New Ontology

Nicolai Hartmann's New Ontology

W. H. Werkmeister

The Florida State University Press
Tallahassee

Library of Congress Cataloging-in-Publication Data

Werkmeister, W. H. (William Henry), b. 1901
  Nicolai Hartmann's new ontology / W. H. Werkmeister.
    p.   cm.
  Includes bibliographical references and index.
  ISBN 0-8130-1008-X
  1. Hartmann, Nicolai, 1882–1950—Contributions in metaphysics.
  2. Metaphysics—History—20th century.   I. Title.
  B3279.H24W47   1990
  111'.092—dc20   90-39459
                                                                  CIP

Florida State University Press
© 1990 by the Board of Regents of the State of Florida
∞ Printed in the U.S.A. on acid-free paper.

The Florida State University Press is a member of University Presses of Florida,
the scholarly publishing agency of the State University System of Florida. Books
are selected for publication by faculty editorial committees at each of Florida's
nine public universities: Florida A&M University (Tallahassee), Florida Atlantic
University (Boca Raton), Florida International University (Miami), Florida State
University (Tallahassee), University of Central Florida (Orlando), University of
Florida (Gainesville), University of North Florida (Jacksonville), University of
South Florida (Tampa), University of West Florida (Pensacola).

Orders for books published by all member presses should be addressed to University Presses of Florida, 15 NW 15th Street, Gainesville, Florida 32611.

Address editorial inquiries to the Florida State University Press, 303 Dodd Hall,
Florida State University, Tallahassee, Florida 32603.

Everyone finds in his time a situation of knowl-edge and of asking questions into which he grows and in response to which he begins his own thinking. He takes over the great problems as they have emerged in the historical situation.

Nicolai Hartmann

"Selbstdarstellung" in *Philosophen-Lexikon*

Contents

Introduction

TO UNDERSTAND WHAT IS MEANT by Nicolai Hartmann's *new ontology* it is necessary to review briefly what traditional ontology has been.

The idea of an ontology goes back, of course, to antiquity. Parmenides, for example, boldly declared that "there is Being and nothing else besides Being," that it is "one, unchanging, eternal."[1] In the *Phaedo* Plato argued that coming to know "things in themselves" is but "recollection"—an argument that is basic to Book VII of the *Republic*. Aristotle defined metaphysics as "a science which investigates Being as Being and the attributes which belong to it in virtue of its own nature."[2]

The theme recurs in the worldview of Anselm of Canterbury as an argument for the existence of God and in the writings of Thomas Aquinas,[3] the most influential representative of Scholasticism.

Ontology as a doctrine of Being had thus been long in existence

1. Parmenides, *On Nature*. See Eduard Zeller, *Die Philosophie der Griechen*, 6th ed. (Hildesheim, 1963), vol. 1, chap. 1.

2. W. D. Ross, *Aristotle Selections* (New York: Scribner, 1927), 53.

3. Thomas Aquinas, *De Potentia Dei*, III, 5c. See also his *Summa Theologiae*, I, the argument of the "Five Ways." See also Josef Schmitz, *Dispute über das Teleologische Denken: Eine Gegenüberstellung von Nicolai Hartmann, Aristotles und Thomas von Aquin* (Mainz, 1960).

when it was canonized by Christian Wolff (1679–1754) and Alexander Gottlieb Baumgarten (1714–1762). In his *Philosophia Prima Sive Ontologia* (1729) Wolff saw all universals, condensed as *essentia,* as the form-giving substances that determine the inner nature of things and are comprehensible in concepts. He argued in effect that, alongside the world of things (including man), there exists a realm of essences that, timeless and nonmaterial—a realm of perfection—is the realm of a higher Being, and with this thesis ontology became deductive.

Kant's *Critique of Pure Reason* put an end to all of this. Kant argued that any reference to "Being" is but "the positing of a thing, or of certain determinations, as existing in themselves"; he argued that, "logically, [Being] is merely the copula of a judgment" (A598).

But the tradition lived on.

As recently as 1912, P. Coffey, reflecting in general the orientation of the philosophy of Louvain, developed ontology's basic theme as "the study of the first principles of Being in themselves."[4] It pertains to "the being and becoming of reality, its possibility and its actuality" (*Ontology,* 23). "The notion of Being, spontaneously revealed by the human mind, is found on reflection to be the simplest of all notions" and "the *first* of all notions in the logical order, i.e., in the process of rational thought" (32). It is so simple that, "strictly speaking, it cannot be defined." It is not absolute "nothingness" but is rather "whatever can be an object of thought" (35). That is, it has no specific characteristics.

Kant's *Critique of Pure Reason* presumably put an end to all of this. Kant had regarded his first *Critique* as "a treatise on the method of cognition, not as a system of metaphysics" (Bxxii). Hegel repudiated this Kantian position. The Hegelian dialectic, as developed in the *Science of Logic,*[5] entails a position in suspense beyond idealism and realism. It is a complete abandonment to the object—a sensitive and progressive conforming to it, which in its detailed analysis of categories is actually a radical turning of Kantian idealism into an ontology.

Since 1927 Heidegger's *Sein und Zeit* has been the center of much philosophical discussion. As "*Erste Hälfte,*" however, the book was

---

4. P. Coffey, *Ontology or the Theory of Being* (London: Longmans, Green and Co., 1912), 21.

5. *Science of Logic,* trans. W. H. Johnston and L. G. Struthers, 2 vols. (New York, 1929).

intended as an introduction to an ontology, and I find his *Die Grund-probleme der Phänomenologie*[6]—which includes the missing *Dritte Abschnitt* of *Sein und Zeit*—to be the more important work. Its 466 pages are devoted to wide-ranging problems of ontology as reflected in the works of numerous thinkers of the past, and as entailed by the problems of "temporality" to which *Sein und Zeit* merely refers in its concluding questions. In the *Grundprobleme* Heidegger's basic theme is that "Being is the genuine and sole theme of philosophy" (15). "Being," he states, "is always the Being of something that *is*—of *Seiendes*," and therefore is "approachable only by starting with something that *is*—with *Seienden*." This means that, in phenomenological reduction, we "must turn from any determinate comprehension of what-is [*von Seiendem*] to the comprehension of the being of that *Seiende*" (29). Although Heidegger thus turns away from Husserl's phenomenological reductionism, the method of ontological investigation which he means to employ is still "a phenomenological construction" and is not concerned with the manifold forms of the *Seienden* but with the abstract understanding of Being (30).

Kant had argued that Being is not a real predicate and that "perception . . . is the sole character of reality" (*Critique of Pure Reason*, B273). Heidegger admits that "in its negative meaning" this thesis cannot be challenged; but in a positive sense it is unclear and questionable, for it neglects the distinction between perception and what is being perceived. "Nothing less is here at issue than *the mode of Being of perception in general, i.e.,* its ontological essence" (*Gesamtausgabe*, 24:77).

The subject which experiences perceptions experiences itself as *Dasein*[7]—as "being there"; and as *Dasein* it "exists in the mode of

6. Martin Heidegger, *Gesamtausgabe*, vol. 24, ed. Friedrich Wilhelm von Herrmann (Frankfurt: Vittorio Klostermann, 1975).

7. The term *Dasein* was first used by Hegel. In his *Wissenschaft der Logik*, vol. 1, *Werke* III, 2d ed. (Berlin: Duncker und Humblot, 1841), he wrote, "*Dasein* ist bestimmtes Sein; seine Bestimmtheit ist *seiende* Bestimmtheit. . . . Es hat die Form von einem Unmittelbaren" (106). And "Das *Dasein* erscheint daher als ein erstes, von dem ausgegangen werde."—In the Johnston/Struthers translation titled *Science of Logic*, vol. 1 (New York: Macmillan, 1929), chap. 2, *Dasein* is rendered as "Determinate Being." Page 121: "Its form is something immediate." And pp. 121–22: "Determinate Being [*Dasein*] appears as something primary and as something from which a beginning is made." Heidegger quite obviously uses the term *Dasein* in this Hegelian sense.

being-in-the-world" (Heidegger, *Gesamtausgabe*, 24:234). The world
is not merely present in our perceptions; it *is there,* just as the *Dasein*
that we ourselves are *is there,* i.e., it exists. Its *mode of Being* is *Dasein*
(237). With the existence of *Dasein* there is given also "the objectification of Being as transcendental science or ontology" (466).

Just as Heidegger modified in a specific way the position of his
mentor, Edmund Husserl, so Nicolai Hartmann changed radically the
subjectivistic Kantianism of his teachers at Marburg, Hermann Cohen
and Paul Natorp; he did so by adopting a position "this side of idealism
and realism."[8]

In a slender volume entitled *Neue Wege der Ontologie*[9] Hartmann
argues that "the old theory of Being depends on the thesis that the
universal . . . is the determining and form-giving inner aspect of
things" (11), and that an inner vision or intuition gives us direct insight into the form-determining aspects of reality. With this thesis the
"old ontology" becomes essentially teleological and deductive. But this
schema of thought proves itself untenable, for it is simply not true
that "all categories of Being are principles *a priori*" (13). The whole
contrast of *a priori* and *a posteriori* is merely an epistemological one.
"In so far as we come at all to a knowledge of categories we obtain it
not in an *a priori* way" but only "through an analysis of the objects"
through which alone "we comprehend categories of Being" (17). "The
way of the new ontology is thus, first of all, an analysis of categories"
that "presupposes the whole extent of experience" (18).

The analysis of this content Hartmann supplies in a series of mas-
sive volumes: *Grundzüge einer Metaphysik der Erkenntnis* (1921; 551
pages), *Zur Grundlegung der Ontologie* (1935; 322 pages), *Der Aufbau der realen Welt* (second edition, 1949; 616 pages), *Möglichkeit
und Wirklichkeit* (1938; 481 pages), *Philosophie der Natur* (1950;
709 pages), *Das Problem des geistigen Seins* (1933; 482 pages), *Ethik*
(1926; 746 pages), *Aesthetik* (1953; 476 pages), and three volumes
of *Kleinere Schriften* (1955, 1957, 1958). These volumes contain all

8. Nicolai Hartmann, "Diesseits von Idealismus und Realismus" (1924) in
Kleinere Schriften 2: 278–322.
9. *Neue Wege der Ontologie*, 3d ed. (Stuttgart: W. Kohlhammer Verlag,
1949), 8. Translated by Reinhard C. Kuhn, under the title *New Ways of Ontology*
(Chicago: Henry Regnery Co., 1952). See also "Die Wiedergeburt der Ontologie" in *Nicolai Hartmann, Der Denker und sein Werk*, ed. Heinz Heimsoeth and
Robert Heiss (Göttingen: Vanderhoek & Ruprecht, 1952), 131–43.

previously published articles. (*Ethik* has been translated into English by Stanley Coit in three volumes under the title *Ethics*. See the Bibliography for complete publishing information for the works of Nicolai Hartmann.)

In what follows I shall provide for the English reader a detailed account of Hartmann's empirically based analyses of the categories involved in various strata of reality—an analysis which is indeed a "new ontology."

* * * * * * *

Nicolai Hartmann, born in 1882 in Riga, Latvia, was educated in St. Petersburg (Leningrad) and Dorpart, and received his Ph.D. at the University of Marburg. He remained on the faculty of that university from 1920 to 1925, when he was appointed professor of philosophy at the University of Cologne. From 1931 until 1945 he was Ordinarius (Chairman) of the Department of Philosophy at the University of Berlin, where I became acquainted with him.

Hartmann was so deeply engrossed in his work and so absorbed in basic problems that what happened around him never seriously distracted him. Proof of this detachment from events of the day can be seen in Mrs. Hartmann's "Nachwort" to Hartmann's posthumously published *Aesthetik*:

He began writing the manuscript on March 9 (1945) and completed it on September 11. It was the time of the encirclement and occupation of Berlin, a time of general famine, insecurity and confusion. But the complete isolation from the outside world favored his concentrated work. Day by day in the midst of this catastrophe he wrote his pages.

In this book of 476 pages there is not one word about what was happening in Berlin, at the university, and to his own home. Throughout the entire Hitler period he was concerned exclusively with basic problems of philosophy.

As a student at Marburg, Hartmann came under the influence of the neo-Kantians Paul Natorp and Hermann Cohen. His first book, the formidable (512 pages) *Platos Logik des Seins*,[10] reflecting Natorp's

10. Giessen: Töpelmann, 1909; hardcover reprint, Berlin: Walter de Gruyter & Co., 1965.

Platos Ideenlehre, is a *hymnus demonstrativus* of Cohen's "philosophy of origins." Hartmann's inaugural dissertation of 1909, "Des Proklus Diadochus Philosophische Anfangsgründe der Mathematik,"[11] reflects Cohen's thesis that the method of mathematics is to be followed in dealing with all basic theoretical problems. Even in 1912, on the occasion of Cohen's seventieth birthday, Hartmann was still an apologist for the Cohen system. His "Systembildung und Idealismus"[12] proves it.

What liberated Hartmann from the Marburg version of neo-Kantianism was his intensive study of post-Kantian German idealism. His two-volume work *Die Philosophie des Deutschen Idealismus*[13] can leave no doubt about this. Hartmann himself states in the "Vorwort" that it was "after more than twenty years of struggle" that he achieved an understanding of Hegel's ultimate meaning, and that he had become convinced that "the more critically we examine Hegel's position the more we can learn from him" (2:vi). At the end of his volume on Hegel, Hartmann wrote:

> It is always tempting to view Hegel in terms of his own categories as a historical phenomenon. One then sees him as a stage on philosophy's way to truth . . . : a stage which is the completion of a long way and, at the same time, the first step in a new path. . . . However, one will not find the key to this transition within the system itself. That system is not only complete in its categories; it is also a pioneer in categorial analysis. (2:389)

In this new analysis of categories Hartmann himself took the first real step beyond Hegel. The result is his "new ontology."

Edmund Husserl had argued that certain general types of 'essences' could be "bracketed" so that they made possible a direct intuition of them.[14] But while it is true that phenomena are in some sense directly

11. *Philosophische Arbeiten*, IV, 1 (Giessen: Töpelmann, 1909).
12. *Philosophische Abhandlungen*, Festschrift für Hermann Cohen, Berlin, 1912. See also Joseph Klein, "Nicolai Hartmann und die Marburger Schule," in *Nicolai Hartmann, Der Denker und sein Werk*, 105–30.
13. Vol. 1: *Fichte, Schelling und die Romantik*, 1923; vol. 2: *Hegel*, 1929 (Berlin: Walter de Gruyter & Co.).
14. Edmund Husserl, *Ideen zu einer reinen Phänomenologie und Phänomenologischen Philosophie*, vol. 1 (Halle, 1913). For a brief discussion of Hartmann's relationship to Husserl see Michael Landmann, "Nicolai Hartmann and Phenomenology," *Philosophy and Phenomenological Research* 3 (1942/43): 393–423.

given, they are merely modes of the appearance of objects and not the objects themselves. Phenomenology thus provides no criterion for distinguishing between appearance and reality.

Undeniably, man exists in manifold relations to a world, relations to which he is adjusted and to whose influences he responds. He thus stands upon a broad context of Being—a context which obviously exists even without him. He has his own Being within that world; and the world has its own Being with and without him. Man's very existence thus leads to a problem of Being, and therefore to an ontology. In attempting to understand man, philosophy must turn to ontology—but to a *new* ontology.

The facts leading to ontological problems are undeniably real. We encounter them in all aspects of our existence—in the world around us and in ourselves as well. Living in a world of things, we cannot escape what *actually is*—*das Seiende*—as modes of Being. All search for principles in daily life as well as in our sciences is concerned with various modes of Being, and must begin with them. The orientation of our ordinary attitude toward things is also the path to an ontology whose mode is that of science. It is the point of view from which Hartmann starts his analyses, for it is in this world that we encounter such heterogeneous entities as matter, living organisms, consciousness, and human spiritual life. All of these represent modes of Being, and Hartmann's ontology deals with them all.

1

The Epistemological Basis of Nicolai Hartmann's New Ontology

We regard it as Nicolai Hartmann's most magnificent achievement to have viewed the phenomenon of cognition again from that aspect from which alone it can be viewed—the aspect of Being. Cognition is Seiendes. *It is embedded in Being, as is everything which* 'is'.

Katharina Kanthack
Nicolai Hartmann und das Ende der Ontologie

BASIC TO HARTMANN'S EPISTEMOLOGICAL POSITION are his formidable *Grundzüge einer Metaphysik der Erkenntnis*[1] and its supplement, the equally formidable *Zur Grundlegung der Ontologie*.[2] In addition there are several minor publications, most of which are included in the three-volume collection of *Kleinere Schriften*.[3]

In the Preface to the first edition of the *Grundzüge* Hartmann speaks of "the task of this book" as an attempt to develop a philosophical position that will transcend all conflicting points of view of philosophical tradition. This is, of course, a formidable task, but it is Hartmann's conviction that Aristotle's procedure of "discussing problems without trying to solve them at any cost"—i.e., *aporetic* as a method—is "the natural, the only basic procedure in philosophy."[4] It culminates in an

1. Berlin and Leipzig: Walter de Gruyter & Co., 1921; enlarged 2d ed. 1925. Hereafter referred to as *Grundzüge*. For critical commentaries see Joseph Klöster, "N. Hartmanns kritische Ontologie," in *Philosophisches Jahrbuch der Görres-Gesellschaft* 41 (1928): 405–31; 42 (1929): 24–41.

2. Berlin and Leipzig: Walter de Gruyter & Co., 1935. Hereafter referred to as *Grundlegung*. For comments, see Joseph Geyser, "Zur Grundlegung der Ontologie. Ausführungen zu dem jüngsten Buche von Nicolai Hartmann," in *Philosophisches Jahrbuch der Görres-Gesellschaft* 50 (1937): 9–67.

3. Berlin: Walter de Gruyter & Co., 1955 (vol. 1), 1957 (vol. 2), 1958 (vol. 3).

4. *Grundzüge*, 8. It was, of course, Socrates who first saw philosophy as an aporetic. See Plato's *Theaetetus* 149A. Plato himself used the method exten-

analysis of categories which, for Hartmann, turns into a new ontology.[5]

Let it be noted at once that both the cognizing subject and the object cognized are *Seiendes*, that both are embedded in Being, and that ontology is therefore basic even to cognition. And let it be noted also that "cognition is not a creating or a bringing forth of the object—as idealisms old and new tend to persuade us—but is a comprehension of something which exists prior to the cognition of it, and is independent of cognition."[6] "If there is nothing that exists in itself, then there also is no cognition; for in that case there would be nothing that could become known" (*Grundlegung*, 162). But this means that "cognition is a transcendent act—an act which reaches beyond the limits of consciousness."[7] What exists (*das Seiende*) is indifferent as to whether and to what extent it is being made an object for a subject. It makes no sense to regard the shifting representations of things in consciousness as differences in the existence or nonexistence of the things themselves or of their being this way or that. The world remains what it is, and what really changes in it does not depend on the subject's knowledge of it. What changes in accordance with the attitudes of the subject are but images of the world ("Erkenntnis," 133). This means that in order to comprehend what really is the case or what actually happens in the world we must approach the problem of cognition from the point of view of our natural attitudes toward things. We must commit ourselves to a "natural realism." When we do this, the cognitive relationship fits readily into the rest of the relations of Being within the world. It stands in line with actions, with loving and hating, with expectation and fearing, with all harsh encounters with things. Johannes Thyssen regards this Hartmannian thesis as "a realistic deviation from *Husserl's* phe-

---

sively. For an appreciative evaluation of Hartmann's recourse to aporetic, see Gottfried Martin, "Aporetik als philosophische Methode," in *Nicolai Hartmann, Der Denker*, ed. Heimsoeth and Heiss, 249–55.

5. Nicolai Hartmann, *Neue Wege der Ontologie*, 3d ed. (Stuttgart: W. Kohlhammer Verlag, 1949). See in particular chap. 2: "Das Erfassen von Seinskategorien," 11–20.

6. *Grundzüge*, 1. See also Nicolai Hartmann, "Zum Problem der Realitätsgegebenheit," in *Philosophische Vorträge der Kantgesellschaft* 32 (Berlin: Pan-Verlag, 1931).

7. Nicolai Hartmann, "Die Erkenntnis im Lichte der Ontologie," in *Kleinere Schriften* I: 128.

nomenology,"[8] and in a sense this is correct. What Hartmann aims at is a phenomenology of cognition as analysis of the essence of what is real, and this means that the initial analytic work must in principle remain "this side" of all theories and attempted solutions and must be restricted to a description of facts.

1. Natural Realism

And what are the facts?

The most obvious fact is that in all cognition a subject and an object stand to each other in a specific and indissoluble relation. The characteristic of this fact is a "primordial distinction" (*Urgeschiedenheit*). Neither one of the relata can be taken out of the relation without ceasing to be either a subject or an object. Although the relation is two-sided, it cannot be reversed. Being a subject for an object is radically other than being an object for a subject. Their functions within the cognitive relation are irreversible. Seen from the side of the subject, the act of 'comprehending' is a reaching out into the heterogeneous sphere of the object. In its being comprehended, the object remains that which stands over against the subject. It is *Gegenstehendes, Gegenstand*. In cognition nothing new comes into existence in the object. Within the subject, however, an awareness of the object arises, and with it an 'image' and/or a 'conception' of the object. Insofar as cognition is a phenomenon, it is "pure consciousness of the object"—and is neither consciousness of the subject nor of the act of *cognizing*. The object alone and as such is being comprehended (*Grundzüge*, 43–44). "Everything in experience testifies to the presence of the object, and all scientific endeavors seek to penetrate into it" ("Erkenntnis," 126). "There simply is no cognition the entire meaning of which does not consist in a relationship of consciousness to something which in itself is extant—*ein Ansichseiendes*."[9] In cognition, it is the subject that makes

8. Johannes Thyssen, "Zur Neubegründung des Realismus in Auseinandersetzung mit Husserl," in *Zeitschrift für Philosophische Forschung* 7 (1953): 147. See also J. N. Mohanty, "Nicolai Hartmann und die Phänomenologie," in *Symposium zum Gedenken an Nicolai Hartmann* (Göttingen: Vandenhock und Ruprecht, 1982).

9. Nicolai Hartmann, "Wie ist kritische Ontologie überhaupt möglich?" in *Kleinere Schriften* 3: 209. Reprinted in *Kleinere Schriften*.

that which exists in itself into an object,[10] but it does not create what exists.[11]

No one who is aware of a thing—who sees it, touches it, handles it—imagines that it comes into Being in the seeing, touching, handling, and that it ceases to be as soon as one looks away or no longer touches or handles it (*Grundlegung*, 163). However, even merely intentional objects—thoughts and representations—'are' something and can become objects of possible cognition; for they are in themselves what they are, and are not merely objects of that cognition whose contents they happen to be (155).

This immediate knowledge of the in-itself-ness of the object is the basic aspect of natural realism, a realism that is not a theory or doctrine but is the basic experience upon which all human activity in the world rests. Every conception of the world that deviates from this realism must account for that deviation by way of special theories. But even then it can not suspend natural realism as basic phenomenon (*Grundzüge*, 163). "The thesis of natural realism is thus the true *exemplum crusis* which separates points of view into those which can and those which can not be maintained. It must be accepted as the *a priori* valid universal form of our actual consciousness of objects in general" (135).

Wilhelm Grebe has commented at length on Hartmann's commitment to "natural realism" and supports it,[12] as does Arnulf Molitor.[13] Hans Wagner, on the other hand, maintains that "it is not quite correct to regard Hartmann's position as realism."[14] But Wagner reacts to Hartmann's interpretation of the *a priori* rather than to his commitment to natural realism; and this position is indeed not the position of traditional realism. But leaving aside for the moment the problem of

10. Nicolai Hartmann, *Möglichkeit und Wirklichkeit* (Berlin: Walter de Gruyter & Co., 1938), 439.

11. Nicolai Hartmann, *Das Problem des Geistigen Seins* (Berlin and Leipzig: Walter de Gruyter & Co., 1933), 118.

12. Wilhelm Grebe, "Der natürliche Realismus, Eine Untersuchung zum Thema: Philosophie und Wirklichkeit," in *Zeitschrift für Deutsche Kultur-Philosophie* 5 (1939): 169–208.

13. Arnulf Molitor, "Bemerkungen zum Realismusproblem bei Nicolai Hartmann," in *Zeitschrift für Philosophische Forschung* 15 (1961): 591–611.

14. Hans Wagner, "Apriorität und Idealität. Vom ontologischen Moment in der apriorischen Erkenntnis," in *Philosophisches Jahrbuch der Görres-Gesellschaft* 56 (1946): 321.

a priori cognition, we can agree with Joaquin Arago's well-supported judgment that Nicolai Hartmann was "without doubt the most resolute fighter in the movement towards realism."[15]

As far as Hartmann is concerned, "the really essential point is that our natural as well as our scientific orientation, just like our ontological one, understands its object as an independent something which exists in itself" (*Grundlegung*, 53). Faith in the reality of the world is undeniably part of the phenomenon of cognition, but reality is not a mere phenomenon. Our "natural realism" is for Hartmann a position "this side of idealism and [metaphysical] realism," for it is "a fact which we encounter in our daily living."[16]

2. *Dasein* and *Sosein*

It is in this connection that Hartmann comes to terms with Heidegger, who, in *Sein und Zeit*, had conceded that "the question of the meaning of Being . . . is indeed *the* fundamental question";[17] that "basically all ontology, no matter how rich and firmly compacted a system of categories it has at its disposal, remains blind and perverted from its ownmost aim, if it has not first adequately clarified the meaning of Being, and conceived this clarification as its fundamental task" (*Sein und Zeit*, 15/34).

15. Joaquin Arago, "Die antimetaphysische Seinslehre Nicolai Hartmanns," in *Philosophisches Jahrbuch der Görres-Gesellschaft* 67 (1950): 179.

16. Nicolai Hartmann, "Diesseits von Idealismus und Realismus," in *Kleinere Schriften* 2: 278–322, 287.

17. Martin Heidegger, *Sein und Zeit, Erste Hälfte*, 4th ed. (Halle an der Sale: Max Niemayer Verlag, 1935), 5. Translated by John Macquarrie and Edward Robinson, under the title *Being and Time* (New York: Harper & Bros., 1962), 24. Let it be noted that this work, specifically identified in the German edition as "*Erste Hälfte*," was meant to be an introduction to a major work in metaphysics. On May 30, 1937, Heidegger told me that the manuscript of that work "has been completed but the book will not be published during my life-time because in this 'Heroic Age' I have suffered enough as the philosopher of *Angst*—in a complete misunderstanding of my position." In the course of our discussion Sartre's "atheistic existentialism" was referred to. Heidegger stated with emphasis: "*That* I have never intended!" Upon my asking him to characterize briefly his ultimate position, he said: "It is the awaiting of the coming of God." When, after Heidegger's death, I inquired about the manuscript of the work he had referred to, I was informed that no such manuscript had been found in his *Nachlass*. But we now have part of it as vol. 24 of the *Gesamtausgabe*, referred to in the Introduction.

Heidegger argued, furthermore, that "fundamental ontology, from which alone all other ontologies can take their rise, must be sought in the existential analysis of *Dasein*," for in *Dasein*'s own existence the meaning of Being is disclosed. "The ontological analysis of *Dasein* is [therefore] what makes up fundamental ontology, so that *Dasein* functions as the entity which in principle is to be interrogated before-hand as to its Being" (14/34f.). And this *Dasein* Heidegger identified at once with the existing human being in whose reflections upon his own existence Being is revealed.

Reacting to this Heideggerian position, Hartmann points out that here all *Seiendes* is from the very beginning seen only in relation to man. It is always specifically his own Being relative to which the Being of things and of other persons is understood. As Heidegger himself put it: The world is always "specifically my own"—"*die 'je meinige'*" (83–88/114–122).

With this approach, so Hartmann points out, the question concerning the *Seiende as Seiendes* has been sidetracked. What is now intended is merely the *Seiende as it exists for me*—as it is given to me and is understood by me. The basic ontological problem has already been prejudged. If one were to agree with this approach, the results would not be obtained through an analysis of Being but would be entailed by a biased asking of the question.

This fact is not altered when the cognitive relation is replaced by a broader conception of *Dasein*'s relationship to the world. The relativity of the *Seiende* to man is and remains the same, no matter how more specifically its givenness is interpreted. The crucial mistake in Heidegger's starting point is that *Being* is confused with the *givenness* of Being. The result is that all further determinations disclosed in Heidegger's "existential analysis" are but aspects of the givenness of things. One could not object to this if, at every step in the analysis, that which is given were distinguished from the *modus* of its givenness, and if in this way the problem of Being were at least afterwards faced once more. But this development is lacking in Heidegger's published works. In fact, the *modalities of Being* are displayed as *modi* of givenness.

Still, in Hartmann's view,

Heidegger has given us a valuable contribution to an understand-ing of the relationship of man to his world in the analysis of *Zuhandensein*—the 'being-at-hand'—which reveals clearly the context of Being of man and things. A thing as a tool or object-for-use is what it is only in the hands of a human being, and only through its being used.

But, so Hartmann continues,

because of this fact, the thing ceases to be merely an object of nature, for there is reflected in it the synthesis of nature and man. In its dynamics, nature follows even here its own laws; but it is being elevated beyond the mere context of nature by virtue of the special application which it finds.[18]

On the subject-side,

the dealing with and handling of things leads to the context of life. . . . Man 'makes uses' of things. He uses them for his purposes as he finds them, and then applies them. He even uses them up, wears them out. But he also first forms them for his use. They enter as his own into the sphere of his person; they belong to him, receive their shape from him for his purposes. Every human being has such a sphere of things around him. Clothes, furniture, house, tools—these and many more—belong to that sphere, but it would be a mistake to think that in their being-for-me, in their being 'my things', there were not also a being-for-themselves for the things. Their being-for-me consists not simply in their being 'my representations'. It exists irrespective of whether or not I have a conception of it. (*Grundzüge*, 212)

Seen without interpretative prejudice, being-at-hand (*Zuhandensein*) is but a very specific nondissolvable givenness of the reality of the world, which, as world, is in itself what it is. Granted that the being-at-hand of things is a fundamental form of their being given; and granted also that this givenness discloses the reality of things "in use" (as it does in tools and in what is achieved with tools), and that it thus testifies clearly to the totality of the actual context within which alone their use is possible; for none of this can be doubted. But neither can it be

18. Nicolai Hartmann, "Naturphilosophie und Anthropologie," in *Kleinere Schriften* 1: 225f.

doubted that things which serve as tools exist prior to their being used as tools; that they have a *Dasein* or *Vorhandensein*—a *being there*—prior to their being-at-hand, prior to their *Zuhandensein* (Heidegger, *Sein und Zeit*, 63–88/90–122).

Katharina Kanthack maintains that "Hartmann does not see 'correctly' the meaning of being-at-hand because he takes it to be equivalent [*gleichsetzbar*] with what is actually existing [*dem Vorhandenem*]." [19] But in this she is mistaken; Hartmann simply maintains that, "understood ontologically," what-is-at-hand (*das Zuhandene*) is, of course, given only within the context of being-for-me. But from this we cannot conclude that what is thus given does not exist in itself also—"dass es garnicht vorhanden 'sei'," for only that can be at-hand (*zuhanden sein*) which first is at least existent (*vorhanden*). How could you make a tool out of something which does not exist?

> The world is given to me not merely as "environment," and certainly not as 'merely mine'. It is rather the one real world in which all persons and everything which is at-hand for them are located. But if this is so, then the world so disclosed is in the strict sense a givenness of reality [*eine Realitätsgegebenheit*]. (*Grundlegung*, 214)

In Heidegger's philosophy two other terms play a prominent role. One is *Sorge,* the other is *Angst.* They are interrelated and are crucial as revelatory of man's being-in-the-world. But the usual translation of *Sorge* as *care* does not give us the basic meaning of the German *Sorge.* That meaning is best expressed in the verb form *das Sorgen,* which relates it at once to *Angst*—anxiety and fear. "*Im Sorgen*"—in being anxious about something, in fearing something—the character of the transcendent act is clearly manifest as teleologico-prospective. It belongs together with willing, striving, doing, and acting no less than with expecting, fearing, hoping. "In its broadest meaning *Sorgen* remains an undifferentiated, diffuse total attitude on the part of the subject towards what is approaching in time; but it lacks the specific character of an act" (214). Still, as Heidegger points out, *Sorgen* is a "being-ahead-of-oneself" (*ein Sich-selbst-Vorwegsein*), and anxiety is

19. Katharina Kanthack, *Nicolai Hartmann und das Ende der Ontologie* (Berlin: Walter de Gruyter & Co., 1962), 161.

"a fearing in the face of something threatening" (*Sein und Zeit*, 431/ 390). What is philosophically important as far as *Sorge* and anxiety are concerned is thus what is valid with respect to all prospective acts. These acts are concerned with the future—with obtaining the necessities of life, with taking care of needs (one's own and those of others), with working toward what is desired, with actively preparing for what is to come, with living up to accepted responsibilities, and so forth. In all of these acts, as Hartmann points out, their transcendent character is obvious. They are concerned with what is coming as something which in itself is real—"a full-weighty [*vollgewichtiges*], real Being-in-itself" (*Grundlegung*, 215).

But anxiety is also the most illusory and ontologically the most ambiguous of all prospective acts, for "it falls victim to every illusion— be it one of tradition or be it a self-created one." And "he who is filled with anxiety is from the very beginning incapable of a sober view of life . . . , of seeing *Seiendes* as it is" (197f.).

For Hartmann's position more important than *Sorge* and anxiety are various human acts that culminate in work. As he sees it, the basic phenomenon of work (*Arbeit*) is neither economic nor sociological but ontological, for work is a transcendent act of a specific kind. It is a real performance within the realm of reality, a dealing with things and means, and an application and a using-up of things. Beyond this, labor has a goal-object that it tries to realize and that in the process of realization is made into a real thing. At the same time, however, labor is always labor 'on something'. It encounters something that is already present (*Vorhandenes*) and the *Sosein* of which labor modifies. Moreover, because of the goal it tries to attain, labor is ultimately also related to 'somebody'—the person for whom the work is being done, be that oneself, some other person, or even a community of persons. As a real act of a real person, labor is thus related to reality in a fourfold way; and insofar as there is a knowledge of these relationships in the consciousness of the laborer, there is in labor also a fourfold reality: the reality of the laborer, of the material worked on, of the tools used in doing the work, and of the person or persons for whom the work is being done (216).

Moreover, in working, man is constantly forced to measure himself against things. He 'experiences' himself in the energy applied, both mental and physical; and he experiences the things in their resistance to his labor. Both experiences are inseparably bound together, and both are an experience of reality. Here is the proof, as Hartmann sees it, that in work and, in general, in dealing with things I experience the world not simply as 'mine'—as merely a content of my own consciousness—but in the hardness of its own reality.

> Here power stands against power. And in the phenomenon of labor we have the universal proof that the sphere of reality is in itself homogeneous in the sense that everything real in it is ontically equivalent and, in its mode of Being, constitutes one unified world. (216f.)

Parallel to, and in some respects more important than, man's dealings with things is the individual's encounter with other human beings, individually and in communal situations. No one can deny here the transcendency of the acts of contact with real entities. Persons and their acts have no higher 'reality' than have things and their interrelations, but they belong to a 'higher stratum' of reality. They have an incomparably more complex structure than have mere things, and in this sense they are higher formations of reality. The basic ontological fact is precisely this *unity* of the mode of Being despite the manifoldness of strata of reality and of human relevance (203).

Hartmann's position here is reminiscent of William James's thesis that "the parts of experience hold together from next to next by relations that are themselves parts of experience." The directly apprehended universe needs, in short, no extraneous transempirical connective support, but possesses in its own right a concatenated or continuous structure.[20]

Hartmann regards this "natural realism" as basic to any theory of cognition. But Joseph Geyser has argued that the thesis of natural realism may already be an interpretation of Being.[21] And in some sense Geyser is right, for at every cultural level man has certain preconceived ideas concerning the nature of things that confront him. The fact remains, however, that at every level of his existence and cultural

20. William James, *Essays in Radical Empiricism* (New York: Longmans, Green and Company, 1912), xii–xiii.

21. Joseph Geyser, "Zur Grundlegung der Ontologie. Ausführungen zu dem jüngsten Buch von Nicolai Hartmann," in *Philosophisches Jahrbuch der Görres-Gesellschaft* 49 (1936): 3–29, 289–338, 425–465; 50 (1937): 9–67.

development man firmly believes in the reality of the world in which he lives, and in the reality of things within that world—no matter what his definition of reality may be.

Hartmann speaks of his own starting point in philosophy as "a natural tendency of cognition which at all times reveals itself as realistic."[22] And this "natural realism" entails the fact that "cognition is a transcendent act" (*Grundzüge*, 259).

Any act of consciousness that does not comprehend something that exists in itself may be an act of thinking or of the imagination, perhaps even an act of judgment; but it is not an act of cognition. The being-in-itself of the object is essential to the cognitive relation but is not affected by the *act* of cognition (44).

The representation of a thing in consciousness is, of course, not the thing itself, but only the thing as seen, touched, and meant. This means that as far as the subject is concerned, everything in cognition pertains to the thing *as object* only. Our everyday experience, however, is testimony to the fact that the thing itself is what is to be comprehended; scientific research is proof of this (Hartmann, "Erkenntnis," 126; *Grundlegung*, 54).

It is evident, furthermore, that in cognition the relation of subject and object cannot be reversed. Being an object for a subject is quite different from being the subject for an object, and in itself the object is what it is. Although the subject's comprehension of an object may contain aspects of spontaneity on the part of the subject, the subject does not determine the nature of the object itself in any way. Receptivity with respect to what is given in cognition and spontaneity with respect to the image of the given are by no means mutually exclusive. Cognition is, in any event, a transcending determination of the subject by an object. Even ideal objects, such as mathematical propositions, and feelings and attitudes—insofar as they are objects for a cognizing subject—are independent of the acts of cognition. It is in this independence, not in any 'psychologically external' over against the 'inner' aspect of a subject, that the cognitive meaning of transcendence consists (Hartmann, *Grundzüge*, 47).

---

22. *Grundzüge*, 198. For a comment on this approach see Hinrich Knitter-meyer, "Zur Metaphysik der Erkenntnis. Zu Nicolai Hartmanns *Grundzüge einer Metaphysik der Erkenntnis*," in *Kant-Studien* 30 (1925): 495–515.

3. Modes of Cognition

It cannot well be doubted that all cognition is bound to a cognizing subject. And it is equally beyond all doubt that cognition cannot be reduced to merely mental or logical problems, for it depends on the subject's being aware of a relation to objects that transcends its own mental events.

Cognition actually involves three aspects of experience, aspects that are heterogeneous and transcend the act of cognition. On the object-side, the relation of subject and object borders on the logical and the ontological, for the in-itselfness of the object can be an ideal as well as a real one. On the subject-side, cognition borders on the mental, i.e., on the realm of psychology. And with respect to the relation between subject and object, the act of cognition, involving intellectual integrity, borders on the moral (*Grundzüge*, 43ff.).

The cognitive relation itself occurs in two distinct modes: the *a posteriori* and the *a priori*. The former begins with sense impressions—with seeing, hearing, touching—and culminates in a conceptual comprehension of individual objects and their apparent characteristics. As Hartmann puts it: All comprehension in which an individual object is given is *a posteriori*. Here something is being comprehended as belonging to what is given. What is comprehended in this way is, of course, valid for other cases also. If so, cognition is in effect a generalization based upon individual instances.

The *a priori* mode of cognition is concerned with the universal essence of what is given. Insofar as essence is ontologically primary relative to any given instance, comprehension of this "essential *prius*" is indeed "cognition *a priori*" (44).

We must note, however, that the *a priori* element in cognition has generally and unjustly been limited to form, lawfulness, and synthesis, and has been taken to be a function of the subject. As such it has been associated primarily with thinking and judging. It is Hartmann's conviction, however, that *a priori* cognition must be traced back to "an independent autonomous source of cognition in general" ("Diesseits," 301). As he points out: "All *a priori* cognition of what is real is 'objectively universal'. . . . Every judgment to which it leads pertains to a totality of possible real cases" (*Grundlegung*, 277). What Kant meant by the universality and necessity of synthetic judgments *a priori* characterizes exactly all genuine apriority.

A priori cognition is unquestionably a fact in our sciences. The best example is, of course, mathematics. "Its perfection and exactness are pure apriority."[23] It is evident, however, that nothing which is understood to be strictly universal and necessary can be derived from experienced individual facts (Hartmann, *Grundzüge*, 339).

Since Plato's time *a priori* cognition has been regarded as an inner *Schauen*—an intuiting.[24] In this sense it is perhaps best known in the Kantian interpretation of the spatiotemporal aspects of perception. But, as Hartmann has pointed out, the *a priori* element in cognition "has unjustifiably been misplaced into functions of the subject; and within those functions has unjustifiably been identified with thinking and judgment" ("Diesseits," 285).

It is Hartmann's achievement to have freed the concept of apriority from its traditional and seemingly indissoluble association with rationalistic and idealistic motives, and to have attempted to comprehend it "in its basic metaphysical significance."[25] As Ingeborg Wirth has noted, "In Hartmann's philosophy a realistic conception of cognition and an epistemologico-theoretical concept of the *a priori* stand in correlation."[26] In the *Vorwort* to her book she raises the question of "whether or not [Hartmann] is able to explain the co-existence of realism and apriorism." But Hartmann is quite clear on one point: In the whole realm of cognition "one can never know *a priori* whether something really exists or not, but only how that is constituted which has already been attested to as being real" (*Grundzüge*, 242). The miracle of *a priori* cognition is precisely this: that "without direct relation to given instances it comprehends something which exists in itself [*ein Ansichseiendes*]" (319).

23. Nicolai Hartmann, *Philosophie der Natur* (Berlin: Walter de Gruyter & Co., 1950), 400.

24. Nicolai Hartmann, "Zur Lehre vom Eidos bei Plato und Aristoteles," in *Kleinere Schriften* 2: 164. See also the relevant parts of Nicolai Hartmann, *Platos Logik des Seins* (Giessen: Töpelmann, 1909; hardcover reprint, Berlin: Walter de Gruyter & Co., 1985, 512 pages).

25. *Grundzüge*, 9. See also Hartmann's "Über die Erkennbarkeit des Apriorischen," in *Logos* 5 (1914/15): 290–329.

26. Ingeborg Wirth, *Realismus und Apriorismus in Nicolai Hartmanns Erkenntnistheorie* (Berlin: Walter de Gruyter & Co., 1963), 4. For a different response to Hartmann's interpretation see Hans Wagner, "Apriorität und Idealität. Vom ontologischen Moment in der apriorischen Erkenntnis," in *Philosophisches Jahrbuch der Görres-Gesellschaft* 56 (1946): 292–361; 57 (1947): 431–96.

All cognition *a priori* transcends any given case and does not wait for a particular object to be given. It knows in advance how the object must be constituted in some respects; for what is given in *a priori* cognition is a universal character trait or essence, a *Sosein* without regard to its presence in any particular real instance. Insofar as such characteristic traits are what is ontologically primary, cognition of them is indeed cognition *a priori*. To put it differently: Cognition *a priori* comprehends only what is universal—the law, and the thoroughgoing determination of possible objects. It is not concerned with individual objects as such but is "a higher form of intuition in which consciousness comes into direct contact with the essence of things" (*Grundlegung*, 223).

Hartmann thus repudiates the idealistic interpretation and frees the *a priori* from its traditional rationalistic motives. He speaks of a "*Neugestaltung des Aprioritätsbegriffs*" (*Grundzüge*, 9)—a disclosure of the basic metaphysical meaning of the *a priori* as "a higher form of intuition in which consciousness comes into direct contact with the object" (*Grundlegung*, 223).

In order to understand this we must view the *a priori* in its basic *ontological* meaning.[27] It then becomes clear that *a priori* cognition is possible if the principles of the subject are at the same time principles of the object, i.e., when the categories of cognition that are valid for all subjects are valid also for the objects of cognition, and are thus also categories of Being that are valid for both the subject and the object. The categories must therefore be a 'third'—something in addition to subject and object—through which the objects are determined. Kant stated this in his "highest principle of synthetic judgments" when he said: "The conditions of the *possibility of experience* in general must at the same time be conditions of the *possibility of the objects of experience,* and therefore have objective validity in a synthetic judgment *a priori*."[28]

What this principle clearly expresses is the universally sufficient and necessary condition that alone makes *a priori* cognition objectively valid, i.e., valid for transcendent objects. And it is a principle that

27. *Grundzüge*, 9. For a comment on this thesis see Joseph Klösters, "Die Kritische Ontologie Nicolai Hartmanns und ihre Bedeutung für das Erkenntnisproblem" (Ph.D. diss., München, 1927; privately printed in Fulda, 1928).

28. Immanuel Kant, *Critique of Pure Reason*, A158/B197, trans. Norman Kemp Smith (New York: Macmillan, 1929), 194.

permits a realistic as well as an idealistic interpretation but depends on neither. It is a position strictly "this side of idealism and realism" ("Diesseits," 278–322).

This assertion of the identity of the principles of subject and object is a first and critical minimum of a metaphysical hypothesis that is both necessary and sufficient to account for the fact of *a priori* cognition and for objectively valid categorial analyses. Chapters 2, 3, and 4 will provide proof of this fact.[29]

As far as cognition *a posteriori* is concerned, the question is: How can perceptions reveal the characteristics of actual things? The transcendence of things is and remains in principle an opposition to the subject, and the relation of comprehension is and remains a transcendent act on the part of the subject. Our empirical knowledge of real things is thus no less metaphysical than is *a priori* cognition. In fact, it is even less understandable because of the immediacy and self-assurance with which consciousness takes its own contents as objectively valid. It is this self-assurance that is the problem (*Grundzüge*, 368).

For all empirical cognition, including that of our sciences, perception is the ultimate witness of fact. Even more fundamental than mere sense impressions, however, is our interaction with things. Here perception is not a matter of problems but a solution, a fulfillment of anticipatory thought (369). Thinking remains limited by perception. It can interpret perceptual content and can learn to subsume it under laws, but it cannot dissolve that content without a remainder. It can neither create nor destroy it. Moreover, perception itself is independent of all judgment. Here the autonomy of the *a priori* is confronted by an obvious autonomy of the sensory content, the *a posteriori*.

But perception is not an indifferent *x* lacking determination. It is something which in manifold ways "experiences" the object, and is a factor which supplements the *a priori*. Cognition is evidently bound to an object in two ways—ways that are compensatory in revealing different aspects of the object.

Perceptions are an immediate testimony of reality (371f.). Whatever qualitative aspects may be involved (and there may be some question about them), perception is under all circumstances a consciousness of

---

29. For a preliminary orientation see Hans-Joachim Höfert, "Kategorialanalyse und physikalische Grundlagenforschung," in *Nicolai Hartmann, Der Denker und sein Werk*, ed. Heimsoeth and Heiss, 186–207.

reality; and insofar as any judgment is a judgment about reality—i.e., insofar as it distinguishes between reality and nonreality—it depends on support in the testimony of the senses.

A *priori* cognition pertains in principle only to the universal and necessary. Its application to reality, however, presupposes perception as the point of reference of all contents and relationships. Kant's definition of reality through reference to perception must be understood in this sense, as must also his famous "restriction" of the use of categories to objects of possible experience. As Kant himself put it: "The conditions of sensibility constitute the universal condition under which alone the category can be applied to an object" (*Critique of Pure Reason*, A140/B179; 182).

The fact that perceptions are in some respects subjective does not eliminate their objective kernel, their justified, irreplaceable testimony of a reality that is independent of the content of consciousness. This objective kernel is revealed irrefutably in the procedures of our empirical sciences—in observations and experiments, both of which are primarily testimony of our senses. No matter how much subjectivity there may be in sense perceptions, perception is and remains a source of knowledge, and it is also testimony of the reality of objects known. That the qualities immediately given in perception cannot be ascribed directly to things but are subject to interpretation does not in the least affect their reference to reality. All interpretation remains bound up with materials given in perception that are to be interpreted. The subjectivity of perceptions does not destroy the significance of them for cognition, not even for scientific cognition. At most it can but set limits to it.

Very important, however, is the so-called 'relativity' of perceptions, that is, that they occur only in individual subjects and have no intersubjective validity (as cognition a *priori* has). Cognition a *posteriori* thus pays for the advantage of an immediate certainty of *Dasein* with the disadvantage of individual relativity (*Grundzüge*, 373).

It is not true, however, that in perception everything without exception is *a posteriori*, whereas in thinking all is *a priori*. We find numerous *a priori* elements in perception also. Kant had already seen some of them in the spatiotemporal aspects of perceptions,[30] but there

---

30. *Critique of Pure Reason*, A24/B39; A26/B42; A30/B46; Smith translation, 71, 74, 77, respectively.

are many more. For example, there is the relation of yellow and orange, and of the complementarity of red and green, which can be intuited *a priori* as a relationship that is not a matter of reflective judgment but one of the perceiving consciousness prior to all judgment.

The problem which we face here is this: Either the transcendence and reality of the object are an illusion or our comprehension of the object in sense perception is illusory. Perception presumably connects two basically different worlds: the world of space-time events and the temporal but nonspatial phenomena of consciousness. What is involved here is the well-known 'psychophysical' problem, which clearly indicates the metaphysical character of the situation. It is not simply the problem of perception only but, ultimately, the problem of consciousness and of the Being of things.

In our natural attitude toward things we see here no particular difficulty. We simply accept the interaction of 'body' and 'mind'. Philosophical reflection shows, however, that this interaction is a crucial problem, for we do not understand how a bodily process can call forth any occurrence in consciousness (*Grundzüge*, 380ff.). In perceptual experience two types of phenomena are obviously involved: the physical processes in the various organs upon which perceptions depend, and the mental processes in consciousness involved in interpreting the content of perceptions; and these processes are and remain heterogeneous even when a precise relationship exists between them.

Despite this basic duality, the unity of body and mind is obviously present in the very essence of a human being. However, the *hiatus irrationalis* of this duality is not one of factual duality but one of our understanding only. Behind the apparent dualism of physical and mental processes stands an ontological unity of the psychophysical Being —i.e., the empirical subject. How processes that have a bodily beginning can end as processes in consciousness—or vice versa—is simply incomprehensible. Here is an absolute limit of cognition where all categorial conceptions fail us. The unitary essence of the psychophysical processes belongs to an ontological basis not available to us in cognition, for those processes are at the same time metaphysical and metapsychical—i.e., they belong originally to a shared basic stratum of Being of which only certain aspects—the physical and the mental— are encountered as phenomena.

To attempt to explain this basic stratum of Being would be just as nonsensical as to deny it (*Grundzüge*, 380–82). The inescapable idea of an ontological unity and its transcausal type of determination is not a hypothesis but the inescapable minimum of a metaphysics that strives to formulate the problem of perceptual experience. All we can do is to see the basic psychophysical relation in general as the counterpart of a basic categorial relation that plays the same role in perception that that relation plays in cognition *a priori.*

That, despite its irrationality, the conception of a basic psychophysical relation is a fertile idea is obvious; for if such a relation does exist, then the empirical element in our cognition of objects can be an independent and irreducible factor which no cognition *a priori* can disregard.

Perception has always been looked upon as a 'being affected' by an object, and the evidence of our natural encounter with things supports it. But such affection is ontologically possible only if, in addition to the basic categorial relation, there exists also a basic psychophysical relation. After all, cognition is a mode of Being, and consciousness is a *Seiendes* embedded in the sphere of the *Seienden* in general (380–90). The condition of the possibility of cognition must therefore in some way also be part of the system of conditions of Being. Within a certain range every change of the *Seiende* must in some way also signify a change within the cognizing subject. The more complete this functional relationship is, the more perfect is the range of reactions of the subject, and the more of the *Seiende* is represented in it. This means nothing less than that the cognitive contents of consciousness —however limited and subjective they may be—must have a strictly lawful functional relation to the structure of Being, and must thus in a very definite sense be 'true'. How this functional dependency actually comes about need not be knowable. It suffices to realize that the subject's reaction to an object is understandable as a transcausal determination; this fact of determination differentiates the specifically *a posteriori* cognition from any cognition *a priori.*

Moreover, the 'subjectivity' of perception and the skeptical argument based upon it find here their refutation: They are contradicted by the ontological relation of subject and object.

For cognition to be possible, however, the reaction of the sensory consciousness to the characteristics of the object must be subordinate to a very firm law of transformation. That is to say, they must have a common ontological modus that is rooted in the all-encompassing sphere of Being (385). This presupposition is the ontological minimum entailed by the problem of cognition.

A precise conception of what is sensorially given is possible only when one distinguishes it strictly from everything else that is given—such as mathematical propositions, in which an ideal Being is given, not the actual reality of an object.

Although what is given through the senses is always an indication of reality, it is neither the whole of reality nor an unexceptionable proof of it. As content of consciousness, the given corresponds only to a limited segment of the real. 'Real', in the full ontological meaning of the term, is only the concrete Being of the object itself, which is indifferent to its being known or not. What is real always exists and is an object of possible cognition, but in itself it is not what is given. If the evidence of our senses were a complete cognition of reality, the sensuously given would also be the real; and this is evidently not so. After all, many elements of *a priori* cognition are intertwined with what is given in sense perception and cannot be separated from it. A large part of the categories of cognition, for example, are present in perception. They are what combines heterogeneous sense data into the unity of objects. Although the testimony of the senses is indicative of ontological reality, it is not sufficient as an adequate cognition of that reality. Sense data are but tokens for the cognition of objects. They are but the primary—i.e., the lowest and not further analyzable—stratum of cognition (393).

We must note, however, that in the testimony of the senses there is also something universal. 'Red', for example, is always the same for all red things and for all subjects who see it. 'Red' is thus also universal, regardless of its differentiations as to intensities and nuances—which themselves are universal. The same is true of 'sour', 'cool', 'hard', and 'loud'. In fact there are no sensory qualities that are individual in themselves. All are universal—as Aristotle already knew. The fact is that the content of sensory cognition can be universal without the cognition of it being a cognition of universals. In other words, what is known directly in our sensory experiences may well be something universal, but it is known only in given specific cases and *not as* universal. The transcendental relationship of subject and object is found exclusively in what is individual—i.e., in the occurrence of sense data and their unique constellation in a given situation (395–97).

4. Emotional Transcendent Acts and the Problem of Reality

Up to this point we have dealt with cognition as if it were the only transcendent act of the subject. But cognition is actually only one of a group of acts that includes various forms of human activities and emotions: handling objects, dealing with other people, ventures of various kinds, success and failure, hoping and disappointments, fearing and being affected in various ways by objects and events. Such experiences are in actuality generally interrelated. What is important for philosophical analysis is that in their very nature all of these experiences are transcendent events: They all involve objects and events whose occurrence transcends the confines of subjective consciousness, and are part of an objectively existing real world but are knowable by the subject (*Grundprobleme*, 185). What all of these experiences have in common is that, in themselves, all of them are not yet a cognition in the true sense. They are not simply "acts of observation" but are events in which one is "involved": One encounters the objects and/or situations, and one is affected by them. The experience is as yet not cognitive in the strict sense but is without doubt the most convincing evidence for the crucial importance of realism in experience. Turned into the metaphysical, this fact has given rise to the idea of 'fate'—and does so even in our times. The metaphysical meaning given to it is "the best proof that experiencing is not comprehension (cognition, understanding)" (*Grundlegung*, 191), for the context of the real relations upon which the idea of fate depends is here fundamentally misunderstood.

Closely related to the phenomena of action is the awareness of resistance encountered in them. This awareness is distinctly other than a "purely receptive experience or enduring," for it involves an awareness of the desiring, the striving, and the willing as well; and the enduring is not identical with them. It is true in general that in all experiencing, aspects of the spontaneity of the person are involved and reveal themselves as existential aspects (*Wesensmomente*) in the form of 'being affected'. The task we face is not to isolate but to clarify the aspects that are always involved in the totality of an experience.

Once we have become aware of the aspect of resistance, we cannot disregard the fact that it is precisely in the resistance that "the givenness of reality takes on a firmer [*verdichtete*] form." What is essential here is that "this reality is encountered at all levels of human acting, from the lowest to the highest, without the importance [*Gewicht*] of the real resistance markedly changing" (200). Only the severity of being affected changes, and this change pertains only to the difference of the levels of existence at which the resistance is encountered.

Consider an example. "I intend to move a stone and experience the resistance of its weight; I intend to fight somebody and experience his counter-attack; I want to appropriate someone else's property and experience the counter-move [Gegenschlag] of the law; I want to convince somebody and experience the resistance of his independent thinking. All of these cases show the same experience of the same real resistance; for real is not only the weight of the stone—equally real is the defense of the one attacked; the power of the existing law, respectively of its appointed representative; and just as much also the spontaneity [Selbsttätigkeit] of the other's thought" (202).

It is thus a mistake to regard the senses alone as disclosing the givenness of the reality of things and events. Encountering resistance is always already a basis of experience that includes what is being perceived. Perception already falls within a "preparatory [vorbereiteden] basis of a more primitive but stronger experience of reality" (203). Even seeing is basically not primary, for the naively experienced resistance is at once generalized and need not be specifically "interpreted into" what is seen. This is also the reason why of all the senses the sense of touch is preeminent in providing "certainty of reality [Realitätsgewissheit]."

The concept of reality now requires further clarification. Although for naive experience, things are the most obvious representatives of what is real (for they are constantly encountered in the world we live in), they are not all there is in the world. Wherever the reality of things is at issue, there is also, and connected with it, the reality of the human situation, of conflicts, destiny, even the reality of the course of history. This fact enhances the problem of reality, for it "pertains simultaneously and in equal immediacy to the Being of things and of human beings, the Being of the material and of the spiritual world, and this with the inclusion of everything which according to an order of stratification in the world lies between them" (Grundzüge, 405ff.).

The concept of reality basic to Hartmann's ontology is thus from the very beginning an enlarged one, in contrast to all other interpretations that are oriented merely toward things. But it is precisely this "natural realism" that understands the world in which we live as one manifold whole containing in various and complex interrelations what is heterogeneous: the living and the lifeless, things, mental processes and the spiritual. The same mode of Being encompasses both matter and spirit, just as matter and spirit show the same basic aspects (*Grundmomente*) of individuality and temporality. Even spiritual Being originates and vanishes in time, is in all particularization unique, and, once vanished, cannot return. Only spatiality separates the spiritual from what is of the nature of things. The basic error of all materialism is to regard only what is spatially external as real. "Magnitude, measurability, visibility do not characterize the real; what does it is becoming, process, uniqueness, duration, succession, simultaneity" (415f.).

This ontological conception depends entirely on the unity and uniqueness of real time, although the unity of this time has often been denied. What is essential of real time (*Realzeit*) is that it encompasses without distinction everything real, irrespective of its kind or stratum of reality, be it natural or historical, material or spiritual. An analysis of time that ignores this phenomenon of unity is false, and the categories of reality depending upon it are a mistaken ontology of reality. It pertains to the lower strata of reality only, leaving the mode of Being of the higher strata not understood.

The traditional isolation of the problem of cognition removes it from its natural basis in human experience. That basis is the context of the phenomena of living. In actual life we find no isolated cognitive relation, and in some sciences we find only an approximate one. The pure 'subject-object relation' is ontically secondary, one of an abundance of primary relations to things, persons, situations in life, and events. The 'objects' are not primarily what we understand but what concerns us in the practical aspects of living, something with which we must "come to terms." Pure cognition is secondary; it begins as included in the broader context of living. And limited as human anticipatory projections of future happenings may be, they at least enlarge our awareness of the world we live in. But this anticipatory projection is by no means a purely cognitive one, and it is limited even more than is the emotional adjustment to what is coming; for we are aware of the fact that something is coming although we do not know precisely what it is. Knowing that something is coming, we are certain of it even though we do not know, or do not know exactly, what it is. We adjust to it even when it is the unexpected, the surprising, the inexplicable. Our emotional-receptive acts are thus supplemented by the emotional-anticipatory or prospective acts. They are not less transcendent than the former. Acts of this kind are all basic types of expectation, of presentiment and composure, which anticipate the actual experience. The characteristic of these acts is precisely that they transcend the restrictions of the present moment.

But it is characteristic of the human individual that in what actually concerns him at any given time he or she lives essentially also in what is yet to come. "Prospective-transcendent acts are nothing other than the special forms of the general and habitual adjustment toward what is coming. The impossibility of escape, of avoidance, of getting out of the stream of events—connected with the narrower limits of parrying, modifying and deflecting it—gives what is approaching its frightening [*ungeheures*] importance as reality before it has become real" ("Erkenntnis," 136). And it gives the anticipatory acts their importance as testimonials of reality.

Here we are not concerned with cognition but with attitudes. It is precisely the impression of the expectation which forces reality into consciousness, for this impression is uncertain only with respect to the content of what is approaching. It is accompanied by the greater certainty that the course of events will bring forth the full and irrevocable character of what is approaching. In the "prospective act of expectation" we thus have evidence of reality of a unique value. The act itself is certainly a "most real mode of the actual adjustments in life, of the dealing with precisely the same coming real situations [*Realverhält-nissen*] which anticipation reveals to consciousness. In having to come to terms [*im Fertigwerden-Müssen*] lies the whole hardness of the real" (*Grundzüge*, 420–29).

But man lives not only in an awaiting of what is approaching but also in an active anticipation of the future. For his initiatives, only the future is open. What in the stream of events is experienceable can no longer be modified, and what is still modifiable is not experienceable. We can, of course, long for the impossible; but to will it, knowing that it is impossible, would be insanity. Willing always includes the transcending reality of the act concerned with realities. It includes the power to affect, to guide events. In this sense, volition and action—and their manifestations—belong homogeneously to the real context of events and are at the same time our knowledge of this fact; for all acts as such are basically part of the context of reality that is the world. Action is but a "participation" in that world. "All human action pushes into a context of reality which already has its firm determinateness.

Within that context it finds its means, but also the limits of what is possible" (411–36).

But man's actions are not limited to things as real objects; they extend to persons also. Here a new aspect of reality emerges, for the individual human being encounters the specific counteractions of the other person. As Hartmann sees it, "it is an inescapable [*unaufhebares*] elementary phenomenon that an action and a will receive their value-aspect [*Wertprägung*] precisely through what in the real world they do with respect to real persons" (437). But persons and their acts have no 'reality' higher than that of things and their interrelations. They merely belong to "a higher stratum of the real" and have an incomparably richer structure. Their mode of Being is, however, the same. Persons and things are together in one real world and in one real time. "The ontologically basic phenomenon of reality as such is precisely the unity of the mode of Being within the manifoldness of the height of Being [*Seinshöhe*] and human relevancies."[31]

It is in this perspective that we must view the details of Hartmann's "new ontology."

5. Ideal Objects

All objects of the emotional-transcendent acts are something real—with the possible exception of the feeling for values. *A priori* cognition, on the other hand, is concerned with ideal Being rather than with given real *Seienden*. The basic question is, of course, Is there ideal Being at all? (*Grundlegung*, 242).

In our ordinary or natural attitude we are essentially oriented toward real things and regard the ideal as 'unreal'. We are not sure whether or not behind it there is a *Seiendes* which is independent of our consciousness. No emotional-transcendent acts disclose one. Nor does ideal Being on its own part act in any observable way; it is not encountered in space or in time. In its own way, however, it is present in our dealings with what is real. As Hartmann puts it: "Its subsistence and sway are unobtrusive so that a special orientation of consciousness is required to notice it at all" (*Grundlegung*, 244).

31. "Erkenntnis," 133. For a discussion of this point see Hermann Wein, "Der Streit um die Ordnung und Einheit der Realwelt. Für und Wider Nicolai Hartmann," in *Philosophia Naturalis* 5 (1958/59): 174–220.

Ideal Being is perhaps best known in mathematics, where we speak of "mathematical existence." For example, we assert that 'between two whole numbers there exists an infinite series of fractions'. Such statements are not only in form existential judgments but are such also as far as their content is concerned. They assert what there *is* or *is not* in a specific sphere of knowledge. And consider also such statements as '3^6 is equal to 729' or 'Pi equals 3.14159. . .'. Such judgments do not say 'I think so' or 'I must think so', but assert 'it is so'. That is, they assert that the objects referred to are in themselves such that they actually possess the character ascribed to them. "They express a Being, not a thing" (245).

It may be objected that we find such judgments only in our thinking; that they are merely a matter of logical positing. But, surely, the judgments themselves contain nothing pertaining to the judgment as such or to a positing. They simply assert objective relationships. In the statement of the judgment these relationships are already distinguished from the statement as such. Mathematics thus silently "presupposes the Being of the objects with which it deals in its judgments" (249). The objects as such are independent of thinking, judging, and cognition. Only on the basis of this presupposition does it make sense at all to speak of the truth or falsity of mathematical judgments. The objects of mathematics share with real Being this character of 'in-itself-ness'.

Hartmann deals extensively with other interpretations of mathematical objects (250–57), stressing the fact that cognition is "not a production of contents or of merely 'having' contents, but is in its very essence an 'understanding' of something which in-itself *is*." As cognition, "pure mathematics" must be genuine understanding; and this is possible only when the mathematical 'entities'—numbers and their relations, spatial relationships and their configurations—have a 'Being' independent of consciousness and comprehension. Purely subjective cognition does not do justice to this character of mathematics.

But there is also other ideal Being—for example, the "intersubjective universality of the *a priori*." It can be shown, Hartmann points out, that where the apriority has "real cognitive character" it already presupposes "a common relationship between subjects and existing facts"—that the cognition depends upon a "transcendent apriority." The intersubjective agreement is, in that case, already the consequence of an object understandable to all because the object has a specific character (*Sosein*) which "can be seen only as it is, and not as it is not" (258).

However, this "imminent apriority"—be it subjectively ever so general—is without further analysis not simply an 'ideal apriority'. Its universality can also be a mere prejudice.

What justifies us in regarding mathematics as "genuine understanding of Being" is the necessity that it imposes upon our thinking, which here encounters "a power over which it is not the master." It experiences an unyielding nature of objects with which it deals. But since the laws of mathematics are valid also for the real things in our real world, they are at least indirectly laws of reality. And laws that, at least potentially, are also laws of real relationships cannot be purely subjective or simply laws of consciousness. They must have a character of Being of their own (263).

But mathematical principles and laws are also valid for facts and events in nature. Nature is in itself quite obviously "mathematically arranged." And this fact is "the true and sufficient basis for our knowledge of the in-itself-ness [*Ansichsein*] of ideal objects" (265).

However, "ideality in the ontological sense is something entirely different; it has a mode of Being *sui generis* besides that of the real" (266). To demonstrate the relative independence of ideal Being, Hartmann develops three arguments: One is based on the nature of apriorism, one on the position of pure mathematics relative to the applied, and one on the indifference of mathematics and of essences in general with respect to the real.

1. "All cognition *a priori* of what is real is 'objectively universal'." Understanding of this universality is not a matter of statistics but of the essence of things. The triangle, the circle, the ellipse, for example, are in themselves characteristic singular ideal essences, and are "this side" of all forms and manifoldness of the real things directly contemplatable. All our understanding of the ideal objects of mathematics is thus experienceable. The fact that pure mathematics is applicable to real relations in nature assures us of the in-itself-ness of ideal objects (279). In fact, it assures us that "ideal Being functions within reality as a kind of basic structure. Consequently, the real world is in an inner dependence upon it" (280). And this relationship is not reversible. In a purely formal sense we may speak of a priority

of ideal Being over the real. However, ontologically speaking, this is not so. It is true, rather, that ideal Being is the lower or, as it were, the incomplete mode of Being. Only the real is the complete mode (282).

To be sure, no material triangle is mathematically exact; and neither are the laws of mechanics perfectly exact. It is impossible to deduce the empirical observations with exactitude. The reason for this is that empirical facts are never simple instances. Knowledge of the mathematically basic laws thus always presupposes a comprehension "this side of the real." All mathematical objects have an "ideal in-itself-ness," and its laws are understood "strictly *a priori*" (285).

2. In addition to the mathematical proper we encounter other forms of the ideal within the world of facts. Hartmann here gives Husserl credit for having done pioneer work by analyzing essences, laws of essences, and contexts of essences within the realm of the real (287). The crucial point is that these essences and their interrelations are not abstractions but are found in the nature of the real—as the 'essence' of the real. The ontological relation is that of the ideal being present in the real. This uniqueness of the phenomenological analysis is not abstraction but "positive comprehension of the essential structure" of the real (291).

The only and ultimate appeal to the certainty of the 'evidence' revealed in this "intuition of essences" is the "silently made presupposition [*die stillschweigende Voraussetzung*] that it itself is infallible" (294). However, at least a "relative criterion" of its truth is available; for, surely, where something is misunderstood, there must to begin with be something that can be misunderstood; and it must in the strict sense be something in itself.

3. In addition to the mathematical there are the laws of logic, which also are valid in the world we live in. To be sure, these laws are first of all (*von Hause aus*) laws of *ideal* Being. But their important aspect is that they are valid with respect to *real* Being. And this fact remains paradoxical so long as we understand the laws of logic to be merely laws of thinking. Their ideal in-itself-ness proves itself to be valid for both the structure of the real and that of our thoughts. "As ideal-ontological

basis of laws [*idealontologische Grundgesetzlichkeit*] the logical is determinative in two directions: in that of thinking and in that of real Being" (303).

The possibility of our natural sciences and of a coherent consciousness of reality in general is actual only on the presupposition that the laws of logic, as ideal laws of essences, are identical for thought and reality (304).

Values play a special role in our experience. They do not directly determine the real but are only indications of what is valuable and what is contrary to values. The mode of Being of values reveals that of ideal Being. Values are "the ideal objects for value-feeling acts." Reaction to values is "genuine vision [*Schau*] of an ideal Being in itself [*ideal Ansichsein*]."[32] The "realm of values" is thus a "homogeneous part" of ideal Being.

Ideal Being, then, can be found in the basic structure of everything real. But this does not mean that all ideal Being is in itself already part of the real structure of the world. And neither does all real structure in the world consist of ideal Being. Ontologically speaking, the whole sphere of the ideal is indifferent to the sphere of the real. But the two spheres do not exist independently, nor do we encounter them in mutual isolation. They are simply different modes of Being. What distinguishes them radically is the fact that everything real is individual, unique, destructible; whereas everything ideal is universal, returnable, always existing (*Grundlegung*, 314).

6. *The Criterion of Truth*

Cognition—be it *a priori* or *a posteriori*, be it a matter of judgment or of perception—requires a *criterion of truth* which assures us that what is given in consciousness corresponds to what is real in the object. Because subject and object are both embedded in Being, the truth is a transcendent relation having ontological status in itself (*Grundzüge*, 405ff.). It consists in a relation within Being. But only situations and subjects are real, and the difference between 'true' and 'not true' exists only with respect to cognition.

32. *Grundlegung*, 308. See Eva Hauel Cadwallader, *Searchlight on Values: Nicolai Hartmann's Twentieth-Century Value Platonism* (Washington, D.C.: University Press of America, 1984).

Skeptics have at all times regarded truth as merely relative; but they have overlooked the fact that it is opinion, not truth, which is relative, and that the exchange of opinion in order to convince others is in itself the strongest confirmation of man's belief in the unity and absoluteness of truth.

The validity of true insights is, of course, not restricted to an individual subject. On the contrary, a proposition that states what actually is the case remains true even if no one thinks it. Its validity is nontemporal, eternal, and absolute—although being aware of it is not.

We must realize, however, that truth is not its own criterion, and that to accept something as true is in itself no indication that it actually is true. But since truth is a relation between a person's belief and an objective reality, the criterion of truth can consist only in a special relation between a cognitive idea and the object cognized. That is, it can be only a relation in addition to the cognitive relation itself. The question is, How is this possible?

Since the criterion of truth is a possible corrective for an actual cognitive content, it must be independent of that content. And this is possible only if there are at least two ways of obtaining testimony of one and the same transcendent object without either being an absolute comprehension of it. But this implies that there is no absolute criterion of truth, and that absolute certainty is an ideal only (*Grundzüge*, 415 ff.).

In actual cognition we are rarely, if ever, concerned with isolated instances. What we have to deal with are larger contexts of experience and, ultimately, an all-encompassing context within which relative incongruities find their correction in the compensatory relations of heterogeneous sources of error. In the integrative process of the total context of experience this relative criterion of truth may approach absoluteness. In principle, however, "man can expect no more than an approach to certainty" ("*Erkenntnis*," 136).

The criterion of truth here meant lies neither in consciousness nor outside it, but lies within as well as outside it. As intrinsic to the complex content of cognition, it lies within consciousness. But insofar as that content pertains to the transcendent objects as a totality, the criterion is rooted in the objects. We must note, however, that the agreement or nonagreement of the content of consciousness with the transcendent objects can be ascertained within consciousness. No additional relationship is required. But a criterion is still needed.

The basis of such a criterion is given in the interrelations of *a priori* and *a posteriori* cognition (*Grundzüge*, 420–29). If in any given case these two modes of cognition are not in agreement—if, for example, the temporal sequence of sensory data is not in agreement with the larger context of *a priori* relationships, such as causal interrelations —then one of the modes of cognition must necessarily be in error. Since, because of the heterogeneity of their respective functions, the testimony of the senses and any *a priori* anticipation in terms of laws can hardly contain the same error, their mutual agreement is at least indicative of a transcendent agreement. That is to say, the agreement of the heterogeneous contents of the two modes of cognition is thus a positive—even if only a relative—criterion of truth.

But we must also take into consideration that in actuality we are never confronted by an isolated testimony of the senses nor by an isolated *a priori* insight. Both experiences occur only within a complex context of sense data and *a priori* interrelations; both are thus part of a potentially unlimited and uninterrupted cognitive context by virtue of which the relative truth-values of both modes of cognition at least approach the character of an absolute criterion of truth—but without ever actually attaining that status.

What is important here is that the cognizing subject is not only aware of the inadequacy of this criterion but is capable of striving for greater adequacy (430–36). Put differently, what is inadequately known need not be untrue; for even an incomplete or insufficient cognition may well be true, and the subject may recognize such insufficiency. The insufficiency itself means that the object is more than what is known of it, and all cognition has the tendency toward total comprehension of the object. This means that the subject has a knowledge of not knowing—a knowledge about the unknown—and this is a form of anticipatory knowledge which the subject experiences as a problem.

It is of the essence of all really secure knowledge that it is bound to both poles of cognition, the *a posteriori* and the *a priori*. In the coordination of them—and only in this—is rooted any possible criterion of truth. What is decisive here is the aspect of *a priori* cognition, for its principles are conditions not only of an actual experience but of all possible cognitions, and thus pertain even to what is as yet unknown. They form a kind of anticipation of possible objects whose reality remains questionable until sensory experience confirms it.

We must note also that *a priori* insights involve one another; that they are embedded in a *complexus* of relationships which is independent of the limits of any particular cognition and exceeds them. We face here not a construction on our part but the Being of relationships relative to which we have the freedom to accept or not to accept it. The facts transcend mere cognition and point to a realm of categories of Being within which the individual categories are conditioned by their relations to others.

But if a specific segment of the categories that are determinative of objects stands in mutual relationship to all other categories, then what is *a priori* knowable of any object involves aspects which are unknown and perhaps unknowable; this fact we recognize as an awareness of the irrational (437).

As cognition advances, the subject's conception or 'image' of the world—that which depends upon the subject—changes; but "the world remains the same" (437).

2

The Structure of the Real World

DECISIVE FOR HARTMANN'S PHILOSOPHICAL POSITION is that "the cognitive relation is basically a relation of Being—a real relation of real *Seiendem;* that it is but one of many relations through which consciousness is bound to a surrounding world. It is by no means the primary or basic relation but belongs with volition and action, with hope, fear, and worry to a group of transcendent acts with which it is firmly connected in our everyday living, and relative to which it attains independence only at the level of science.[1] In other words, cognition is a mode of relatedness of consciousness to something that in itself is real,[2] and any theory of cognition must ultimately be an ontology of cognition.[3]

From this perspective it is quite clear that something that exists can be an object for a subject by standing 'opposed' to it and that 'being

1. Nicolai Hartmann, *Neue Wege der Ontologie* 3d ed. (Stuttgart: Kohlhammer Verlag, 1949), 107.

2. Nicolai Hartmann, "Wie ist kritische Ontologie überhaupt möglich?" in *Kleinere Schriften* 3: 269.

3. *Grundzüge*, 16. For a commentary on this interpretation, see John E. Smith, "Hartmann's New Ontology," in *Review of Metaphysics* 7 (1954): 583–601. See also Ingetrud Pape, "Wirklichkeit—dem Begriff und der Sache nach," in *Symposium zum Gedenken an Nicolai Hartmann* (Göttingen: Vandenhoeck & Ruprecht, 1982), 24–39.

in itself' means nothing other than being independent of the subject (Hartmann, *Grundlegung*, 153). But it is the unique character of the world that it encompasses *Dasein* and *Sosein*—existence and specific characteristics (91). And this fact is basic to any analysis of categories, for categories are not concepts of the understanding—as Kant had it —but are determinants of the specifics of Being.

The world we live in is stratified in its unity. We can readily discern strata of material reality, of organismic existence, of consciousness, and of rational or spiritual Being. It is crucial for cognition to determine "if and to what extent the strata are dependent upon one another, and what the nature of this dependency is. If we are successful in demonstrating a connectedness of the strata, and the specifics of that connection, then we also understand something of the integrated unity of the world" (*Neue Wege*, 50). That the stratification is real cannot be denied. Human beings are proof of it. We ourselves are stratified reality.

1. The General Concept of Categories

As Hartmann sees it, categories are "the silent presuppositions" that we accept in our interpretations, explanations, and evaluations of objects. Kant had specifically identified twelve. Hegel had many more. But it can readily be shown that there is an as yet undetermined number, for every field of inquiry has its own categories.[4] And this means that the analysis of categories must be concerned with the *structure of Being*—not simply with our modes of thinking.

What makes the analysis of categories possible is the basic principle of all *a priori* cognition, which, as we have seen, asserts that the conditions of the *possibility of experience* are at the same time the conditions of the *possibility of the objects of experience*.

Since the world consists of integrated structures at different levels of Being, it has always been tempting to look for its basic categories either at the lowest or at the highest level. The result has been the development of speculative forms of materialism, idealism, rationalism, and theism. But in their one-sided orientations, all of these have been distortions of reality. The *new* ontology, Hartmann insists, must

---

4. Nicolai Hartmann, "Ziele und Wege der Kategorialanalysis," in *Kleinere Schriften* 1: 91f.

break with all of this, and it must also break with the tradition of constructing speculative systems. Its first task must be to clarify the essential character of each of the interrelated strata, and then to deal with their interrelations. For this purpose the traditional categories of form-matter, potency-act, idea-thing, *essentia-ens,* and others are hardly adequate. To realize that the unity of the world is a specific order of interrelated strata is but the beginning of an understanding of the whole.

It is tempting to regard the stratification of reality as the result of a development—as a genesis. But the riddle of the origin of the world— of this universe of galaxies and cosmic interrelations, of plants and animals and human beings—is shrouded in a mystery that is far removed from what is actually given. It is and remains one of the unsolvable metaphysical problems.

The stratification of Being itself, however, is a fact, and is observable in the world around us. The order of rank from the merely material to the spiritual is undeniable, and an analysis of categories must clarify the relationships involved. Hartmann's attempt to do so is developed in great detail in *Der Aufbau der Realen Welt,*[5] which, in effect, is the development of a new type of ontology—of an ontology whose first task is to clarify whatsoever exists *as existing;* and whose second task is to deal with the modes of Being of the existent and with their interrelations. We must keep in mind, however, that the categories pertain not to *Dasein*—not to existence as such; but to the *Sosein* of what exists—to the forms, structures, and contexts that are characteristic of what is real (*Aufbau,* 15).

2. The Fundamental Categories

We encounter what is real in the highly complex sphere of our everyday living. We experience it as something that presses in on us and is important to us. It is only natural, therefore, that the first group of categories include the categories of things and of our practical concerns; and that by inquiring into the constitutive principles of Being as thus encountered we inquire also as to how far these principles are specifically related to our everyday activities.

5. (Meisenheim: Westkulturverlag Anton Hain, 2d ed. 1949. [First edition: Berlin: de Gruyter, 1940.]) Hereafter referred to as *Aufbau.*

Two characteristics are common to all categories of Being: They are *universal,* and they have the character of *determinants* (42). This means that in some respects categories are similar to essences. They have no temporal existence and are transindividual, encompassing an infinity of specific manifestations. But they must not be confused with ideal Being. The latter has specific categories of its own.

Although categories are determinants of Being, they do not determine in the way in which causes do; neither do they determine as grounds of reason, and especially not as purposes (66–78). Instead, categories are principles that have no independent existence but "have a being only for others." Their 'being' is completely contained in the determinateness or characteristics of the concrete *Seiende*—of what exists.

Various philosophical 'isms' have singled out specific groups of categories as determining all phenomena, no matter how heterogeneous these are. Materialism thus submits life, mental activity, and everything else to the category 'matter'. Biologism imposes the categories of organismic existence upon the phenomena of consciousness and of spiritual existence. And psychologism interprets morality, cognition, and social and historical relationships in terms of the categories of the mental. But 'isms' such as these, and others that might be mentioned, distort the picture of the actual structure of the world we live in.[6]

A serious investigation of that structure must also reject any attempt to explain the lower strata in terms of the higher, or to impose teleological or spiritual categories upon the merely mechanical aspects of reality. A metaphysic "from above" is just as bad as a metaphysic "from below" (*Aufbau*, 85–97). Our first task must therefore be to examine the categories that are characteristic of each stratum of Being. Only when this has been done is it possible to understand the relationships of the categories of the various strata with respect to one another.

3. Changes in the Structure of the Strata

What, specifically, is meant by categories?

It is Hartmann's position that any theory of categories based upon

6. See Heinz Heimsoeth, "Zur Geschichte der Kategorienlehre," in *Nicolai Hartmann—Der Denker und sein Werk*, ed. Heinz Heimsoeth and Robert Heiss (Göttingen: Vandenhoeck and Ruprecht, 1952), 144–172.

a "principle of formalism" has from the very beginning the disadvantage of not being able to deal effectively with the content of our actual experience (98–106). When one asserts that as far as the categories are concerned *everything is mere form,* one transgresses the natural limits of fundamental cognition. The philosophy of Duns Scotus, asserting that in the last analysis purely formal elements constitute individuality, illustrates the point. The inevitable result is that the whole range of the limitless manifoldness of real instances must be duplicated in the purely formal realm of ideas, and such duplication is essentially no longer a reference to principles. It has completely absorbed the concrete. But even for Kant, space, time, and the categories are "pure forms," and the empirical imperative of morality is a merely formal law.

Hartmann concedes that there are manifold formal elements in the categories; but, he maintains, the categories themselves cannot be reduced to what is merely formal. This is so with respect to the categories of Being as well as with respect to the categories of cognition. The issue is not one of "form and content" but one of "form and matter"; for at the various levels of Being specific aspects of the substrata are constitutive in the same sense as are the categories, and these aspects must be taken into consideration when we deal with what is encountered in the world. There we find a manifoldness of different strata which involve a plurality of categories.

The categories of Being are not 'applied' to what is encountered in the world. They are the determinants of the concrete reality and, in this sense, are inherent in the things themselves. Only the categories of cognition are 'applied'. This distinction between categories of Being and categories of cognition is crucial for Hartmann's position. And we must guard against the widespread idea that categories are concepts. To be sure, we do have concepts of categories, but our concepts of them are not the categories themselves. They are merely attempts to fixate the categories definitionally.

The categories themselves are principles that are determinative of objects and events, and are therefore necessarily contained in them. It is not in the power of things to be otherwise than they are. Nor is it in the power of the cognizing subject to comprehend things otherwise than as determined by the categories intrinsic to them. Concepts are ontologically secondary. As determinants of things, the categories are primary. Aside from the things which they determine, there is nothing to which the categories belong or to which they can be related. To hold that not only the cognition of objects but the objects themselves have their determining principles in the subject is the basic prejudice of all forms of idealism (111–19).

Hartmann's thesis is that categories cannot be derived from the forms of the understanding (as Kant tried), for they are determinants intrinsic to the *content* of cognition and can be identified only as structural aspects of the objects themselves and their interrelations— of aspects that are independent of the degree of our comprehension of them. Insofar as the categories are to be known at all, they must be seen as the intrinsic determinants of the things themselves (144). This means that only an analysis of the structure of objects will reveal the categories that are intrinsic to them.

What alone makes an analysis of these categories possible is, of course, the basic principle of all *a priori* cognition, referred to in chapter 1; this principle entails a position "this side of idealism and realism."[7]

The fact that in cognition the subject and the object stand in opposition to each other cannot be abrogated. But, as we have seen, this opposition is ontologically not fundamental. The one real world is a world of things and persons, and the sphere of cognition is but one partial aspect of that reality—a specific relation of *Seiendem* with *Seiendem*. To be sure, there are different levels of cognition, ranging from mere sense impressions to conceptual interpretations; but all of them are modes of comprehending objects that exist in themselves. In this respect, the ontological orientation of our ordinary everyday view of the world and of our practical endeavors fuses unchanged and without specific demarcation into the scientific or purely cognitive attitude. The subject-object relation remains what it is, and the common function of the various levels of cognition is but to comprehend what is given.

At the same time, however, the subject is spontaneous with respect to the images and concepts of the structural patterns found. Perception, for example, individualizes. It divides the continuum of the *Seiende* and brings about a kind of isolation of the individual objects. Scientific cognition, on the other hand, with its emphasis on concepts, laws, and principles, opposes such isolation by stressing *continua* and attempt-

---

7. Nicolai Hartmann, "Diesseits von Idealismus und Realismus," in *Kant-Studien* 29 (1924): 160–206. Also reprinted in *Kleinere Schriften*.

ing to reconstruct the given as a whole. But only where the different modes of cognition are interrelated—only where they supplement one another—is the one-sidedness overcome. And in this supplementary relationship alone is there a chance for cognition to become a criterion of truth—even if only a relative one (*Aufbau*, 170ff.).

Cognition entails an internal relation also with respect to ideal Being. It consists not only in the fact that all cognition of reality contains an element of ideality, but also in the fact that even the naive consciousness of situations reveals characteristics pertaining to real things. Even what Hume called 'association' is far from being explainable as a product of association. It contains *a priori* elements which can be directly discerned in relations such as similarity and contrast, and in spatial and temporal associations.[8]

At the highest level of cognition, an essential lawfulness prevails—a lawfulness pertaining exclusively to the context of the experiential content. To be sure, thinking is a process and, as such, has its own laws; but what is characteristic of thinking is that it is simultaneously under two orders of law: the laws of the psychological process of thinking, and the laws of the content of thinking, i.e., the laws of logic. The two sets of laws do by no means always harmonize. They are generally rather in conflict. But the laws of logic can have truth-value only when the correctness of an argument reflects the actual relations of the *Seiende* referred to in the premises. This means that the laws of logic must ultimately be grounded in basic laws of Being. To put it differently: The relation of universals and particulars, upon which the laws of logic depend, must be a relation within Being (*Aufbau*, 172–218).

'Nature' and 'Spirit' are two heterogeneous realms of the *Seienden* that are superposed within one and the same real world. And that world involves at least four levels of reality: the spiritual, the mental, the organismic, and the purely material. This distinction reveals a relationship of superposition—a difference in structural elevation, in laws, and in categorial forms.

4. Categorial Laws

A theory of categories that does justice to the phenomena must at least recognize the distinctions—but must also recognize the interrelations of Being that transcend them.

8. *Grundzüge*, 48, 80, 209; chap. 1.

For Hartmann, there are only three 'cuts' (*Einschnitte*) in the real world. The most obvious one is that between nature and spirit. The great riddle here is how this 'cut' can go through the center of the human being without destroying it (196).

A second 'cut' is that between lifeless matter and living organic nature.

The third 'cut' is that between spiritual Being and mental acts.

We thus find four main levels of what is real, and understanding the unity of the world can but mean to understand the world in its structure and stratification. What makes this possible is that, from structure to structure, we find the same relation of the higher stratum resting upon, and being conditioned by, the next lower. Despite this fact, however, the higher stratum has in each case its own mode of Being and its own type of laws. This relation of the strata characterizes the basic unity of the real world. In other words, the structure of the real world is a sequence of supportive strata—each stratum having its own laws and its specific categorial structure.

There are, however, also categories of such generality that they are common to all strata. Their ontological significance lies in the fact that they are the unitary basis of the real world as a whole. They are the "fundamental categories" that are basic to both the real and the ideal worlds. And these categories are the special concern of a universal theory of categories.

The categorial manifoldness of the world is evident in two respects: in the distinctness of the various strata and in their rank. In this structure, cognition is ontologically secondary. It presupposes the *Seiende* that is its object; but it is itself also a *Seiendes sui generis* and can occur only in strata of a specific height—i.e., only where there is a consciousness which transcends mere mental associations. After all, cognition is a specific function of spiritual Being, and must be understood as included in that specific stratum of the world.

5. Categorial Stratification

In *Der Aufbau der realen Welt* Hartmann begins his analysis with the antithetical categories encountered at all levels of reality—categories that together form a broad basis of possibilities of existence. He distinguishes two groups of such categories. Within each group the categories are appositional but not contradictory. Both members of the opposing pairs are positive and form genuine polarities such that between the members of each pair a whole dimension of gradations is possible (223).

The following list illustrates Hartmann's point, but the groupings are only tentative and may require modification.

> I. 1. principle–*concretum*
>   2. structure–*modus*
>   3. form–matter
>   4. inner–outer
>   5. determination–dependence
>   6. quality–quantity
>
> II. 7. unity–manifoldness
>   8. harmony–conflict
>   9. opposition–dimension
>   10. discretion–continuity
>   11. substratum–relation
>   12. element–structure

These categories are so related that in every pair each category presupposes its counterpart, and is presupposed by it. Form, for example, presupposes matter, and matter is what it is only as matter of some form. Dependence presupposes determination, and determination is what it is only with respect to something which is dependent. Similar relationships exist with respect to all other pairs given (230–31).

In addition to this correlation there is also the inner connectedness of categories in the form of a transition from any particular category to its correlate. There are two types of such transition. One is the relativization of the opposites with respect to each other. It is exemplified in the case of matter and form, for all form can itself be matter for a higher form, and all matter can be form for a lower matter. "But the contrast of matter and form remains perfectly preserved in this kind of relativization" (233). An atom can thus be matter for a molecule, but it also is form for its nucleus and electrons.

In the real world there thus prevails a multidimensional manifoldness from the lowest stratum on up to the highest forms of spiritual Being. This manifoldness constitutes the countless variations within our world. It also exemplifies the manifold interrelations (237). Recognizing these interrelations is the first step leading into the intercate-gorial relationships characteristic of the structure of the world (240).

The table of categories (given above) already shows clearly a strict correlativity of categories. There is also a second type of inner rela-tionship of the categories, which consists in the steady transition from one extreme to another. But this transition is nothing other than a relativization of the opposites with respect to each other. It is a rela-tionship which occurs in two forms. In one form the relationship is such that one of the opposites remains constant while the other dimin-ishes. In the relationship of matter and form, for example, we find a stratification in which the absoluteness of the contrast ceases while the direction of the relationship remains constant. This kind of rela-tionship also prevails with respect to structure and element; for every structure can itself be an element of a more inclusive structure, and any element can itself be already a structure (249). "The sequential character of such relationships is actually a basic principle that is de-terminative of the structure of the real world in all its strata and as a whole. It is the principle in accordance with which the manifoldness of the *Seiende* is stratified throughout" (250).

The situation is similar with respect to the relations of determina-tion–dependence and unity–manifoldness.

The second type of transition is one of one-sided diminution. It is exemplified in the contrast of substratum and relation (251). The boundary case is the substratum in the narrower sense, which itself is not relational and can be only a relatum for possible relations.

In considering the various types of interrelationships of the cate-gories we must keep in mind that all *Seiendes* has two "Seinsmomente" —two aspects of Being—*Dasein* and *Sosein*. "Every *Dasein* of some-thing is itself also a *Sosein* of it; and all *Sosein* of something is itself also a *Dasein* of it. This relationship is the inner law of the aspects of Being—of the *Seinsmomente*. It may be formulated as the continuously moved identity of *Dasein* and *Sosein* within the whole of the context of Being" (254).

When one considers only an isolated part of *Seiendem*, then *Sosein* and *Dasein* are quite distinct. But we must keep in mind that "what-soever exists has its own *what* in and through which it *is*—and each *what* is in its own way something that *exists*."[9]

9. *Grundlegung*, chap. 19; especially p. 136.

We must note that only the interrelationship of all the categorial pairs listed above determines a given *concretum*. In the analysis of reality it is impossible to discern a single category without bringing a whole series of others into the picture; for only together do they determine anything which is concretely given. Only together do they constitute the categorial basis of all *Seienden,* and only in what is concretely given are the categories interrelated. They have no connection with one another except as common determinants of what is given as a *concretum* (*Aufbau*, 264). In themselves they have no existence. And they are not the implicates of some logical or epistemological principle.

6. Modification of the Contrasts of Being in the Strata

Categories serve as determinants of the various strata of Being. Some of them do so without being appreciably modified from stratum to stratum. Others reflect even the slightest difference in the characteristics of different strata. But it is a fact that categories do transcend individual strata, and that some recur in most or even in all of them (*Aufbau*, 267). The relation of 'principle' and '*concretum*', encountered at all strata with slight modifications, illustrates the point. But the term 'principle' must not be identified with the term 'universal'. It must be taken in the sense of Kant's "highest principle" as the condition of the possibility of what is given.

Even then, however, it is never just one principle that is the complete determinative ground of what is concretely given. All principles are interrelated in determining what is real, and the concretely given must not be confused with material reality. The strata of organismic existence, of the mental, and of the ideal must also be taken into account. A modal analysis will then show that the mode of Being and the intermodal relationships, despite some variations, are fundamentally the same in the various strata. This is true, in particular, of the modes of Being of reality and ideality. The intermodal relationships are not limited to the materially or spatially given (275f.).

We must note also that relation is a fundamental category, and that all isolation is secondary and exists only in cognitive abstraction. Within each stratum and in the interrelationships of the strata in their totality the primary fact is *context*. We find it in the interrelations of structures and forms no less than in the interdependencies of the various strata, and in the relationships of the real and the ideal (280f.).

Within the context of the various strata we encounter that which offers itself as a stratified dimensional "*something*." It is here that the problem of substance arises, for we are here concerned with what persists as a basic element in the various relations. That is, we are here concerned with the substrata of the relations. But we must not confuse substrata with material substances. At the level of the mental, for example, all materiality ceases—along with spatiality. Mental acts and their contents constitute a complexus of relationships that is different in kind from mere matter, and that arises above and beyond all materiality. It is and remains an irreducible 'other'.

Every real structure is internally a matter of relations. Hartmann distinguishes three types of such relations: (1) the rigid relations that constitute and assure the constancy of what is given as a type; (2) the loose relationships that differ from case to case and determine in each case the individuality of the given; and (3) the broad relationships that connect the *Seiende* of heterogeneous strata, and which can themselves be either typical of a group or unique for an individual (283).

Let us consider in this perspective the stratification in its totality as encountered in the world. At every level, matter and form are so interrelated that the same *Seiende* is matter in relation to higher forms, and is form in relation to lower structures. Hartmann speaks of this interrelation as the "law of over-forming" (*Gesetz der Überformung*) (287). We must note, however, that in the real world the sequence of matter and form is not schematically simple. We find here 'cuts' (*Einschnitte*) where the relationship of form and matter is interrupted by the appearance of new strata. The most important of such cuts is that between merely organic and mental existence. Although in the organism the dynamic structure of atoms and molecules is preserved, the acts and contents characteristic of conscious existence and of mental life generally no longer contain the spatial forms and processes of merely organismic existence. Here a new sequence of over-forming begins— one which, in effect, is a superstructure resting upon the organic.

A similar cut is encountered when we consider the mental and the spiritual strata. The mental acts themselves, though indispensable to the result, are themselves not elements of the content of language, knowledge, law, and art. Although supported by, and in essential respects dependent upon, mental acts, the spiritual and cultural realities with which these acts are concerned are not reducible to the merely mental: The history of culture proves it. Surely the greatest transformation of the concept of form has occurred in our natural sciences. The *substantial forms* of the old physics, which never quite accounted for processes in nature, have given way to the conception of *laws* that are determinative of the processes in question (288).

It is a truism that no structure or world can be understood as mere unity, for unity is an empty concept without its counterpart of the many. Not even a point, as an inkmark on paper, is a mere unity. Only unity and manifoldness together *are* something. And only in this togetherness do the unities themselves become manifold—one unity differing from all others. This manifoldness of the types of unities is characteristic of the world as a whole.

Even more important than this is the fact that all changes, processes, and events in the world are themselves unities whose character is best expressed in the laws that govern them. Unities in this dynamic sense are encountered not only at the level of mechanical and organismic processes. They are in evidence also in the development of a human being from its conception to its death, including its mental and spiritual development, as exemplified in the process of history as a whole (293f.).

The dynamic unities of the purely material world are characteristically mere structures. The interrelations of their parts is no special problem. The unity of living beings, however—in their ontogenetic development, and the unity of the species despite the changing individuals representing it—involves a special problem. Even more mysterious is the situation at the level of consciousness, which, as far as its content is concerned, is a ceaseless stream of events, of impressions and thoughts, and yet in itself is a unity—my consciousness or yours. Not less mysterious is the unity of the person as an acting and morally responsible agent. Finally, that which for perception is but the unity of an image is for comprehension the unity of a concept and becomes the unity of a theory for a whole field of inquiry. And all of these strata have their specific categories (297).

Among the categories which change least from stratum to stratum, Hartmann identifies direction and continuity as dimensions of the given. Actually, however, every dimension is already a continuum. But it is also more than a continuum, for it is a substratum. In the qualitative relationships, for example, to which all measurements and mathematical determinations pertain, the dimensions presuppose nonmathematical substrata, such as distance, duration, velocity, and weight.

That is, behind the dimensions of quantitative determinations lie the realities that are measurable.

Furthermore, it is typical of all *Seiendes* that there are no isolated dimensions. All manifoldness in the world is multidimensional, the interrelations of its components being disclosed in the interrelations of the constitutive categories (302).

7. Determination and Dependence

Determination is a form of relation. At the same time, however, it is more than a mere relation. There are two aspects to it: one that determines and one that is being determined. The most important forms of determination are the patterns of series in which the determination is being transmitted from one member to another, and in which the direction of the determination is preserved in the continuous transition from earlier to later. The determination of this kind is exemplified in the connectedness of the *concreta* such that one exists 'because' of the other (*Aufbau*, 309).

As a rule, however, the ontic relationships are such that the determination depends upon a whole sequence of factors which function as codeterminants. Only when all of them are given—i.e., when the series of determinants is complete—does what is determined by them come about. And nothing that is thus determined can be other than it is.[10]

Perceptual experience reveals what is 'actual' but does so without revealing the necessity for its being what it is. Even an experience involving the interrelations of events still has far to go to comprehend the necessity behind the actual.

Of all types of determination we know immediately only two: the causal nexus in the realm of the physically real, and purposiveness in the realm of our own actions. In general, however, the modes of determination are more diversified. We can distinguish at least eight of them (*Aufbau*, 314–16).

1. The simplest of the modes is the physical nexus of causality
   —the dependence of what is later upon what is earlier in an

10. Hartmann gives a detailed analysis of this fact in *Möglichkeit und Wirklichkeit* (Berlin: Walter de Gruyter & Co., 1938). See especially p. 205: "The 'adequacy' of the real ground is the very same as the completeness or 'totality' of the real conditions."

immediate time sequence. Since for every cause there must be a preceding one, the causal sequence comes out of an infinite past and moves into an infinite future.

2. At any given stratum of reality there occurs also a determination known as reciprocal action of the simultaneously existing realities.

3. In the realm of organisms we find a subtle purposiveness of the partial functions with respect to one another. It is exemplified in the self-regulations of the whole, and in the development of the organism from an initial *complexus* of genes. Although this form of determination looks very much like purposive determination, the purpose-setting consciousness is lacking.[11]

4. There are mental events with their progression and mutual interconnectedness. Their determining factors emerge out of an unconscious background. When this emergence comes into consciousness, it takes on the form of purposive action. How it determines anything prior to becoming conscious activity is as yet unknown.

5. At the level of personal spirit we find the finalistic *nexus* proper —i.e., we find purposiveness. It begins with the projection of a goal, proceeds to the choice of means, and ends in the actual process of realizing the goal. Since the first two phases of this process are typically events in consciousness, the finalistic *nexus* of determination can occur only where a goal-setting and means-selecting consciousness is present.

6. Among the many forms of spiritual determination, the determination through values is perhaps the most unique and noteworthy, for values themselves are not real powers. From them there proceeds only an 'ought-to'—a challenge or demand (*eine Anforderung*). Values thus determine only indirectly, and only insofar as a real will decides in their favor.[12]

11. For a discussion of these problems, see W. H. Werkmeister, *A Philosophy of Science* (New York: Harper & Bros., 1940; paperback reprint, Lincoln: University of Nebraska Press, 1965), chap. 10: "Interpretations of Life," 317–65.

12. Hartmann is here in essential agreement with Max Scheler's position as developed in *Der Formalismus in der Ethik und die Materiale Wertethik*, 4th ed., in Max Scheler, *Gesammelte Werke* (Bern, n.d.). For a discussion of Scheler's point of view, see W. H. Werkmeister, *Historical Spectrum of Value Theories*,

7. Determination through values thus presupposes still another mode of determination: the decision of the will for or against a demand; for or against an *ought*. This new factor consists in the self-determination or autonomy of the will.

8. In the life of a community and in history there are even more complex forms of determination. Here some of the lower modes interpenetrate at least in part and are often in conflict with the higher ones. The goals that human beings set for themselves and on behalf of which they take the initiative are not always harmonious or realizable: Conflicts prevail. The tendency of human beings to direct and form the historical process is, nevertheless, an essential factor within that process.

But it is characteristic that from organismic reality on up, not all conflicts are resolved, and that incalculably much is destroyed by inner conflict. As far as categories are concerned, this means that harmony is something other than conflict; that both stand in opposition in the world and tend to replace each other. In a very naive form, Empedocles expressed this fact when he declared "hate and love" to be the moving forces in the world (*Aufbau*, 324). Here the contrast of the two categories is acknowledged.

It must be noted, however, that this conflict increases notably in the higher strata and that, corresponding to the increasing magnitude of this conflict, higher forms of unity emerge. But not all conflicts are dissolved in harmony. Especially in the realm of human existence—in the prevailing ethos, in history—no resolution of the conflicts is given. Its realization is a task for man.

8. Element and Structure

It is clear from the outline just given that in the higher strata of reality, articulation increases and ultimately dominates (*Aufbau*, 329–41). This domination depends on the occurrence of relatively closed structures that, despite their inclusion in the ongoing process, have a certain independence relative to that process. The facts are best described as an interrelation of element and structure.

---

vol. 1 (Lincoln, Neb.: Johnson Publishing Co., 1970), chap. 11: "The 'Emotional Intuitionism' of Max Scheler," 287–313.

Within a given structure, the elements themselves are not as determinative as are their interrelations. A structure is always a system of relations and determinations. All natural structures, however, are integrated processes; and since processes do not occur without forces behind them, all structures in nature are also systems of dynamic impulses and drives. In such structures the elements are as much components of the processes as they are merely structural parts. Elements should therefore not be thought of merely in analogy to material particles. The universal mode of Being is actually a Becoming. There are no absolutely static structures in the world. All actualities are structured processes or components of processes, and are results of the driving powers that determine the processes. The facts are obvious in the case of organic structures whose special mode of Being is the process of life. But the facts are clear also in the higher structures of mental life—of consciousness, of the ethos of man, of communal living, and of history. In all of these strata, the unity of structures rests upon the interplay of manifold and partially opposed tendencies. But the way in which a process-structure maintains itself within specific limits of stability differs greatly from stratum to stratum.

As far as purely material reality is concerned, modern science has revealed that even atoms are complex dynamic systems whose external forces are the internal forces of molecules. At the molecular level the equilibrium of forces is quite different from that of the inner atomic forces. But the purely physicochemical structures are also exemplified in our solar system and, beyond this, in the galaxies and systems of galaxies. The sequential order of such dynamic structures gives us a certain integrative view of the universe that despite all manifoldness of structures is relatively uniform as a dynamic whole.

The living organism, however, is a structure of an entirely different kind. It is a structure of processes determined in a radically new way. Let's face it: Life is a deep riddle. It has the form of a process with its own inner periodicity of beginning and end. Basic here is the process of metabolism—a process in and through which the organism maintains itself. But metabolism itself is the counterplay or mutual opposition of two processes: one a building up, the other a retrenching—two processes that are complementary functions within a unitary event. In fact, the life of an organism depends on the complex equilibrium of many interacting partial processes that are characteristic of life; and their interactions depend on the self-acting regulation of the equilibrium of the whole.[13] The organismic structure itself is stratified. The smallest units of anything living approximate the magnitude of large molecules. Even unicellular organisms already involve an amazing differentiation of fundamental structures. But beyond this, the partial functions which various cells perform in multicellular organisms is indicative of a new kind of determination. Still another, and even more important, kind of stratification is manifest in the role that individuals play in the 'life of the species'. This superposed structure, the species, has no visible form nor is it a system of forms. The species is, however, a system of processes. The elements here are the living individuals whose birth, development, and death provide the stability of the life of the species.

In the realm of nature, structures thus have a certain predominance, but it is otherwise in the higher strata of Being. Man's consciousness and, beyond mere consciousness, the moral person are characterized by their inwardness, their unity and determination, and by their relationship to the surrounding world—all of which involves more than mere structure.

Above the stratum of the individual human being we again find real structures, and structures of two main types: the type of community and the type of the objective spirit. In the community the individual persons with all their manifold tendencies, interests, demands, and dependencies are the elements. But the form-giving reality that raises the community above the level of a biological species consists in morality, law, the state, and all other forms of social development. All of them are created by human beings as spiritual beings.[14]

9. External and Internal Forces

In the stratification of reality the external forces of the lower existents are at the same time internal forces of the higher structures (*Aufbau*, 341). This is quite obviously true at the level of atoms and molecules. But it is also true at the level of organismic existence where the individual cells are at the same time essential inner functions of the multicellular organism, and where the individuals, through generating new individuals, perform the most important inner function of the

13. For a detailed analysis of organismic existence see *Philosophie der Natur*, part 3, chaps. 45–64.
14. A detailed analysis will be given in chap. 5.

life of the species. In the human community the external actions of the individuals, although not determinative of the social structure as a whole, obviously stand in unique interactions with one another in such a way that the individuals contribute to the whole, and that the whole affects the actions of the individuals. In other words, there is a particular form of interaction such that the individuals, as internal factors, do not simply determine the structure, but instead the structure retains an independence that is broadly determinative for individuals.

But there also exist more precise forms of the inner-outer relationship of elements and structure: the living organism, for example. The development of the individual in embryogenesis is a highly complex process that is uniquely directed from within. The specific pattern of chromosomes, as given in the DNA molecule, is something other than a mere collocation of individual factors and forces. What is still largely unknown is how such internal determinative factors can form a unity *sui generis* that cannot be dissolved into individual elements without destroying the whole (347).

At the level of human existence the 'inner world' centers in the actuality of self-consciousness (348–50). It is a limited but genuine inner aspect that directly discloses the manifold relations in which the personal self stands to the external world. These relations consist in experimenting, in hoping and fearing, in loving and hating, in yearning and desiring, in willing and acting. In brief, the unity of the self consists in a whole series of transcendent acts. Orienting oneself in an environment, comprehending and mastering actual situations, assuming responsibility and accountability, and all other moral value aspects are objects given in an awareness of what is external to oneself. But the inner reality of man's consciousness is in itself a sphere in which what it includes has its own mode of Being. It is of a nonspatial, nonmaterial, dynamic nature. And each human being has his/her own inner reality that never passes over into someone else's mental life. All relations among individuals must occur indirectly via the 'externalization' of what is 'inner'. No one can transmit his feelings to another if the other cannot on his own part feel the same way. No one can communicate his thoughts to another if the other is not able to attain those thoughts in his own thinking, for understanding another person is but to think that person's thoughts too. However, the inner reality of the individual transcends itself in its actions. It extends itself in its 'externalization' into the world. In the life of the community, however, the structure as a whole affects the individual's 'inner' reality through its norms and demands. In the last analysis, what is decisive is one's place within the context of the real world (352).

10. The Problem of Categorial Lawfulness

After a discussion of specific categories—such as positive-negative, identity-difference, general-individual, and quality-quantity—Hartmann turns to an important analysis of what he calls "the categorial laws" (*Aufbau*, 412ff.).

His first point is that "categorial laws themselves have the character of categories," but that, in a sense, they are more fundamental than even the basic categories of Being. The reason for this is that categorial laws are primarily laws of the categories themselves and are not directly laws of the concrete content of experience. That is, the categories themselves stand under laws in the same sense in which what is concretely given stands under categories. In other words, the categorial laws are principles of principles and do not directly affect the basic relation of principles to what is concretely given.

But since the categorial laws are what is universal in the categories, they cannot be discerned without a prior analysis of the categories; for what is universal with respect to the categories can be seen only when the categories are considered in their manifoldness and their mutual relations, and these cannot be known *a priori*. Under these circumstances, Hartmann insists, it may not be surprising if a proof proper of the categorial laws cannot as yet be provided; only progress in the analysis of the categories themselves may lead to such a proof.

The realm of categories is a multidimensional manifoldness and cannot be reduced to a simple lineal schema. We must take into consideration not only the differences in 'height' of the various strata of Being, but also the coordination of the categories within the strata of the same height. In the superposition of the strata a law of the stratification of categories can thus be seen—a law that, on its part, is also rooted in a principle.

In considering the different interrelations that are obviously involved, four principles of categorial laws may be discerned (418f.):

1. *The Principle of Validity.* Categories are what they are because they are principles of something concrete. They are nothing without the concreta, and the latter are nothing without them.

As principles the categories are determinative of the specific aspects of the concreta and of their interrelations.

2. *The Principle of Coherence.* Categories do not exist individually or by themselves, but only within the context of a categorial stratum. They are bound and codetermined by the context of a given stratum. In their interrelations they determine the characteristics of any given stratum.

3. *The Principle of Stratification.* Categories of the lower strata are largely retained as supportive of the higher strata. But specific categories of the higher strata are not contained in the lower ones.

4. *The Principle of Dependence.* Dependence is one-sidedly that of the higher categories upon the lower. But this is only a partial dependency that assures the independence of the higher categories within broad areas. Each stratum has its own characteristic modes of determination which can be neither explained by nor reduced to the modes of determination of the lower strata.

The first of these principles pertains to the Being of the categories, asserting that this Being consists in nothing other than being principles "for something"—for some concretum that because of the categories is what it is. The relationship is irreversible. The categories make concreta determinate.

The second principle expresses the fact that various categories have validity for different strata of reality. Categorial validity is a determination of concreta that is irreversible as well as irresistible. The categories of any particular stratum of reality determine everything but only what belongs to that stratum. The princple thus entails a specific limitation of the validity of categories. But this fact is by no means self-evident and can be substantiated only by a further analysis of the interrelations of the various strata of reality.

The stratification of reality as a whole is not determined by the categories that are specifically valid for each stratum, for what is involved here is a "categorial coherence" that transcends individual strata. An understanding of the stratification can therefore be attained only through an analysis of the intertwining of differently dimensioned determinations.

Let us remember that the categories of any particular stratum are closely interrelated. Each category is "bound to" all other categories of the same stratum and does not exist in isolation. Hartmann states their relationship in four specific laws (433f.).

1. *The law of connectedness.* The categories of any given stratum do not individually determine the concreta of that stratum, but do so only together in categorial interconnection. The categories constitute a unity of determination in which some individual categories may well be more prominent than are others, but no isolated categories determine what exists.
2. *The law of the unity of a stratum.* The categories of any given stratum form within themselves an indissoluble unity. There are no isolated categories, and their joined determination of the concreta is rooted in their own interrelations.
3. *The law of the wholeness of the strata.* The unity of a given stratum is not a mere sum of its categories but is an indivisible totality that has priority over the individual categories involved. Its wholeness consists in the codeterminateness of all its members.
4. *The law of implication.* The wholeness of a stratum recurs in every one of its members. That is, each individual category, although it has its own specific character, implicates the other categories of the same stratum. The coherence of the stratum is completely reflected in every member of it as well as in it as a whole.

Some explanatory comments about these four laws may well be in order.

The 'law of connectedness' asserts the basic interrelations of the categories which together determine the concreta of any particular stratum of reality. The law itself can be fully understood only by way of a thorough analysis of the concretely real in each stratum. Such analyses will be given in detail in chapters 5 and 6. We must note here, however, that the connectedness of the categories in the determination of concreta pertains only to what is a matter of principle as far as individual instances are concerned. It is what is common to all actual existents within a given stratum and therefore gives each stratum the categorially unified character that differentiates it from every other stratum. The law of connectedness is thus in effect the *basic* law of all stratification (436ff.).

According to the second law, the unity of any particular stratum of reality is what it is because of the basic relatedness of the categories that together determine the concreta of the stratum (440ff.). There are no isolated categories within any stratum and therefore no isolated categorial determinations.

The categories of any given stratum stand in "inter-categorial relations" to one another—a fact that gives each stratum its own unified character. The interrelations of the categories are nothing other than the structure of the articulated but indissoluble unity of the stratum itself (443f.).

The fourth law states that "every individual category implicates (*impliziert*) all other categories of the same stratum" (445f.). 'Implication' here does not, of course, mean 'logically implies'. It is rather an ontic relationship that is basic to any given stratum.

In order to see what Hartmann means here, consider the following pairs of categories: unity–manifoldness, opposition–dimension, continuity–discretion, substratum–relatum, element–structure (451f.). Every manifoldness presupposes unities and is itself a unity, and every unity encloses something manifold and may itself be an element within a higher manifold. Every opposition indicates a dimension of possible degrees, and every dimension presupposes the opposition of directions. Every discretion presupposes the basis of a continuity, and every continuum is a substratum of possible discretion. Every substratum is a relatum of possible relations, and every relation is the relation of substrata. Elements are what they are only as parts of a structure, and a structure presupposes elements of which it is the connectedness. And it must be noted that such relationships of coherence preclude that any one of the categories involved dominate over all others. What prevails is a mutual conditioning that suspends all superordination. But proof of this can be obtained only through a detailed analysis of the categories themselves. What is meant can be indicated when we consider the categories that are determinative of organismic reality. We then find that the organism is a twofold structure: a structure of forms and, at the same time, a structure of processes. Although we may not understand the individual laws involved in these two aspects, there can be no doubt that, basically, they constitute only one system in which everything mutually presupposes everything else.[15]

---

15. For a detailed analysis of organismic existence, see chap. 3, sec. 16.

Something similar is encountered at the stratum of consciousness and its categories. There exists no consciousness that is merely perceptive or merely thinking, and that is not also feeling, desiring, being interested. This unity of consciousness is simply given. No psychology can seriously attempt to isolate the various manifestations.[16]

A third example of coherence is found at the stratum of personal spirit. What we encounter here is the interdependence of our consciousness of values, of freedom, of self-determination, of foresight and purposive activity. Only together do all these aspects constitute the categorial basis of the *structure of acts* that *is realized in action*. In the case of historical events, furthermore, many strata of Being and their groups of categories are superposed so that in a merely summary view everything seems to grow hazy.[17]

11. The Laws of Categorial Stratification

The sequence of strata from the purely material to that of the personal spirit and beyond is the structure proper of the world we live in (*Aufbau*, 472f.). The laws that are determinative of this stratification are the laws of the structure of reality. But the stratification is a relationship of a very special kind that pertains to both the content and the determinative relations of the various strata. The general fact is that "every stratum of Being has its own categories." But this is not the whole story, for the relationships of the strata are actually given in two parallel phenomenal series—one depending on the given concreta, the other on the categorial structure (474).

Briefly stated, the principle of the categorial stratification of the whole of reality is that the categories of the lower strata recur to a large extent in the higher strata. The reverse, however, is not the case: The higher categories do not recur in the lower. Hartmann formulates this basic relationship in four laws of stratification (475f.):

1. *The law of recurrence.* Lower categories recur in the higher strata as partial aspects of the higher categories. This relationship is irreversible. Higher categories do not recur in the lower.

16. For a detailed analysis, see chap. 5, sec. 2.
17. For a detailed analysis, see chap. 5, sec. 3.

2. *The law of modification.* In their recurrence at a higher stratum the categorial elements are modified in manifold ways.

3. *The law of the novum.* Because of the recurrence, every higher category is composed (*zusammengesetzt*) of a manifoldness of lower categories but is not simply a mere sum of them. On the contrary, a distinct and specific *novum* determines the role which the recurring categories play in modified form in the higher strata.

4. *The law of the distance of strata.* Recurrence and modification of the categories are not simply continuities but occur in leaps. Every higher stratum involves a *novum* which contains the modified categories of the lower strata but has specific categories of its own.

Some comments concerning these laws may clarify their meaning.

The superposition of the strata is given in a broad range of phenomena. Organic life, for example, is not contained in the dynamics of purely physical processes. Mental life transcends mere organismic existence. Sociohistorical reality transcends the mental. But the strata, although quite distinct, are nevertheless definitely connected in a specific and definite order. This order of their connectedness is comprehensible only in terms of categories whose interrelations are determined by the laws of recurrence and modification (479ff.).

Note that the direction of recurrence cannot be reversed. The living organism is much more than a mere mechanism; nevertheless, it contains the laws of the purely mechanical. As a spatiotemporal process, life is materially grounded and causally determined. It is enmeshed in the universal transformation of physical energies. And mental existence is something other than organic life but is never found separated from it.

The law of recurrence does not assert that all lower categories recur in the higher, but only that some do. How many and which recur the law does not say. What it does say is that a reverse recurrence does not occur, and that this fact is sufficient to disclose a strict, univocal, and one-dimensional connectedness from the lower to the higher of the strata of Being within the structure of the world as a whole.

But we must not confuse dependence of the strata of Being with their containing all of the lower categories (482). It is perfectly true, for example, that mental Being does not exist without organic life as its basis, but this fact does not mean that the structures and laws of the organism must be contained in mental life. It simply means that there are some categories of the organism—and even more of what is merely material—that do not recur within the complexus of categories of mental existence. The situation is similar in all relations of the lower to the higher strata.

But there are categories which actually recur in all strata. Fundamental categories are of this kind (483f.). Time and process, for example, recur in all strata. There are not only purely physical processes but organismic and mental ones as well. Life is a process, and so are man's activities—his reactions, his strivings and actions, his experiencing, learning, and investigating. All of these have the character of processes. So do social, political, and historical events—the great spiritual movements, the changes of worldviews, of valuations, and the like. All of these processes are temporal, running their course in the very same real time—and thus presupposing it. There can be no doubt that time and change are common to all reality, no matter how different and seemingly incomparable that reality may be otherwise.

If all categories were of the same kind as time and process, the law of recurrence would be universal; however, this is not the case. There are categories that do not recur in all strata of Being. There are categories that can be traced through several strata but not through all. A crucial example is the category *space*. While temporality includes mental and spiritual reality as well as the material and the organismic, spatiality does not prevail beyond the organismic stratum. The same is true of substance. Physical laws of nature still form a basis of organismic reality—even though higher laws are here superposed upon the merely physical—but both the laws of physics and the laws of organismic existence cease to be valid at the limit of the merely organic. Beginning with mental existence, entirely different types of laws hold sway, as can be seen quite clearly in the contrast between the laws of logic and those of perception and conceptual representation. The character of the superposition of strata is not the same throughout reality (485ff.).

We have already seen that all structures can be matter for higher structures, just as all matter can be structure of a lower matter, as is the case of atoms and molecules. But this relativization of matter and structure is not uniform through all strata. It breaks off at a certain height and then begins anew. Such a break is clearly observable between organismic and mental existence. The special forms and the spatiotemporal processes of the organism do not constitute the 'matter' of mental life. The latter rises above mere organismic existence, but it does so as a 'superstructure' that leaves the matter of all lower strata behind. The contents of consciousness are formed of other elements. The relationship of the mental world to organismic existence and to all the strata of nature is not a relation of simple modification but one of 'building beyond' (*Überbauungsverhältnis*). This difference in the stratification of the real world is fundamental (*grundlegend*). It is precisely at the boundary between the organic and the mental that spatiality and merely material substances—together with the laws of physics and chemistry—definitely cease to be constitutive categories. Up to this point all the lower categories recur in the higher strata; from here on up an essential part of them remains behind. When we disregard the fundamental categories of all Being, very few others recur in the complexus of categories of the higher strata. Although categories of bodily existence are without exception valid within the stratum of organic reality, very few of them—time, process, causal relations—recur within the complexus of categories of mental and spiritual reality.[18]

Above the level of mental life, no pure relationships of 'overforming' are found. The mental acts, for example, are not elements in, but only bearers of, spiritual contents. Spiritual Being proper, despite its close relationship to the mental, is not simply a structure having the mental as its elements. It is a radically new stratum, though it rests upon the mental.

A similar but perhaps more evident relationship of "building over" (*Überbauen*) is found in the relation of the objective spirit to the personal spirit. Basic elements of the latter are consciousness, will, anticipation, purposiveness, and freedom of action. These categories, though, do not carry over into the realm of the objective or communal spirit. There is no common consciousness above the consciousness of the individuals; and since will, activity, and freedom are bound to the consciousness of individuals, they do not recur at the higher stratum of the communal spirit. To be sure, there are common interests, common valuations, common demands; but decision, initiative, and action are always manifestations of the individual human being—even when the individuals decide and act in common.

18. An analysis of the problems involved here will be given in chap. 4, sec. 4.

It is obvious that superposition in the structure of the world is not limited to the boundary of the organic and the mental. In fact, we encounter two radically different superpositions. Only one of them is so constituted that the entire categorial structure of the lower stratum is taken up into the higher. As far as the other superposition is concerned, only some of the categories of the lower stratum enter the higher strata; the others are left behind.

To characterize the differences, Hartmann uses the term "*Überformung*" (brought into higher form) to designate cases in which all the categories of the lower stratum recur in the higher—even when they are there placed into a subordinate role. He uses the term "*Überbauung*" (build over it) to designate cases in which at least some of the lower categories do not enter into the realities of the higher stratum (*Aufbau*, 489).

Since new categories occur at every level, the complex of categories becomes ever richer as we consider ever higher strata of the world, and the relationships of the strata cannot be described in a single formula.

12. Categorial Recurrence

The recurrence of categories reflects nothing less than the unity and inner connectedness of the world despite all stratification. The main binding force is provided by the fundamental categories time and process. But despite their merely partial recurrence in the higher strata, other categories also contribute to the structural unity of the world— a fact that leads Hartmann to speak of "a metaphysics of categorial recurrence" (491–98). What does this amount to?

The 'law of recurrence' is obviously a fundamental principle of the structure of the world, and it is so in a sense quite other than that of the 'law of coherence'. Stratification could occur without the recurrence of categories; but a connectedness of the strata could not. Without the recurrence of categories, the world would be a multiplicity of heterogeneous strata that in the last analysis would have nothing to do with one another. But the real world—the world we live in—has a unity that is neither the unity of a single explanatory principle nor the unity of one unitary center. The form of its order is stratification, and the form of its context is the recurrence of categories. Recurrence thus attains an importance that makes it the decisive factor for a whole series of metaphysical problems.

The first aspect of metaphysical significance is the recurrence of the categories themselves and its irreversibility. Reversibility is impossible, because it would mean that the higher is contained in the lower, the more complex in the simpler, which would be inherently contradictory. Stratification comes about only because the higher strata contain a plus of categorial determination that exceeds the determinations characteristic of the lower strata.

If there were no recurrence of categories, organic life, for example, would exist freely and by itself, without a basis in nonliving nature; consciousness would occur without an organismic basis; and spiritual reality could exist without the mental. The ontological importance of the irreversible recurrence of categories is thus undeniable.

This stratified unity of reality is exemplified in man himself. All the lower categories are constitutive aspects of his organismic existence. In him everything that belongs to the lower strata recurs. Even his mental life is bound to his body and cannot be isolated from it. But it also cannot be reduced to mere organismic processes or to merely physicochemical elements. Communal and historical spirit does not contain even the mental acts per se. And it surely is not an organic process or a physicochemical structure. Still, the community as well as its history are all of this taken together.[19] A people has its 'living space' (Lebensraum); its organismic process of the life of successive generations; its own mental activity; and above all of this, the life of the spirit is raised into the realm of human cultures. Their histories are as much a stratified process as is that of the individual human being. But the heterogeneity of mental life vis-à-vis the organic processes does not disappear. The great 'incision' (Einschnitt) does not disappear. How such heterogeneous strata of Being can be so closely connected in one and the same human being is precisely the great metaphysical problem.

The reverse of the recurrence of categories is found in the 'law of modification'. As they recur in the higher strata, the categorial elements are modified in many ways and become part of the "complexus of wholeness" of the higher strata. The wholeness is reflected in each of its constitutive categories.

The result is that a new structure occurs from stratum to stratum. Consider, for example, the changes of meaning of 'unity' and 'manifoldness'. There is the mathematical conception of 'one' and of

19. For a detailed analysis, see chap. 5, sec. 3.

'many'. But the unity of a thing and the manifoldness of its attributes are already something other than the mathematical conceptions. And something else again is the unity of physicochemical processes in their varieties. Quite other still is the much higher unity of the living organism and the manifoldness of its forms and processes. And incomparable to all of these is the unity of consciousness—despite its being interrupted in sleep—and the diversity of its acts and experiences. Beyond this there are the unity of the person, the unit of a community, of a state, and the unities of languages, of the sciences, and of prevailing law; the unity of the ethos of a people and that of a work of art. The basic categorial element—unity—is the same; but it recurs in always different forms. Its otherness is determined by the character of the specific stratum in which it recurs, for in each stratum many other categories enter into the structure and determine the type of unity that prevails.

Causal sequences show a similar type of modification. The continuing context of dependencies at the lowest stratum goes from earlier to later with the flow of time. But quite a different type can be found at the level of organismic existence where unfolding and development are form-building and form-eliminating events. In the continuity and relative constancy of species, genus, and order we encounter a whole system of discretions that are unknown in the lower strata of Being.

When we consider mental life, we find a very special kind of discretion. The organism passes on its own life through heredity. But no one passes on his own consciousness. Consciousness comes ever new into existence in every new individual. Within the individual, however, consciousness is not less a continuum than is the vital process. But the most remarkable and perhaps the most complex continuum is found in historical events—a continuum that in itself is also stratified, and whose real structure is determined by the interactions of very different modes of determination, from physical disruptions and infectious diseases to new insights and inventions.

13. The Law of Modification and of the Novum

When we compare the various strata we find that behind the modifications of the categories there is still something else—something through which the modifications are determined in essential respects. Because of the recurrence, every higher category is, as far as content is concerned, composed of a manifoldness of lower categories but is not simply the mere sum of them. The higher category is always something more. It contains a categorial *novum* that is specific for the higher stratum, and relative to which lower categories are variously modified. Without the occurrence of such categorial *nova* the richness of forms and modifications of the various strata of reality is incomprehensible. The new combinations and modifications of the recurring categories are a function of a higher structure that is as original as are the elementary categories it includes. Hartmann has summarized this fact in the "law of the *nova*" (*Aufbau*, 499).

This law is not a limitation of the recurrence of categories but a positive counterpart to it. It does not hinder the recurrence of lower categories within the higher strata but opposes to it the categorial independence of the higher stratum that may entail some modifications of the included lower categories. But without the occurrence of the *novum*, the differences in height of the strata of Being would not be possible.

The *novum* is unique for every stratum. This means that there is also a *novum* in the stratification itself. The two characteristics—coherence within a given stratum and coherence of the stratification as a whole—are intertwined. The relationships of the strata reveal not only an intermingling of recurrent categories and their coherence, but also a far-reaching interpenetration of the strata themselves. The heterogeneity of the strata does not preclude their interpenetration within a higher totality. Only together do they constitute a multidimensional realm of categories.

However, we actually know the distinctions of the strata not from the relations of the categories but exclusively from the concretum—i.e., from the structural distinctions of the actual strata of Being. It is the concretum, the *Seiende* as such, that in its total reality as realm of phenomena reveals the stratification of Being. The rest is interpretation and disclosure of the categories encountered in the given. The various categorial laws that Hartmann has formulated—as well as the individual categories—can be disclosed only through an analysis of the concretum. This, of course, entails an element of the hypothetical, but the basic problem remains the same, for the categories are given with the concretum.

When we examine the stratification of the world, we find that spatiality and inert matter do not recur beyond the stratum of organismic reality (512f.). They are encountered neither in the realm of the mental nor in that of the objective spirit. It is true in general that the higher up in the range of strata a category is first encountered, the more limited is the possibility of its modification as to extent and quality; for the determinative character of individual categories is ever more subordinate to the *novum* of the higher stratum. The limitation in the recurrence ceases when we consider not the strata of Being in general but the specific concreta as given. Of these, the higher ones—the human being, the community, and history—are themselves stratified realities that contain the complete categorial stratification from below.

It is possible, of course, to contemplate *in abstracto* the two highest strata as if they had no foundation in the lower. Such an abstract view of them is actually encountered in philosophy no less than in the various sociocultural sciences. However, viewed ontologically, there is no *real* consciousness and no *real* spiritual realm separated from the lower strata. A merely phenomenological investigation brackets, as it were, the reality encountered by considering only the specific characteristics of the phenomena. But, surely, we know real consciousness only as 'supported' by a living organism—just as we know the organism only as 'supported' by the stratum of inorganic reality. Understood categorially, the profound otherness of consciousness vis-à-vis the organism is only the obvious manifestation of a powerful categorial *novum* which cannot be dissolved into the categories of the merely organic.

The same is true with respect to spiritual Being (514)—and not only with respect to personal spirit, but also with respect to the historically objective spirit that, as *this particular* real spirit, is yet always supported by nonspiritual reality—by the whole array of the lower strata of Being. After all, the objective spirit is real only where there are real human beings whose spiritual life constitutes it. Objective spirit is related back to actual consciousness and presupposes its categories in its own Being. Since actual consciousness does not exist without the living organic bearer, and since the organism does not exist without a supportive physicomaterial Being, the whole stratification of the lower categories is already presupposed in spiritual Being and in its categories.

What is important here is that between the strata of Being there exists a relationship of conditions that makes the whole *Dasein* of the higher strata dependent upon the lower. But just as no one can seriously maintain that this dependence of the higher upon the lower could explain spiritual Being in terms of the lower, so no one can seriously doubt the dependence of the higher upon the lower. That is, in the stratification of the world there coexist an elementary dependence upon lower strata and the undiminished independence of the higher strata relative to the respective lower ones. The dependence is as one-sided as the recurrence of elements is irreversible. The ontic importance —although not that of meaning and significance—corresponds precisely to this irreversibility. The categories, as the simpler ones, are in a strict and clearly discernible sense a 'basis' for, a 'foundation' of, the higher structures—of structures that presuppose and 'rest upon' them.

This irreversible relationship can be summarized in four propositions (519f.):

1. There exists a categorial dependence of the strata such that the categories of the lower strata are foundational to the higher ones. This relationship is irreversible.
2. This dependence of the higher strata upon the lower is real not only where the recurrence of categories is continuous, but also where it breaks off. Even then the higher stratum 'rests upon' the lower, which, in itself, is a stratum of determinative principles. In no case is the higher stratum basic to the lower.
3. Wherever in the stratification of reality we find a recurrence of categories, the lower categories are only 'matter' for the higher. The higher categories cannot modify the lower but can "build over them."
4. Because of their *novum* the higher strata are 'free' and autonomous relative to the lower strata. But this freedom is *above* rather than *within* the lower strata. Since the lower stratum is merely an element in the higher, the freedom of the higher is unrestricted by the lower.

Taken together, these statements disclose the inner dynamics of the stratification of Being. But they define only one—albeit complex— inner relationship. That there should be a dependence and at the same time an autonomy seems in a purely formal sense to be contradictory. That this contradiction is only an apparent one constitutes the real essence of the interplay of dependence and freedom. Both come to their full significance only when they are taken together. Here lies the metaphysically crucial importance of the relationship of the various strata. Everything else stands or falls with it.

But if one does not wish to harbor metaphysical prejudices, one must refrain from speaking of this forming of higher strata as a 'development' or an 'unfolding', for development and unfolding presuppose a given 'inner something' that can develop or unfold. Development and unfolding are not creative of something new. The slogan "creative evolution" (Bergson) is intrinsically a contradiction (532).

For describing the actual growth of lower forms of Being into higher ones, all images and comparisons fail. Conceptions such as 'preformation' and 'epigenesis'—which for a time were slogans of opposing theorists—are essentially nothing but the crude schemata of one-sided modes of viewing the facts in which the ontologically most significant aspects are completely disregarded—the facts, namely, of the basic relationship of principles to the concreta as that relationship is manifest in the ways just described. In the concretum the higher forms of Being come into existence secondarily, whereas as far as the categories are concerned (which themselves have no temporal being), the stratification preexists. But even this is not an adequate description of the facts. The truth of the matter is that there is no image or conception that is adequate to the actual relationships of superposition of the strata of Being and of their respective categories. We face here the basic, unsolvable problems of metaphysics.

In the world as given there is no preformation of stratum to stratum, no unfolding of a preformed reality. There is only an overforming (*Überformung*) of the lower by the higher, and where this fails there is only a building above (*Überbauung*) the lower. As far as these types of relationships are concerned, the Being of any lower stratum is completely indifferent to the strata above it. At no level does the lower have an intrinsic tendency to support the higher or enter into it as constituent element.

In view of these facts, Hartmann regards Hegel's attempt to show that category by category, stratum by stratum, the lower always leads 'dialectically' to the higher as "putting the crown upon romanticism of thought [*Gedankenromantik*]."[20] Here dialectic is not the simple

20. *Aufbau*, 534. For Hartmann's penetrating arguments on this topic, see his *Die Philosophie des Deutschen Idealismus*, vol. 2, *Hegel* (Berlin and Leipzig:

pursuing of implicative contexts but a reconstruction from below of a teleology of forms that is completely determinative from above. The danger is that such an inversion, once it has been introduced and developed into a system, attains an aspect of compulsiveness in thought; and once adjusted to it, thinking accepts its form as a law and becomes captive of a self-created schema of thought. It can no longer think in any other way.

The error in such an orientation is an ontological one. It consists in the radical distortion of the basic law that is determinative of the order of rank and of the sequence of dependencies of the actual strata of Being. Neither that which is superior in meaning and value nor that which is more closely related to spirit generally is ontologically foundational. Insofar as in the stratification of the form of Being there is dependency, the higher is dependent upon the lower, and the lower is indifferent to the higher. Dependency in the world, as this world actually exists, does not have the character of an order of meaning and value, but simply an order of Being—a *Seinsordnung*. And even if this *Seinsordnung*, when seen as a superposition of diverse strata, reveals an order of rank of the strata, it must be understood in its structure and inner dependencies from below and not from above.

What is the case for the structure of the world as a whole is true also for all differentiated gradations of particular structures, events, and relationships of the various strata within that world. The whole sequence of strata reveals clearly and irreversibly the dependence of the higher upon the lower, and the indifference of the lower toward the higher.

But this is only one side of the basic relationship. The other side is revealed in what Hartmann calls the 'law of matter' and the 'law of freedom' (*Aufbau*, 539–44).

What Hartmann here refers to is the fact that the higher stratum depends upon the lower only in certain respects, and that in other respects it has its own form of determination. Categorially understood, this means that the lower is only 'matter' for the higher. It is what is 'built over' by the higher. Although the lower strata are the stronger, the dependence of the higher upon them extends only as far as the determination 'from below' limits the full scope (*Spielraum*) of the

---

Walter de Gruyter & Co., 1929). Also Hartmann's "Aristoteles und Hegel," in *Beiträge zur Philosophie des Deutschen Idealismus*, vol. 3 (Erfurt, 1923), 1–36.

higher forms. In other words, the determination from below is *conditio sine qua non,* but not more than that. As previously indicated, this is exemplified in the relation of the stratum of inorganic matter to the stratum of organismic existence. The atoms and molecules—together with all the laws of physics and chemistry—are preserved in the structure of an organism and in the processes that constitute its life. But the structure of the organism itself and the interrelations of the processes of living are realities of higher modes of existence and cannot be accounted for in terms of the categories and laws of purely physical reality.

The relationships of the other strata of reality show similar aspects of a preeminence of strength and of being fundamental, and a preeminence of height and of specific types of independence—i.e., of "categorial freedom" and autonomy.

We must note, however, that dependence of the higher strata upon the lower is by no means a complete dependence. In fact, the higher up in the strata a given concretum belongs, the more do the lower strata sink to the level of a mere foundation that remains indifferent as to what is above it. This fact entails that, at its own level, the higher stratum has freedom relative to the lower ones. Its freedom is, however, not identical to complete independence. It is autonomy despite dependence upon what is lower. In other words, it is independence within dependence.

The crucial point is that autonomy and a unique lawfulness prevail at every stratum of reality. In each stratum we find a thoroughgoing determination, but one that is unique to that particular stratum. The higher nexus is always a categorial *novum* and, as such, is 'free' relative to the types of determination that prevail at the lower strata.

Of the real determinative connections within the various strata, we actually know only two: the causal and the purposive. Anything between them we can only surmise.

The most obvious form of the causal nexus is mere mechanism—the push-pull type. It prevails at various levels of dynamic relationships and is found even in organic processes. However, its simple linear progression in time is not sufficient to account for the morphogenetic process of organismic existence. Here mere causality becomes a structural element of a nexus in which a preexisting whole gives the direction. Granted that in the developmental process of the individual organism a very real predisposition—originated in time, located spatially,

and bound to specific cells and parts of cells—is the effective determinant; but *how* this predisposition becomes causally effective in the
developmental process of the growing organism can be guessed only
in part.[21] The *appearance* of purposiveness does not in itself justify the
assumption that there actually is purposive action.

The causal processes, however, do not recur in just any of the higher
forms of determination. The truly remarkable fact is that, despite its
openness to acausal forms of determination and its being 'guided' by
them, the causal nexus remains true to itself. Its essence is not changed
by coming under the directive influence of higher forms of determination that give the causal nexus their own direction and let it be effective
for them. They depend upon it as basic to their own ends but do not
disrupt it.

When we consider the stratum of moral and personal Being, we encounter the forms of a nexus higher than the merely causal and the
organismic. It is obvious that 'motives' of the specifically mental stratum play a part in the determination of actions. But it is also clear that
in the consciously responsible decisions of voluntary actions, even the
'motives' of the mental stratum are subordinate matter for the spiritual
stratum. Hence, if the lower determination is codeterminative within
the higher, and if the *novum* of the latter is in every case above the
lower, then there is in the stratification of determinations also a stratification of autonomies. The higher forms of the nexus never entail
the suspension or disruption of the lower. The higher form is always
an *Überformung*, and freedom can occur only in the superposition of
several forms of determination. The uniqueness of each of the superposed autonomies lies in the special way in which the lower types of
determination are "built into" the higher.

The consequences of this relationship are of the greatest significance.
They eliminate the old opposition of determinism and indeterminism.
Determinism takes the lower form of determination to be the total
determinative factor of all strata—including the mental and personal.
Indeterminism disregards the lower chains of determination in favor
of the higher. Both views are quite obviously distortions of the facts.
The multiforms of determination encountered in the real world are
perfectly in harmony with freedom from a determination exclusively
by concreta of the lower levels.

21. For a detailed analysis, see chap. 3, sec. 11.

3

An Analysis of Modalities

BEFORE WE DEAL WITH the realities of the world we live in, it will be well to consider Hartmann's detailed analysis of the modalities and their interrelations in that world.

In the course of the history of philosophy, six basic modalities pertaining to actual and/or possible objects of experience have been discerned. Arranged in a preliminary pattern ranging from the 'lowest' to the 'highest', they are "impossibility, unreality, accidentalness, possibility, reality, necessity."[1]

This arrangement coincides with a similar classification of the validity of our judgments about aspects of experience. However, closer examination reveals an important difference of the various levels of experience. Impossibility, for example, is obviously a kind of necessity, namely, "negative necessity." Accidentalness, on the other hand, is not a form of necessity but is rather a denial of it. And unreality is indifferent to both necessity and the accidental, although it can be what is impossible.

In the case of positive modalities the lower is always contained in the higher. Reality thus always presupposes possibility.

The accidental occupies a special place, for what is experienced

1. Nicolai Hartmann, *Möglichkeit und Wirklichkeit* (Berlin: Walter de Gruyter & Co., 1938), 32ff.

as accidental may in itself be necessary, as philosophical determinism asserts: "Everything real is necessary" (Hartmann, *Möglichkeit und Wirklichkeit*, 35). In this view the accidental is but a modality of comprehension. When it is taken in any other sense, it means an uncaused event, a "not-being-necessary [*ein Nicht-notwendig-sein*]"; and in this sense it is highly questionable because it stands in conflict with the context of actual events and with the laws and dependencies in the real world (39).

The stratum of necessity also involves ambiguities. In one sense 'necessary' means that something is needed for a specific purpose. In our natural sciences, for example, we speak of the necessary conditions for a certain event to occur. But in this sense the term does not strictly mean *necessity*. In the popular sense, on the other hand, the meaning of 'necessary' is 'it cannot be avoided'—like fate or destiny. Here the conception of something being predetermined is basic, and the meaning of necessity is essentially teleological. Its structure is that of a "finalistic determination [*Finaldetermination*]," and thus differs from the necessity meant by causal determination (41f.). The necessity entailed by causality is "real determination [*Realnotwendigkeit*]," but it is not the only necessity in the real world. Organic and mental processes also have necessity of a kind that cannot be reduced to the merely causal form. Neither can personal, spiritual, and historical events be so reduced (44).

Possibility also needs further clarification. In one sense we speak of the *merely* possible. But what 'merely is' is not real, and it is certainly not necessary. Possibility here means a disjunction that is dissolved in the transition to something real. In contrast to this, however, there is also an "indifferent possibility" which is reconcilable with 'being real' as well as with 'being necessary'. This disjunctive possibility refers to a "modality of Being" that is other than the modality of reality but does not preclude it. It is compatible with the real and with the nonreal. It is not a separate modality of Being beside that of reality but "can as condition fuse into the real" (46f.).

Of course, we also speak of "logical possibility," and simply mean 'without contradiction'. But what interests Hartmann is "real possibility [*Realmöglichkeit*]," for "what is without conflict harmonious within itself is for this reason by no means possible in the context of reality [*im Realzusammenhang*]" (49). As Hartmann sees it, "Really possible in the strict sense is actually [durchaus] only that whose conditions have been fulfilled to the very last item. As long as one condition is missing, the matter [Sache] is not possible but is rather impossible. The completion of the conditions here means nothing less than their real presence—that is, their being actually real [Realwirkliches]" (50).

Real possibility in the strict sense is thus never disjunctive, and never a merely partial possibility. In its very essence it is "indifferent and total possibility." And possibility in this sense is, like necessity, always rooted in "a context of dependencies (Abhängigkeitszusammenhang)" (52f.).

1. Basic Laws of Modality

In our daily life, as well as in the sciences, the tendency is to reduce all modalities of Being to available secondary strata—that is, to those of logic and epistemology. Actually the modalities of the secondary spheres are dependent upon the spheres of Being and, in a sense, merely give us a picture of them. When Hartmann considers the situation as a whole, he finds that all modalities can be arranged in a sixfold dimensionality of opposites as follows:

1. Positive and negative modalities
2. Higher and lower modalities
3. Modalities of Being and secondary modalities
4. Modalities of the ideal and modalities of the real
5. Definite and indefinite modalities
6. Fundamental and relative modalities (*Möglichkeit und Wirklichkeit*, 65)

On the basis of these distinctions Hartmann finds it possible to develop a basic law of modalities. But we must here keep in mind that "relationality is not relativity" (71). That is, what is 'relational' consists of relations and has the structure of relations. What is 'relative', on the other hand, stands in relation to something else, is dependent upon it, or is 'relative to it'. It is possible, of course, that the 'relationality' of a structure is connected with 'relativity', in which case its relativity stands in categorial contrast to absoluteness.

In view of these facts, the *basic law of modalities* can be stated this way: "All relational modalities are relative to the absolute modalities." Or, in a more precise form: "Impossibility, possibility, and necessity are relative to reality and unreality" (71).

This law is valid in all spheres of possible gradations of reality. Its validity means that all relational modalities of a sphere are relative (*rückbezogen*) to the reality and unreality of that same sphere. The impossibility of A thus means that A *cannot* be 'real'. The possibility of A means that A *can be* 'real'. And the necessity of A means that A *must be* 'real'. In all three cases it is the *reality of A* that is either impossible, possible, or necessary. This basic modal relationship persists in all strata of experience. The *relational* modalities remain—either mediately or immediately—modal components of reality: its specific aspects and modifications. The *basic* modalities, on the other hand, are simply and in themselves reality and unreality (73).

In all spheres *reality* is the fundamental modality for the *relational* modalities; for "only on the basis of real conditions can something be possible or necessary" (77). "Unreality is but negative reality," for "pure nothingness is nothing at all, and a specific not-being is also a specific Being" (79). The real and the unreal together are "a single homogeneous foundation of Being (*Seinsfundament*) for the relational modalities in which their qualitative opposition disappears" (80). After all, "unreal possibility" is not possibility at all, no matter with which sphere of experience we are concerned. And "unreal necessity" is no necessity. Wherever in a realm of Being accident dominates, there is not only nothing necessary but, strictly speaking, "there is also nothing impossible and nothing possible" (87). Between necessity and fortuitousness there exists a unique relationship such that "there is no necessity without fortuitousness, but there can be no fortuitousness without necessity" (91). And in the real world "neither axioms nor laws nor principles of any kind are necessary." They are at best merely "necessary presuppositions" for our understanding of the world. They represent an "epistemological necessity [*Erkenntnisnotwendigkeit*]," not a necessity within the *Seiende* that is disclosed in cognition (93).

2. The Modality of Reality

Every stratum in the world requires its own modal analysis. What 'is' ideal Being and what 'is' real Being cannot be directly defined. However, since the modalities of the two spheres are different, their difference will give us indirectly the difference between the natures of ideality and reality. This is possible because (a) the modalities of a distinctive sphere are all interrelated in a primary sense (*Intermodalverhältnisse erster Ordnung*), having their own specific laws; and (b) there are modal relations between the modalities of one sphere and those of another sphere. These are intermodal relationships in a secondary sense (*Intermodalverhältnisse zweiter Ordnung*) (105).

How great the difference between strata really is becomes clear when we compare the primary modalities that are dominant in them.

Perhaps the best known of the spheres is the logical, in which necessity dominates. No matter how secondary the sphere of the logical may be in the world as a whole, it is a sphere of relationships—of consequence, dependence, encompassing and being encompassed. In this sphere no isolated concepts or isolated judgments prevail. The modality of a conclusion is always that of necessity. But this dominance of necessity occurs only in the sphere of the logical. In the sphere of ideal Being, it is not necessary that the whole range of relational modalities prevail; and possibility plays a part more important than does necessity. Everything depends here essentially on the noncontradictoriness of the essences.

In the realm of perception (including that of the emotions), the absolute modalities prevail. This is especially evident in our unreflective awareness of objects—as distinguished from understanding and comprehending, which are possible only in context and in terms of it. And with this we come to a stratum where the *relational* modalities dominate (107).

In the realm of reality (*Realsphäre*), the *absolute* modalities clearly dominate. Everything depends on being and not-being, on reality and unreality. Even possibility and necessity exist only insofar as they 'really' are what they are, and that their conditions have actual reality. The real necessity of what is real is conditioned by reality (108). The modalities of Being are essentially other than the modalities of cognition.

3. Modalities of the Real and Consciousness of Modalities

Something can be necessary even when it is not known to be necessary—even when it is not known at all. The conditions prevailing in reality depend neither on the requirements of reason nor on the laws of consciousness. They are independent of all modalities of cognition. In the sphere of reality, for example, there is no disjunctive possibility. When A is real, there is no longer a possibility for non-A (*Möglichkeit und Wirklichkeit*, 112–15).

From what has been said so far it seems possible to formulate several "laws of equivalence" as follows:

1. Negation of the possibility of A is the necessity of non-A.
2. Negation of the necessity of A is the possibility of non-A.
   These two laws indicate a structural basic relationship of the two positive relational modalities with respect to each other.
3. Negation of the possibility of non-A is the necessity of A.
4. Negation of the necessity of non-A is the possibility of A.

Because of their eminently positive result, laws 3 and 4 are of greater significance than laws 1 and 2. But, in any case, with these laws of equivalence the beginning is made for a clarification of the intermodal relations of the real (117).

We must realize, however, that there is no real indifference of modalities. Thus, Hartmann states as a first basic principle:

No modality of the real is indifferent to any other modality of the real. (121)

But since positive and negative modalities exclude one another, there is also a second basic principle:

All positive real modalities exclude all negative ones of themselves; and since exclusion can only be mutual, all negative modalities exclude all positive ones of themselves. (122)

Since each of these laws involves two aspects, we can derive from them four "paradoxical laws of exclusion." Hartmann formulates them in this way:

1. The Being of what is unreal is not possible (unreality excludes possibility).

2. The non-Being of what is real is not possible (reality excludes negative possibility).
3. That whose Being is possible cannot be unreal (positive possibility excludes unreality).
4. That whose non-Being is possible cannot be real (negative possibility excludes reality). (123)

But Hartmann finds still another basic principle:

All positive modalities of the real imply one another, and all negative modalities of the real also imply one another. (125)

When the second and third basic principles are taken together, the intermodal relationships of the sphere become even more unified. And since all categorial coherence of the categories within a stratum has the form of implication, we can assert of the modalities of the real that "each of its two groups is in itself completely coherent; but with respect to each other the groups are completely disparate." In this fact a unique radicalism of the distinction between 'being' and 'not being' manifests itself. And "this radicalism is the first ontological light cast on the essence of reality" (125).

4. Proof of the Intermodal Law of Reality

This proof is based on the two modalities of possibility: the possibility of being, and the possibility of non-being. These possibilities mutually exclude one another:

1. The really possible is that of which non-being is not possible; and
2. that whose non-being is actually possible is in reality not possible. (*Möglichkeit und Wirklichkeit*, 129)

This double proposition, henceforth referred to as 'law of cleavage' (*Spaltungsgesetz*) of possibility, is a law of being; but it is "valid only for the sphere of the real possibility of being [*der realen Seinsmöglichkeit*]." What it means is real possibility (*Realmöglichkeit*) in the here-now-being-possible (*das Hier-und-jetzt-Möglichsein*). It is a specific being-possible, meaning that what is real in full determination of reality cannot at the same time be unreal in that determinateness. And what within the context of reality is unreal cannot at the same time be real. To put it differently: If the possibility of being is actually inherent in reality, then the possibility of not-being is excluded; and if the possibility of not-being is inherent in actual unreality, then the possibility of being is excluded (130).

"This law in its double aspects is of the greatest importance for the total character of the sphere of reality and for the ontological meaning of reality in general. It is the key to the intermodal laws of the whole sphere; and those laws are nothing other than pure modal expositions of being-real [*des Realseins*] as such" (131).

Once something has become real, its reality can never be changed back into nonreality. Such is the "law of the hardness of reality" (132). The meaning of 'being-possible' and 'being-real' thus determines the meaning of temporality, and not vice versa.

The facts indicate that "becoming is a special kind of Being of what is real." It excludes nonbeing just as firmly as does static Being. There is no "merely possible" within the real. "What is possible of being is also real and necessary. . . . Reality is the absolute decision between Being and non-Being. Becoming itself, the real process in which everything begins and ceases, is a completely real becoming [*ein ganz und gar 'seiendes Werden'*] and not just a becoming *toward* Being—as if the weight of reality were intrinsic to the results of the process rather than in the process itself" (151).

But now the question is: What does it mean to say that what is really possible is also actually real?

The popular concept of possibility means in effect that much of what is not real is at least possible. And in this sense we speak of a multitude of possibilities. But this means at best that here we speak of merely partial possibilities. The totality of the conditions is ordinarily not available to us (157). We must keep in mind, however, that only that is actually possible whose conditions to the very last one are real. When even one of them is missing, there is no real possibility. 'Real possibility' means that "the totality of the real conditions" is given (161). In other words, "When the chain of the real conditions of something is complete, then, with the real possibility of it, its real necessity is also given. . . . That is, the conditions of the real possibility of something are at the same time the conditions of its real necessity"

(163). This interrelation of real possibility and real necessity is the immediate result of the totality and identity of the chain of conditions. "Where and howsoever something is really possible it already also becomes necessary" (165). It is simply a law of reality that real possibility implies real necessity (166–69).

These seemingly minor modal interrelations give us an insight into the structure of the world that the "exalted speculative principles" of metaphysics cannot give us (174).

We must realize, however, that the "identity of the conditions" which we find in the realm of the real is rooted in "the law of the totality of real possibility" (176). When all conditions to the very last one are given, A *must* become real. But only within the sphere of the real is what is possible thus limited (179).

5. The Ontological Law of Determination

Everyone is sure that what is real must also be possible, but one does not readily admit that what is real must also be necessary. Our awareness of reality is in this respect inconsistent. And yet, in the context of reality, nothing can be other than it is. Real possibility is also real necessity. This relationship is what Hartmann calls the "*Realgesetz der Wirklichkeit*"—the basic law of reality.

This law reveals the ontological determination of the mode of being of what is real. To put it differently: "The real is the sphere of complete interpenetration [*Durchdringung*] of possibility and necessity" (*Möglichkeit und Wirklichkeit*, 197). And this interpenetration characterizes the whole of actual reality—of *Realwirklichkeit*—as a process in which the possible is made real, step by step, and can become nothing other than what it becomes (201).

Determinism here does not mean something like predestation or finalistic determination, nor even causal determination as we find it in the realm of the merely material—the physical. The causal law is but a special case of the basic law of real determination, which states that "the chain of conditions through which something becomes really possible is also the sufficient ground of its actual reality" (203). And this means that in reality nothing is possible that does not have its sufficient ground in something that is actually real. "Everything real is completely determined by something real" (207).

To state it more explicitly: "What actually is real must at least be actually possible. It is actually possible only on the basis of the complete chain of its real conditions. But on the basis of this chain it is also really necessary and therefore 'can' not be otherwise than it is. It is univocally determined by that chain. This chain of conditions is its suffient ground" (208).

6. Types of the Nexus of Reality

The 'law of real determination' is indifferent to unity or plurality of the *forms* of determination. That in the individual strata of Being different modes of determination prevail, and that for this reason the strata are relatively independent, depends not on the basic form of determination but on the specific categorial structures of the strata. Actually, each one of the strata has its own special law of determination (*Möglichkeit und Wirklichkeit*, 211). But this much seems clear:

1. In all strata of reality determination has the form of a 'nexus' —that is, the interrelation of the real with the real. Everything real is determined by something real.
2. There is no stratification of the *Seiende* which does not involve the dependence of the whole stratum. But this categorial dependence prevails only from the lower to the higher stratum, and not vice versa. The higher strata contain the lower ones as subordinate aspects. But this does not affect the higher type, which is a *novum*, an 'overforming' of the lower.
3. The individual strata are determinative complete. Each is determined by the nexus of reality typical of it.
4. This means that, despite the manifoldness of its strata, the real world remains a closed whole, representing a thoroughgoing interconnection of everything real—and this despite the manifoldness of the forms of determination. (213)

Despite its manifold strata—each with its own form of interrelations—the real world is determinatively homogeneous. It is real in all its strata. But related to the problem of determination is also the problem of freedom. And here everything depends on what is meant by freedom. If by freedom we mean an indeterminateness—freedom in the negative sense—then we do not find it in the real world. But freedom "in the positive sense," as Kant called it—that is, freedom of self-determination—is itself a form of determination and is thus in harmony with the basic law of reality. What freedom means in this sense is that "on the basis of its categorial uniqueness, the will is autonomous." In the real world such freedom is possible only when various modes of determination of the higher strata of reality are superimposed upon the lower strata. And this means that the structure of the real world involves determinations of a complex type (217).

7. The Modalities of Process

Process depends, of course, on the temporality of the real. Past stages in the process "are no more," and future stages "are not yet"; and the position of the present relative to what is future is other than what it is to the past. This entails the unchangeable irreversibility of the flow of time (223). The question is, What is entailed by the "openness" of the future in its indeterminateness?

In every moment of the process a 'manifoldness of possibilities' seems to be given, and this entails a characteristic connection with the idea of partial possibility. The future is viewed as "a manifoldness of eventualities" (224). But the question is, What kind of 'possibilities' are here meant? Real possibility in the strict sense cannot be meant. We can speak of a manifoldness of possibilities only in the sense of referring to an "incomplete complexus of connections" in which the multiple directions of development can be augmented.

In every process the conditions of possible development are antecedent to what is conditioned. As the process advances, 'possibilities' are constantly eliminated. When the 'chain of conditions' is complete, only one outcome is 'possible', and it becomes real. As the process continues, what has thus become real is now a partial condition of further possibilities (227).

In all of this, however, time is uniform and without content—a merely dimensional something and, beyond this, an unrestrictable flow and schema of order in that flow; but it is not 'that which' flows or underlies its order. "Time itself determines nothing; it brings forth nothing and destroys nothing" (230).

The anthropomorphic conception of time involves two basic errors. The first is to regard the future as a "realm of possibilities." The second is to explain differences in modalities in terms of temporality (232f.). The person who wills something and acts believes to face an indetermi-

nateness of 'many possibilities'; and in this indeterminateness he sees
the freedom for his actions. In truth, however, his freedom is something quite different: It lies in his being able to insert his initiative as
a factor into the already existing complexus of factors. And this does
not depend on an indeterminateness of future events but on the indifference of the causal nexus to additional factors of a higher form of
determination (234).

There is, of course, an indisputable dependence of the stages in a
process which coincides with the direction of time from earlier to later.
But in this process a single decision we may make is not alone what
decides the outcome. The whole sequence of supplementary factors
is involved. Only when the various conditions are complete is there
a "final decision in favor of *one* possibility and the exclusion of all
others" (237). And so there is but one *real* possibility—which is "the
possibility of that which in the continuation of the process becomes
real" (239).

8. The Modal Structure of Becoming

The occurrence of isolated processes in the world is highly questionable. Indeed, it appears to be true that all such isolation is purely
subjective in our interpretation, and a mere abstraction. In the real
world all individual processes occur inseparably within one total process (*Möglichkeit und Wirklichkeit*, 240). This is confirmed in the
proposition that the totality of conditions of a process is the sufficient
ground of what happens.

Still, there is also a distinct meaning to the concept of partial possibility. We speak of it when we assert that at a certain stage in the
process, A, some of the conditions of X have not yet become real—
have not yet entered the process (247).

The determinative structure of process prevails not only in the
lowest stratum of reality but is found in the higher and more complex strata as well—in organismic development and in the purposive
actions of human beings (249).

Consider the case of the development of an organism as determined
by the initially given pattern of genes. Although that pattern is already
a real structure, it by no means contains all the conditions necessary for
the development of the mature organism. That development depends

at each stage on external factors also, and thus is involved in the actual process of reality in general.

The same is true at the much higher stratum of the purposive actions of human beings. In the realization of purposive actions, the selection of a purpose and of the means for its realization are certainly part of a real process in a real world—even though both presuppose consciousness and deliberate action as well.

What is really possible even in these cases depends on the realization of *all* the determinative factors in the process. This but confirms the fact that "process is the universal basic form of everything which constitutes the permanency of the real world" (254). And this implies that only that is possible which either is real or will become real. The modal structure of 'becoming'—of process—thus reveals clearly the unimpeded moving forward of the inexhaustible productivity in the onward movement of the process of reality (257).

9. The Realm of Incomplete Reality

Included in this realm are the various regions of volition and action on the one hand, and artistic creation and its objects on the other (258).

The strict interrelation of possibility and reality is a "mere reality-relation [*Realverhältnis*]" in the realm of the real. In the case of "incomplete reality" it must loosen up; and it can do so in two directions: Either necessity dominates over possibility, or possibility dominates over necessity. The first is exemplified in the case of volition and action —that is, in the realm of the 'ought to be'. The second is exemplified in the object of aesthetic vision and creating (259).

In the course of an 'ought to be', necessity dominates over possibility. That which 'is to be' is as yet actually something unreal. But at least part of the chain of conditions that leads to its realization is already given. The 'ought' simply anticipates the process. It posits as necessary what as yet is not actually necessary. In this sense the 'ought to be' is "free necessity"—that is, it is not real necessity (*Realnotwendigkeit*) (263). Nothing is subtracted here from necessity in nature, but something is added to it. Through the will, which decides itself in favor of it, the ideal demand—essentially a commitment to values —becomes a real determinative factor in the complexity of a given situation.

In the final analysis, real necessity is but a special case of necessity in general. It is necessity of the real on the basis of the actual totality of all real conditions. Free necessity, on the other hand, is a case of necessity on the basis of an ideal value (270).

Aesthetic objectivity is the beautiful, not what is actually real. It is "lifted above reality and yet near to it, bound up with it." The foreground of the aesthetic object is real, rooted in the context of the real. Its background, however, "is and remains unreal" (273), freed from the context of reality and its laws. The creative artist does not create beauty but lets it appear in what he or she creates. The artist's exhibition of the beautiful is exhibition 'in' something real, and is therefore limited by the "narrowness of real possibility." And so the great freedom of the artistically possible is freedom "only relative to the narrowness of the possibilities of the real" (276).

10. Modality of the Unreal

In the "logical sphere" we encounter concepts, judgments, and inferences. These are not acts but are "objective structures that have their own laws" (*Möglichkeit und Wirklichkeit*, 270). The best known of these laws are those of identity, contradiction, and the excluded middle. And we recognize here a distinction between apodictic, assertoric, and problematic judgments. While in the real world a necessity prevails throughout, the realm of judgments is open without limit to what is accidental (281).

In the sphere of the logical we find no laws of modality corresponding to laws of real possibility or of real necessity. What is logically possible is not yet logically real, and what is logically real is not yet logically necessary. The logical context is in itself simply indifferent as far as the laws of the connections of real events and their mode of Being are concerned.

The sphere of the logical has always been considered to be a domain of universal and complete order, of universality and lawfulness. But just as in this respect we had to change our view of mathematics, so we also have to change our view of logic—we change it fundamentally (294). Thus, in the sphere of logic the principle of sufficient reason can only mean: "What is logically possible has its sufficient reason. A tautological statement is not worth being made" (294ff.). The "merely assertoric" has no sufficient ground. The principle of sufficient reason thus ceases to be a law of complete determination. Of really strict consequence within the sphere of the logical is only the area of syllogistic inference. Here a sufficient basis for complete determination prevails, but not everything in the logical sphere is thus connected.

We encounter the greatest difficulty in the sphere of logical possibility, for this possibility rests upon mere freedom from contradiction. And the "principle of noncontradiction" is not a specific law intrinsic to determining concepts, judgments, and inferences, but it is a law of ideal Being, where concepts, judgments, and inferences are subject to it (301). The problem of the syllogism is one of logical necessity, but it does not coincide with the realm of judgment. This is the reason why in the sphere of the logical as a whole there remains much that is 'merely assertoric' and 'merely problematic'.

The realm of the logical is actually a "realm in between" (*ein Zwischenreich*). In its absolute modalities it is 'bound to' the real and its constant process, but in its relative modalities it is bound to ideal Being. "It is the imperfect compromise [*Ausgleich*] of both realms within the realm of thought" (309).

11. The Modality of Ideal Being

Ideal Being includes only *essences (Wesenheiten)* and the *context of essences (Wesenszusammenhänge)*. The meaning of 'being real' is here quite other than in the realm of reality, and so is the meaning of other modalities. But 'the realm of essences' is also beyond temporality and individuality of the real. And it has nothing in common with mere positing. "Ideal Being is simply a Being-in-itself and is independent of being comprehended" (*Möglichkeit und Wirklichkeit*, 311). There is a radical difference between ideal Being and real Being—a difference that has led to the belief that only the real has Being and that ideal Being has none.

What is fundamentally characteristic of the real mode of Being is that possibility and actuality—and their negative counterparts—almost alone dominate everything. This means, however, that possibility and necessity (and with them all other modalities) must here have a different character (313).

Let us note first that what is ideally possible already has an ideal existence. Modalities of relation determine membership in the realm and the prevailing laws as well.

But let us also note that, in the realm of essences, possibility does not mean totality of conditions (as it does in the realm of the real) but only freedom from contradiction—albeit within a broadly articulated context. There is no external boundary to this world. Reality fades out behind the relational texture of possibility and necessity.

But even necessity here means something other than real temporal 'following'. Much is here possible that is not "really" possible. And much is logically possible that is not possible in essence. For example, logic can stipulate a 'square circle' and then derive logically certain consequences. But in its essence a 'square circle' is simply not possible. The 'impossibility' of objects like 'square circle' is an impossibility of Being, not of logic (323). Possibility of essences is not simply freedom from contradiction.

Ideal Being is stratified throughout according to the principle of subordination. Freedom from contradiction is but the law governing coexistence in one and the same 'object' (*Gebilde*) or in the very same system of interrelated 'objects' (331).

In the law of possibility, as it prevails in the realm of the ideal, we have the most extreme contrast to reality. In the realm of ideal Being everything "has reality"—even what stands only in disjunctive parallel possibility (332). This changes the intermodality laws fundamentally. Two main points make this clear:

"What is at all ideally possible has co-existence in the ideal sphere; but what has ideal co-existence in the ideal sphere is for this reason alone not yet compossible" (332). Compossibility is obviously a higher modality of ideal Being, not only vis-à-vis possibility in general but also vis-à-vis ideal reality.

In the sphere of ideal Being, the 'real' has the same extension (*Weite*) as the possible. Only what is *merely* possible lies beyond that limit. And as far as Hartmann is concerned, for a revision of the traditionally ontological concepts an analysis of the modalities of ideal Being is the really crucial task; for it means to untangle "an intrinsically complex range of traditional errors within the apparent simplicity of the postulated double equality of ideality and possibility, reality and actuality [*Realität und Wirklichkeit*]. . . . Traditional ontology has posited the difference of the spheres as equal to the difference of the modalities. Because of this 'equalization', its propositions remain ontologically ambivalent even where they are undeniably true" (338).

In the traditional pathos of philosophical thinking we find veneration of, and even devotion to, the realm of essences. The essences appear to be divine or at least related to divinity. Such are the nimbus of Platonism and the dark beginnings of mythic thinking. But "ideal Being is an incomplete Being, one that remains in the mere universal which, in relation to the real, is not the higher but the lower Being" (344). We must here radically learn anew.

The real has always been regarded as the region of the accidental, and the realm of the ideal as that of necessity. The actual situation is just the reverse. Within its range, the real does not contain the accidental but only a single closed context of complete determination. Ideal Being, on the other hand, is not a closed context, not a unified system. Its determinations are multiply parallel, excluding one another so that there is room for the accidental.

12. Problems of Modality in Cognition

Cognition does not have its own mode of Being but belongs entirely to that of reality. Its characteristics are (1) temporality combined with the categories of process coming-into-being and ceasing-to-be; (2) individuality and uniqueness; and (3) completeness of determination within the context of the real. All these characteristics pertain to spiritual Being and its particularities, *and* to the realm of the real (*Möglichkeit und Wirklichkeit*, 358). This unique modus of intermodality relations is found only in cognition.

Cognition involves the subject, the object, a relation between them, and the cognitive image or representation of the object in the subject. But a modality of comprehension is not a modality of the object, nor one of the awareness of an object. What is given in experience reveals itself as a modality of the awareness of reality (363). And here we must distinguish between cognition *a priori* and cognition *a posteriori*. Cognition *a priori* is an insight into possibility and necessity, and is thus not a mere acceptance of what is given. However, it is primarily only an insight into possibility and necessity of essences—as in the case of the logical modalities of consistency and implication (365).

In cognition *a posteriori*, an awareness of reality and an understanding of possibility and necessity prevail. Awareness of reality does not presuppose an awareness of possibility and necessity; but a comprehension of reality presupposes a comprehension of possibility and of necessity. To put it differently: Insofar as comprehension of possibility and comprehension of necessity lead to an understanding of reality, they constitute the process of knowing the real. This twofold statement, Hartmann maintains, is "the decisive basic law of the modality of cognition" (372).

We must realize, however, that, from perception on up to a strictly scientific understanding, cognition is one single uninterrupted context. Pure sensory impressions and pure logico-mathematical thinking are extremes. Real cognition occurs in the manifoldly stratified transition between them (384). It begins with immediate givenness (which is that of reality or unreality), in which what is comprehended is what just happens to be there. From this base, cognition advances via an awareness of possibility and via an understanding of necessity to a comprehension of reality. From this highest phase of cognition the process turns back to the most elementary 'given' in perception. This process involves a specific difficulty, for it is not possible to combine what is perceptually given with the comprehension of reality itself. In a specific sense, therefore, the modality of the accidental, which is characteristic of the unreflective givenness of the real, is, strictly speaking, not a modality intrinsic to cognition; for the givenness of reality is indifferent to an awareness of accidentalness and a comprehension of necessity (387). Actual cognition is the 'roundabout way' (*Umweg*) from a comprehension of the universal to a comprehension of the really individual. "Penetrating comprehension must go this way because the universal on which that comprehension depends is only *a priori* directly available" (392).

As actual cognition approaches a comprehension of real possibility and real necessity, it must leave the cognition of essences with its modalities of the universal, and must return to the positive content of perceptual experience.

But even so we have no ground for believing that a complete comprehension of the actually real (*des Realwirklichen*) is possible, for we know in every case only a fraction of the sufficient reason for something to be real. The analysis of the modalities of cognition thus disposes of the obliteration of the difference between 'real ground' and 'cognitive ground', and of seeing in human cognition a mode of comprehension in which possibility and necessity fuse into one. "An insurmountable boundary has been drawn between human cognition and the chimerical *intellectus infinitus*" (415).

The only criterion of truth that we have in real cognition is 'relational'. It is rooted in the independence and heterogeneity of the two sources of knowledge—the *a priori* and the *a posteriori*. Each has its corrective in the other. Their failures and errors compensate each other because they cannot easily be brought to coincide (462).

In the realm of ideal Being, the absence of contradiction is sufficient indication of the reality of essences (*Wesenswirklichkeit*). In the realm of reality, the accepted laws and even the subsumed givens are questionable. Even a conclusion based upon a complete knowledge of real conditions—even that of the necessity of some specific A with its individual 'here' and 'now'—is in truth seen only within a simplified situation. Logical necessity in an apodictic judgment does not directly imply a comprehension of real necessity; but it does imply the comprehension of contexts that, on their part, depend upon real necessity. And in implying this, the apodictic judgment leads indirectly to a comprehension of necessity in the realm of real cognition. It thus is the natural approach to our knowledge of real necessity (481).

4

Philosophy of Nature

SO FAR WE HAVE SEEN that an understanding of the realities of the world around us depends upon an analysis of the categories that are constitutive of the various strata of reality. Our contact with, and manipulation of, things gives us at least an elementary understanding of these categories; and our sciences give us a clearer insight into the characteristic aspects of at least some strata of the world. But what is distinctive in modern science and what has made it so crucial to our understanding of reality is its mathematical structure, the basic principle being that "real is what is measurable."[1]

But this radical and narrow point of view can prevail only when we deal with inorganic reality. With respect to organismic reality it is a severely limited approach; at the highest level of reality—at the level of consciousness and rationality—it is totally inadequate.

It is of utmost importance, however, to note that even the objects of our natural sciences are not contained within the mathematical structures without a nonmathematical remainder. For every measurable quantity there is always a substratum of a nonmathematical kind. Distance, duration, speed, and acceleration, for example, are in themselves not quantities but substrata of possible quantities. Pressure, density,

---

1. Nicolai Hartmann, *Philosophie der Natur* (Berlin: Walter de Gruyter & Co., 1950), 21. Hereafter referred to as *Natur*.

temperature, radiation intensity, frequency, wavelengths, stress, resistance—all these are something measurable that underlines the measurements. The substratum of the 'measurable' is the precondition of any determination of magnitude.

What is quantitative is not only antecedent to the measuring, but is something other than the measurements. Whether we measure speed in terms of miles or kilometers per hour does not affect speed itself in any way; and what extension, duration, force, or mass really are is not disclosed in mathematical thinking. However, the substrata as the measurable provide the metaphysical background problems for a philosophy of nature. The measurable aspects of the objects of nature are only their rational side, and this can be comprehended mathematically. The laws of nature also can be formulated mathematically. The laws themselves, however, are not identical with such formulations (Hartmann, *Natur*, 23). That is, the *Seiende* itself is not identical with our mathematical description of it; and the so-called *constants* of nature can be ascertained only empirically. It is true that the quantitative side of the objects is also their rational side and can therefore be comprehended mathematically; but the mathematical conceptions can give us no more than the quantitative aspects of what is real.

The realm of nature includes not only the purely physical stratum but also the whole range of organismic existence. What distinguishes living beings from the nonliving is the form-building or morphogenetic process. Organisms—at least the multicellular ones—develop in progressive differentiations and centralization in specific directions—processes that are determined from within the organism itself.[2] That is, the living organism regulates and regenerates itself, and for these two basic facts of organismic existence the physicalistic mode of explanation is inadequate.[3]

We must also note that, beginning at a certain stratum of reality, organisms involve two modes of Being: (1) the life of the bodied organism merely as organic existence, and (2) its intrinsic awareness of the surrounding world, which, at the human level, also involves the immediate awareness of one's own existence. The contrast in the way in

2. Nicolai Hartmann, *Philosophische Grundfragen der Biologie* (Göttingen: Vanderhoek & Ruprecht, 1912).

3. *Natur*, 26. See also W. H. Werkmeister, *A Philosophy of Science* (New York: Harper & Brothers, 1940; University of Nebraska paperback), 322–51.

which these two modes of Being are given is irreconcilable and gives rise to two distinct types of interrelations. If one's interpretation of life centers on the bodied organism, one sees the living being as an object of nature under categories of the physical world. But if one approaches the problem of life from the point of view of the inner awareness of one's own existence, one uses categories of minded existence—subsuming the organism under categories of purposiveness. Both modes of interpretation involve a "boundary transgression," taking but one aspect for the whole (*Natur*, 28).

There are causal dependencies everywhere in organic structures, but does this mean that the category 'causality' is sufficient as an explanation of all organic phenomena? Does it account, for example, for the emergence of consciousness? The answer to this question is obviously negative. However, purposiveness is also unacceptable as an explanation of organismic development because the categorial condition of a purpose-setting consciousness is lacking. But if neither the causal nexus nor the purposive nexus fits categorially the particularity of the processes of life, we must conclude that in the realm of organismic reality a third form of determination prevails. For want of a better term, Hartmann calls it the *nexus organicus* (31). We shall discuss it at the proper time.

1. The General Concept of Categories of Nature

What Hartmann attempts in his *Philosophie der Natur* is an analysis of the categories that are essential to our understanding of nature. He is emphatic, however, in maintaining that there is no *a priori* cognition of these categories, that they cannot be derived from the nature of judgments but must be obtained by way of a meticulous analysis of the given phenomena.[4]

Since all structures and events in nature are at the same time spatial and temporal, a philosophy of nature must begin with an analysis of space and time as the most general presuppositions of everything that happens in nature.

The common and basic categorial aspect of both space and time

---

4. In this connection see Theodor Ballauff, "Nicolai Hartmanns Philosophie der Natur. Zu ihren Voraussetzungen und Grenzen," in *Philosophia naturalis* 2 (1952/53): 117–30.

is that of dimensionality. It must be noted, however, that dimensionality is not limited to space and time but is discoverable in all types of measurement, such as weight, density, force, and speed. These are the substrata of quantity. Still, basic to them all is the dimensional system of space and time. To put it differently: The four space-time dimensions constitute the *basic* dimensions (*Grunddimensionen*) of the world of nature (*Natur*, 46).

However, neither space nor time has a real existence aside from, and independently of, real things and events whose dimensions they are. This fact should not trouble us, for we deal here not with things but with categories; and it is of the very essence of categories that "they have no being other than that of being principles for what is concretely real."[5]

Kant, of course, regarded space and time as forms of "presentation" —space being the form of our "outer sense" and time being the form of "inner sense." But, as Hartmann points out, the fact that space and time, as forms of perceptual experience, are "pure intuitions" does not preclude the possibility that, beyond this, they are also categories of real events in nature and are thus subject to categorial analysis.

In the case of time this is fairly obvious, for in addition to our awareness *of* time there is also our awareness of ourselves as existing *in* time. Our consciousness of the temporality of events around us is not the same as the temporality of our own consciousness involved in observing those events. That is, time is not only a "form of intuition" (as Kant had it), but is also a real category of our own conscious existence. The time in which events actually occur is not the time in which they are experienced or represented by us. But as far as consciousness is concerned, space is only a "form of intuition," for consciousness itself is not spatial. Seen ontologically, it is the "great categorial *novum*" (*Natur*, 56f.).

Descartes regarded spatiality as the basic determining factor of the external world and spoke of *extensio* as the substance of things in contrast to the *cogitatio* as substance of the mind. When we disregard the metaphysics of substance here implied, there remains the categorial conception of space as pure *extensio*. But what does this mean?

It is obvious that both extension and dimension belong to space, but neither one in itself is space. Just as duration is not time but a charac-

5. Nicolai Hartmann, *Der Aufbau der Realen Welt*, chap. 43.

teristic of objects and events in time, so extension and dimension are not space but characteristics of what is extended in space. And in this sense the dimensions of space and time are the substrata of measurements. Only the measurements taken in a specific dimension give that dimension its character as length or angular spread, as plane or volume, as duration or speed. The dimensions, therefore, are the substrata underlying diverse magnitudes and thus constitute the heterogeneity of the measured determinations (63).

But a substratum must not be confused with substance. Extension, for example, does not belong to any dimension per se but to the *Seiende,* to that which is extended. Similarly, space itself is not extended, but bodies and distances are extended in space. And neither is time in itself extended. What is extended here are events in time. Space and time as such are merely "that in which" there is extension.

There is also a difference between the dimension in time and a dimension in space. In time, the opposite of directions, for example, is quite different from what it is in space. In time, a motion is irreversible in direction—from the past, through the present, into the future. But in space a motion is reversible—from left to right and back to left, etc.

In addition to the dimensions of space and time we must also distinguish between *extensive* and *intensive* magnitudes. The former is the magnitude of a speed in space and/or in time. But magnitudes are encountered only where there is something to which the quantitative relationships pertain. In other words, the categorial essence of magnitude lies in the fact that it is a magnitude of 'something'. Measurements and numbers are merely schemata of possible magnitudes. But a magnitude is measurable only as to the degree of its dimension; and the measurement pertains only to the magnitude of that dimension —the kind of measurement being determined by the character of the dimension (67).

The magnitudes in space and time are the basic magnitudes of extension, and thus are the prototypes of what is measurable.

2. Categories of Space

As far as space is concerned we must distinguish between real space, space as mode of sensory perception, and the ideal space of geometry. The differences between them are ontological in character and must be considered in terms of the categories involved.

The simplest and the least burdened metaphysically is the ideal space of geometry (*Natur*, 70ff.). We must keep in mind, however, that there is not just one geometric space. The best known, the Euclidean form, is only one among many. Each has its own system of postulates, its own structures and laws. As far as mathematics is concerned, the internal consistency of a system is sufficient for its acceptance. For a categorial analysis, however, this is not sufficient.

In considering special aspects of geometric space we must keep in mind that the *a priori* certainty of the propositions of geometry depends on the direct comprehension of possible types of spatial relations. The Euclidean and various non-Euclidean geometries illustrate this fact. But this is not sufficient for an assurance of the validity of a particular geometrical space for the events in nature. There is quite a difference in saying that rays of light *in* space are curved and saying that the dimensions *of* space are curved. No matter how many different types of geometry we may construct, the relation of geometry to real space consists in the validity of the geometrical laws for things and their relations in space. If geometry were nothing but a product of the mind, such validity would be completely incomprehensible. It either would not exist at all or it would have to be a miracle.

What, precisely, are the basic characteristics of geometric space? Hartmann distinguishes the following:[6]

1. Geometric space is an ideal space. That is, it is a system of dimensions of extensive magnitudes pure and simple. One dimension does not yet constitute space.
2. Geometric space is homogeneous. All distinctions within it are relative to nothing other than the parts of the ideal space itself.
3. This space is stable, constituting a single and uninterrupted continuum in all directions.
4. The space of geometry is unlimited but has no magnitude; for, strictly speaking, only something *in* space has magnitude—be it finite or infinite.
5. Space itself is not something extended but is only the system of dimensions *in* which something extends.
6. There are no boundaries of geometrical space. There are boundaries only of something *in* space.

6. *Natur*, 75ff. For a discussion of various forms of geometric spaces see Werkmeister, *A Philosophy of Science*, 188–228.

7. Although it determines the kind of measuring devices to be employed insofar as this employment depends on the kind of dimension in which the measuring is to take place, the ideal space of geometry itself does not provide any measures of magnitude.

8. However, geometric space is "isometric." That is, the measure that is valid in one dimension is valid for all other dimensions as well, for every particular dimension we select is, as far as space itself is concerned, purely arbitrary.

9. The dimensions of the ideal space of geometry are not a system of coordinates; for coordinates are a system of lines *within* space relative to which the location of points in space can be determined.

Most of the nine points made with respect to the ideal space of geometry hold also for real space. But there are additional points to be considered (*Natur*, 79ff.). For example, in addition to the aspect of *extension* there is the equally fundamental *direction in* space. That is, every extension has its definite direction. In one-dimensional space there is only one direction. In two-dimensional space, however, there are already infinitely many directions, and their number increases with every additional dimension. Every transition of direction from one dimension into another represents a 'turning' that is related to an axis that has its own definite position and direction in space.

The measurement of an angle is in principle something other than a measurement of length; for the magnitude of the angle does not vary with the lengths of the 'legs' of the angle or with the size of the figure. The measure of extensions, however, increases with the number of dimensions; for there are measures of length, of plane, and of volume. None of these configurations and relationships can be dissolved into something else which is prior to them. They are the ultimates of geometric space.

By *real* space Hartmann means the space in which real things and real thing-relations occur. It is the space of physically real events, and in this sense it is as much world-space as it is our own environmental or 'living' space (83ff.). It is the space in which everything exists, and thus it is the form and categorial condition of the existing world. Even so, however, space as such does not exist. Its reality is that of being the condition under which alone the spatial structures and relationships of real things in the world are possible. It is related to the ideal space of geometry as but a special case of the category 'space'.

Since real space is the space in which the world exists, and since that world is only one, it follows that real space is unique. This does not mean, however, that it must necessarily be Euclidean in character.

A differential aspect of the real space of our world is that it has no more than three dimensions. Why this is so we do not know; we simply have to accept it as a fact (88).

In its three-dimensionality, real space is the universal categorial presupposition of all occurrences of substances and their attributes in the real world. Volume, distance, movement—these are something *in* space. And the relation of force to space is the same as that of matter to space, for force is what affects only *things in* space.

We must note also that real space is homogeneous (92f.). Discernible places in it pertain to what is extended in space, not to space itself. Real space is as continuous as is an ideal space. There are no disruptions in it. It forms a simple three-dimensional continuum. Upon this fact depends the constancy of all spatial movement.

The real space is unlimited. All limitations are limits *in* space, not of space. Real space is also not extended. Extension occurs only *in* space. In fact, space as such has no existence, but is the dimensional condition of the existence and the extension of things. That as such a condition space goes beyond any existing masses and relationships of things is no contradiction. In itself, however, space has no magnitude—neither finite nor infinite—but is a condition for the magnitude of what exists in it.

The three dimensions of the space we live in belong inseparably together. They are analogous to one another and can be interchanged in our interpretation of spatial relationships. What is regarded as 'up' in one situation may well be regarded as 'down' in another. In real space there is no natural point 'zero' from which the three coordinates extend. Nor is there a fixed direction of the axis. Point, line, and plane are, however, not separable from their inclusion in the three-dimensionality of real space.

A distinction must now be made between space and spatiality (103).

Space is basic. It is the categorial *prius*. Without real space there can be no real things. Spatiality, however, pertains to things and their interrelations. It is a consequence of their being in space.

All things in space have magnitude, and the relativity of magnitudes is universal. But this relativity pertains only to what is *in* space, not to space itself. And there is no fixed or absolute point in real space relative to which the positions of bodies in space could be determined. There are no absolute positions, no absolute places, in space. All places are relative to other places that are just as relative. There are only positions relative to what is also relative in space.

The result is that every object in real space has at one and the same time many positions, depending on the group of things to which we relate it. This same relativity pertains to the motions of bodies. That is, the two basic aspects of motions—their direction and their velocity —are relative to the motions of other bodies or systems of bodies that, on their part, have motions that are just as relative. This means that the same material thing may be taken to move simultaneously in different directions and with different speeds relative to different systems of reference.[7]

Since space in itself does not exist, nothing that exists spatially is relative to space but only to something that also exists in space. This means that for all forms and motions of material bodies—for their placement, density, distribution, distances, and interactions— spatiality is the basic categorial aspect. All natural forms and dynamic structures—from atomic nuclei to spiral nebulae and cosmic galaxies, as well as their modifications—are forms of what is spatially extended; and the laws that are determinative for them are essentially of the nature of laws of measurements of extension or expansion in space.

Force, however, is not comprehensible in terms of directions and measurements of extension alone; for force has only an intensive magnitude of weaker and stronger, and moves in dimensions other than those of space—although its effects may well be spatially determinable (*Natur*, 111f.).

In the case of living organisms, spatiality sinks further down to a mere peripheral aspect—although even here it is by no means unessential or replaceable. Like any other dynamic structure, every organism

7. *Natur*, 108. See also Albert Einstein, "Cosmological Considerations of the General Theory," *Sitzungsberichte der Preussischen Akademie der Wissenschaften* (Berlin: Verlag der Akademie der Wissenschaften, 1917); Herman Weyl, *Raum, Zeit, Materie*, 5th ed. (Göttingen, 1923); Alois Wenzel, *Das Verhältnis der Einsteinschen Relativitätslehre zur Philosophie der Gegenwart* (München, 1921); and Werkmeister, *A Philosophy of Science*, 225–28.

has its spatial form. Its form, however, is not pure spatiality. It is the form of a process involving the development of the individual organism —its self-regulation and self-reproduction. This development consti-tutes the distinguishing character of an organic structure in space.

Furthermore, mental life, although it remains bound to spatial exis-tence, has itself no spatial structure at all, and its contents are not spatial entities.

What Kant spoke of as "the form of all appearances of outer sense"[8] and what Hartmann calls "intuitive space" (*Anschauungs-raum*) (*Natur*, 113–135) is the form in which external objects appear in our experience. Although we may distinguish between the space of factual experiences, of movements, and of visual space, all three types fuse into one experiential space, for they all pertain to the same spatial objects or events.

Because visual space discloses at once a whole range of spatial rela-tionships, it is superior to the space of touch, and provides an aspect of inclusive unity. Here, in visual space, the three-dimensional picture of what is 'given' has priority; It is this space that entails the phenomena of perspective—the apparent convergence of parallel lines; the appar-ent reduction of the size of objects in relation to their distance; the distortion of forms in slanting viewing of objects; and other phenom-ena of visual experience. It is characteristic of them all that they are not taken to be illusions but as indicating distances or positions.

Because of its dependence on the body, consciousness is indirectly limited to a specific place in real space and can perceive only relative to this mediated location. To be sure, the subject can change its posi-tion in space, but it can do so only by moving its body to another place. It cannot perceive simultaneously from different positions, and the orientation of the field of vision is always with respect to one's own person.

However, a number of categorial elements of intuitive space cor-respond to those of real space: (1) Like real space, intuitive space is strictly three-dimensional. (2) Perceived objects are limitations in both real and intuitive space. They occupy parts of them, and their dimensions are the substrata of extensive magnitude in both spaces. However, this very fact entails the most paradoxical aspect of space as

8. Immanuel Kant, *Critique of Pure Reason*, A26/B42; Smith translation, 71.

a category of consciousness; for the experience of an extended magnitude appears to contradict the essence of consciousness as a nonspatial reality.

(3) Intuitive space is neither a substance nor an accident of intuited objects. It is only that mode of awareness 'in which' objects appear as extended, as structured, and as localized. But whereas real space is unlimited, the space of perceptual intuition is not; and this is perhaps the most important categorial difference between them.

3. The Flux of Time

Every process in the world occurs in time, and every event has its duration in time (*Natur*, 138). But neither the process nor the event as such is time. Duration in time is related to time as extension in space is related to space. In fact, duration is but extension in time.

Only that which is *in* time—that which exists in time and in that sense is temporal—has full reality. It is of limited duration, has a beginning and an end, and is of the nature of a process. It is also essentially unique and does not recur. In this strict sense, the events in nature, the processes of living and of consciousness, the little occurrences of everyday life, and the great historical and cosmological events are *real*. Despite certain recurring events, all of these happenings are qualitatively unique and nonrepeatable. Since this is so, it is temporality rather than spatiality that is the specific characteristic of reality (138). It is the dimensional form of the inner as well as of the outer world, and of all strata of reality. In brief, temporality is the most elementary category.

But here, too, we must distinguish between real time and time as the "subjective condition of our intuition."[9]

Real time, so Hartmann argues (*Natur*, 144–68), is the time in which real things and thing-relationships come into being and cease to be—in which real events occur. It is cosmic as well as historical. It is characteristic of living, and in it consciousness is just as real as are things. It comes into being in time, and it ceases to be in time. Its processes and states are all in time.

But time itself exists no more than does space itself. Its mode of Being is the same as that of real space—namely, as that of a mere condition of reality. Only things *in* time have existence.

9. Kant, *Critique of Pure Reason*, A35/B51; Smith trans., 78.

The characteristics of time are its one-dimensionality, its progression or flux, and the emergence of an ever new *now* within that flux. Time itself is not a system of dimensions; in it there is only the one-dimensional flow of earlier-later of the manifold and intertwined relationships of real events.

But time is also more than flux; for it is also duration. And this involves the *now,* which, as a particular stage in the flux of time, has special significance. It may be but the particular moment in time for a subject to observe an event. Beyond this, however, there is also the *Now* in the sequence of real events when various processes interact. Such a moment in time is unique and will never return. But that there is a *Now* that has primary rank over all other points in time—the present *Now*—is a nonderivative and irreducible characteristic of real time. It is also inescapable.

In conformity with the one-dimensionality of the flux of time, all real processes in the world, no matter to what stratum of reality they belong, are irreversible. Events in time cannot be made to run backwards—although they may be reversible in spatial or dynamic respects. The so-called relativity of time is but a matter of adjustments of "clock times." [10]

But despite—or perhaps because of—its one-dimensionality, real time provides at least the rudimentary beginning of a system of co-ordinates, for it provides what space does not: a fixed reference point —the *Now*. The one dimension of time can be seen as the abscissa of possible ordinates of other dimensions—as is the case in the four-dimensional system of space-time that is of special significance for the structure and unity of the real world.

Because of its one-dimensionality, time allows only one kind of magnitude—that of temporal extension or duration. Time itself, however, has no duration; only things and events *in* time have that. Still, the *Now* introduces the start of a possible system of positions. We *now* look back upon what has been, and we *now* look forward to what is yet to come. The *Now* is no interruption in this flux of events in time nor of time itself.

Real time is not only one-dimensional, it is also unlimited. All so-called temporal limits are limits *in* time, not of time. Time as such is neither extended nor does it have duration, for extension and dura-

10. See Werkmeister, *A Philosophy of Science,* 202–25.

tion pertain only to something *in* time—such as a process or a specific situation. Although time itself determines the kind of time measurements that are possible—hours, days, weeks, years, etc.—it does not provide specific measuring devices. These we obtain from periodic processes in the real world, such as the motion of the 'hands' of a clock, the alternations of day and night, the change of seasons, and other realities.

We must keep in mind, however, that time is not the same as temporality (*Natur*, 161ff.); for it is temporality, not time, that is characteristic of things, events, conditions, and processes. Time itself has no beginning, no end, and no duration. These are characteristic of temporality, and it is temporality that is the basic categorial characteristic of everything that persists or is subject to change. Temporality is thus basic to everything that is real, including mental and spiritual reality.

But temporality is only a function of time, not time itself. This is perhaps best seen when we realize that, in their most essential aspect, real processes are a function of real time, and that this essential aspect of time is their temporality.

Duration is a form of temporality. But it is not simply some given moment that has duration; for only that has duration whose individual characteristics change while it itself persists despite the changes. The basic phenomenon of temporality thus consists in the persistence or extension of something real in time.

Like everything else, the human being is always bound to the "present moment." It is from here that one sees the world in the temporal, double aspect of past and future, with the present separating them. Time itself, however, is no more separating than it is combining past and future; for togetherness and separation in time are not characteristics of time itself but of things and events in time. In the flow of time all individual moments sink into the past but do not change their temporal positions relative to one another; and no power in the world can separate them or alter their sequential order.

But now a problem arises, for it seems that only what is present actually *is*—is real (165). The present, however—the immediate *Now*—is a mere limit without temporal extension; and since in time (as also in space) only what is extended is real, the temporally extended (that which has duration) cannot be present in any particular given *Now*. In other words, what is temporally real cannot be limited to the present moment.

Still, there is the unique and real Being of that which is in the present —as distinguished from what is in the past or in the future. What is *now* has a "rank of Being" higher than the rank of what is past and of what is future. But, so Hartmann maintains, this is only a ranking "within the Now." In the mode of Being this ranking in the *Now* makes no difference; for what is real has its own temporality, its own transitoriness and uniqueness in time. If that which *has been* were simply non-Being, it would be of no concern to us now. But we are very much concerned with it because we face historical situations that have been formed throughout centuries. And there are also causal sequences of past events. What once has occurred can in no way be made to have not occurred. It remains unmovable at its point in time. We have to live with it, for it is real—even though it is past.

And the future is also eminently real for our practical attitudes. Our setting of goals and striving after them, our adjustments to anticipated events—all of this would be nonsensical if we were not concerned with a full-valued reality that is approaching.

What all of this implies is that the movement of events in the world is not restricted to the ephemeral *Now* but is grounded in the temporal context of past and future that passes through the *Now*. This means that the real context of the temporal sequence of events presupposes the reality of what is past and what is future, without diminishing the special importance of *being-Now*.

The *Now connects* what is past with what is future just as it also *separates* them. It is the threshold over which events move out of the future into the past; and it is precisely this transition that is the mark of reality (169).

Although as a point of transition the *Now* is the basic mode of time, time is characterized also by modes of a secondary order. These include simultaneity, succession, and duration—modes that are intertwined in the manifold forms and relationships of the context of reality (171f.).

Where different processes in the world occur simultaneously, they coincide partially or completely in their duration within the same interval of time. This means that simultaneity involves not merely temporal relations but also that it rests upon a firm context of the category time with other dimensional categories. The time dimension is, as it were, the abscissa of possible heterogeneous ordinates.

The basic characteristic of real time is, of course, succession—i.e., the sequence of moments in a one-dimensional direction. It is the continuum in which all temporal distinctions appear as discretions. But this discretion is not time itself. The ultimate and indissoluble essence of real temporality is the fact that all events, whatsoever they may be, always 'run forwards'. What is earlier cannot be interchanged with what is later. In this fundamental sense, time is the unity of direction of all events. Time itself, however, is not the flow of events. It does not begin, nor does it end.

In the stream of events all occurrences "need time." They occupy or fill a special segment of time. Even the process of shortest duration is not limited to a mere point in time. It, too, has the form of succession, and succession is what 'endures'.

What we generally call an experience of the flux of time is in reality only our experience of events in time. A flux of time is not experienced as something *in* time, for the flux *is* time, and time itself is the flux.

As far as time is concerned, all real processes occur with equal speed. No process can overtake any other or fall behind. They are all carried along in the same constant flux of time. If a man is two years younger than his brother, he remains so throughout his life. The facts are undeniable, but much remains incomprehensible. Life, for example, is not simply a getting older in years. There is also development, creativity, achievement—and these are events of a different kind, for they can be speeded up or retarded. And motion in space admits of an incalculable gradation of speed. The faster movement is that which, in the same time interval, covers the greater distance in space. But there is no temporal overtaking or remaining behind. All difference in speed is merely spatial.

What is obvious in the case of motion in space is also true in all other real processes. They are all carried along by the common flux of time; no event stands still at a single point in time.

This flux of time is the first and most elementary form of real determination in the world (185). And let us note especially that this uninterruptible advance out of the future into the past—this irreversibility of time—is real without being causally determined. From an ontological point of view, the irreversibility of time is the mode of determination that is basic to all others. It is the most elementary determination of the real, and for this reason it is also the strongest. The 'law of the uniform succession in time' is unquestionably the basic law of all real Being. Its correlates with respect to real processes are simultaneity and a strict parallelism in time.

As the dividing point between future and past, the *Now* is an ever advancing point in time that maintains itself despite the flow of time. To be sure, the content of the *Now,* as well as its position in time, is always other; but the *Now* itself remains. It is always *now.* Insofar as anything 'endures'—be it a thing, a living creature, a state, an institution, or a whole culture—it advances with the *Now* in the flow of time. The duration of all that is real consists in the same 'being present' in the moving *Now.* The essential meaning of their duration is to remain identical despite all change.

Consciousness, as manifest in human beings, is involved in time in a twofold way (189). It is involved in real time to the extent that its processes actually occur. But, in being aware of objects and events, consciousness is also aware of the time in which they occur. These two times—the time in which consciousness exists and the time of the events of which it is aware—are not the same. One is real time; the other is perceived time. The former is a category of existence; the latter is one of experiencing.

To be sure, experiencing is itself an event in real time, and is thus subject to the laws of real time. But the content of experience is not so restricted. Although a subject can have an experience only in the actual *Now,* in the present, it can also recall what is past or anticipate the future. That is to say, although actual experience—even the experience of recall and of anticipation—is restricted to the *Now,* the events experienceable are not so restricted but may run through a whole series of *Now*-points, as the future moves into the past.

Consciousness endures by changing; but in order to achieve the synthesis that is representative of process, there must be something in the nature of consciousness that remains self-identical in the midst of these changes. The problem here is genuine. The problem of the 'identity of the self' in the midst of changes is the central problem of mental reality (193).

And still another problem is present. The constantly broadening contexts of experience form a horizon that in its temporal aspects is distinguished from the fleeting content of the momentary *Now.* What is not possible in real time—bringing together in one moment the past and the future of one's own existence—is easily accomplished in representational time. And this unifying act of experiencing events extends even beyond the individual—to family, to friends, to coworkers, and even to institutions. For the mature political and historical consciousness the same phenomenon recurs but is enlarged in the conception of a people as a whole, of a state.

For the individual human being this means a far-reaching elevation above the present moment and beyond the primitive prevalence of the experiential present.

4. Process and Situation

Except for our inner experiences, there are no phenomena that are merely spatial or merely temporal (*Natur*, 216–50); but the difference between space and time is radical. It consists in the primordial heterogeneity of their respective dimensions. That is, it consists in the kind of 'extension' that one and the same reality has in space and time.

We must note, however, that even the four dimensions of the combined space-time system do not include all dimensions. This is so because real time is not merely a cosmological category—as space is —but it is also a category for the higher strata of Being for which space is irrelevant. In these higher strata we encounter a 'broadness' of time beyond its one-dimensionality, for otherwise there would be no simultaneity of representations, of thoughts, of mental events; no narrowness or broadness of consciousness; and especially no interplay of spiritual powers in the historical life of a people.

Time is the basic dimension that connects everything that is real. Through it, the otherwise heterogeneously dimensioned world is bound into unity. All occurrences in the world—no matter of what dimension they be—remain fixed in their respective places in time, and move with it into the past. If they are simultaneous to begin with, they share this simultaneity forever.

We must keep in mind, however, that only together do real time and real space form a system of dimensions within which all real relationships occur. Only together are they the universal preconditions of things and events in the world. Still, the particular character of what occurs in them depends on other principles—principles that determine relationships and interactions, structural forms and laws, and, in part, the character of substrata. In modified form (as in the case of time), these additional principles recur in strata of Being higher than those of physicobiological nature. All of these problems require clarification. What is needed, therefore, is a critical "*Grundlagenforschung*"—a careful and critical analysis of the basic categories that are constitutive of the world we live in.

Kant's theory of categories made substance and causality central. But there are cosmological categories beyond these two. The basic concepts of physics, for example—mass, force, energy, radiation, electric current, electron, proton, and others—indicate clearly that the Kantian conception of categories is at best incomplete. But how is it to be augmented?

Hartmann begins his interpretation by accepting a central group of key concepts: substance, causal nexus, lawfulness, and reciprocal action. But this group must now be supplemented in two respects: toward the more specific and toward the more general.

As far as the supplementation toward the more general is concerned, Hartmann points out that here a category has been overlooked, a category that "stands in the middle between real time and the causal nexus": the category "*process*" (252). A process always moves in the direction of the flow of time but is as yet "this side" of any specific form of determination. It can be determined causally but also in other ways. In fact, causal connections clearly presuppose the categorial aspect of process.

The counterpart of process is "*Zustand*"—the state or situation— at any given moment. This relationship of process and situation is fundamental and gives rise to the conception of 'dynamic structures'—an aspect of reality that in various forms is found at every stratum of our world. Hartmann states this fact in the form of a basic principle: "All structures in nature are intrinsically relational" (254). The relations that form the structures are essential to them.

Since that which is situational is subject to change, and since change itself is a process, the conception of dynamic structures leads in the natural sciences to a replacement of the 'substantial forms' of an older view by the conception of basic laws that imply that all structures in nature are codetermined by the processes that form them. These processes themselves, however, are in part determined by the structures in which they are involved. Atomic nuclei, for example, determine the 'orbits' of electrons within an atom, and atoms determine chemical reactions.

Since 'becoming' (*Werden*) is the universal mode of Being of everything that is real, process is eminently *the* category of reality. We must note, however, that process is not limited to what is spatial. It does not end at the level of organismic existence. Its range is the entire spatiotemporal world (259). We encounter process wherever there is an undisrupted emergence of something out of something else. It is the continuity in the succession of interrelated changes, and in this sense it is "the only real form of Being" (261).

Since process is the continuity of interrelated changes, its presupposition is that in the process something remains identical while its circumstances and conditions change. This presupposition entails the problem of *substance,* which will be discussed in the next section. Let us first consider the fact that what is approaching out of the future is as yet not completely determined in every respect. It contains various 'possibilities'. As the process of its approach continues, some of the initial possibilities are eliminated. In the end, only one of them is realized. At that moment all other possibilities are turned into impossibilities.[11]

5. Substance

We have seen that *Zustand*—situation—is the natural opposite of process. But it is obvious that in its complexity a 'situation' is also the opposite of *substance.*

The conception of substance prevails in traditional philosophy as the principle of 'matter'. Kant stated that "throughout all changes in the world *substance* remains, and only *accidents* change."[12] He also said: "Wherever there is action . . . there is also substance."[13] The Kantian conviction that only what persists can undergo changes, and that its changes reveal its persistence, prevailed in classical physics until recent times.

We must note, however, that substance does not lie outside process but is in it as that which perseveres. But such perseverance is not absolute—perhaps not even in the case of the lowest and most elementary strata of reality. Traditional philosophy has generally spoken of it as 'matter', although the meaning of that term has varied according to differences in philosophical approach. In general, however, what was

11. Hartmann discusses this situation in great detail in his formidable (481 pp.) book *Möglichkeit und Wirklichkeit* (Berlin: Walter de Gruyter & Co., 1938).
12. *Critique of Pure Reason,* A184/B227; Smith trans., 214.
13. Ibid., A204/B250; Smith trans., 229.

meant by 'matter' is the categorial opposite of relation, its meaning being that 'matter' is what retains its identity in a process. It is the indissolubly indeterminate, the persisting, the substratum. But this is precisely what Hartmann means by *substance* (*Natur*, 288). And of substance he says: "It is not singular in essence. There can well be a diversity of substances. Substance need not be infinite. It is divisible. It is not universal and need not be absolute. It has no being other than as a principle; and this means that it has no 'being in itself' " (290ff.).

There is no reason why substance must be *matter* and nothing else. It can be matter, to be sure, but it can also be something else. There is no a priori reason why it should be matter.

What do we actually know about matter? Kant's attempt to account for matter as the result of the interaction of two forces—attraction and repulsion [14]—does not seem quite adequate. Hartmann points out that there are at least three forces involved: impenetrability, inertia, and gravity. But he also stresses the fact that the conception of force is not adequate as a replacement for the conception of matter as the stratum of all reality. After all, force is not preserved but used up in its effectiveness. Granted that ever new forces come into existence as processes go on; but in the transition of old forces into new ones their identities are not preserved. However, the substratum-like aspects in the change of forces and in their relationships become comprehensible in the conception of *energy* as that which maintains itself in the change of events: "It is substance dynamically understood" (*Natur*, 296).

6. Basic Categories

When we now take a closer look at the world we live in, we find that all the basic forms of determination have the character of something like strata—space, time, force, motion, causal nexus, energy, and the like. The exactitude of the laws that are determinative of these strata is rooted in their quantitative aspect. Where this ceases, our comprehension of them also ceases. It is of the essence of quantity, however, to be a quantity of something. All quantities presuppose a substratum

14. Kant, *Critique of Pure Reason*, A265/B321; Smith trans., 279; "We are acquainted with substance in space only through forces . . . attraction . . . and impenetrability or repulsion. We are not acquainted with any properties . . . of the substance . . . which we call matter."

that in itself is not quantitatively comprehensible. Length and weight, duration and work, pressure and density—all of these are quantitatively determinable. However, despite all quantitative variations they remain identical in their essence. Time is time, no matter how short or how long any particular interval may be. And pressure is pressure, no matter what our measurements of it are. In these facts we encounter the limits of the mathematical in our interpretations of nature. No natural science can tell us what space and time or energy in themselves are. To be sure, science presupposes them in its initial stipulations, and it is justified in doing so; for all of these aspects are encountered in nature. This means, however, that here a problem of categories is involved that natural science is incapable of solving. It is a problem pertaining to the ultimate ground of Being and therefore requires ontological considerations.[15]

As far as Hartmann is concerned, Einstein's theory of relativity may be seen as an attempt to penetrate from the traditional quantitative basis of mathematical comprehension of space, time, and matter into the region of the nonquantitative-ontic foundation of all that is physically real. The mathematical value of the theory is not affected by this daring venture, but the justification of its metaphysical consequence is affected. A theory that, starting with the idea of universal measurements, chooses its Archimedean point in what is ontologically secondary, and from there pushes its conclusions into what is categorially primary, commits a borderline transgression, carrying mathematical thinking into the realm of metaphysics.[16]

From an ontological point of view, mathematics is not the highest or the most sublime of the sciences but the most elementary and the lowest. Considered within itself only, it is the most perfect science we have. But this perfection lies only in its exactness and is not a mea-

15. Nicolai Hartmann, "Systematische Selbst-Darstellung," in *Deutsche Systematische Philosophie nach ihren Gestaltern*, ed. Herman Schwarz, vol. 1 (Berlin: Walter de Gruyter & Co., 1931). Reprinted in Nicolai Hartmann, *Kleinere Schriften* 1; 24f.

16. "The theory of relativity is a very simple and eloquent description of the relevant results of measurements and is therefore completely sufficient for the practice of the physicists but is not sufficiently justified for the demands of the epistemologist or the ontologist and metaphysician."—Eduard May, "Die Stellung Nicolai Hartmanns in der neueren Naturphilosophie," in *Nicolai Hartmann, Der Denker und sein Werk*, ed. Heinz Heimsoeth and Robert Heiss (Göttingen: Vandenhoeck & Ruprecht, 1952), 22.

surement of the Being of its object. What is lacking is the richness and character of the substrata of nature. Its object is ontologically the most elementary.

What the natural sciences have for centuries hoped for—to dissolve real processes and relationships into mathematical functions and relationships—has been a self-delusion of mathematical thinking. To be sure, the substrata of the real structures in nature do have their mathematical aspects, and to this extent they are comprehensible with exactitude. But they are *not merely* mathematical. Mathematical formulations are not sufficient for a comprehension of their ontic character. Despite all uniformities of laws, the natural structures and processes are uniquely individual and can be distinguished as individuals. Mathematicism cannot comprehend them in their uniqueness.

In his First Analogy of Experience, Kant has argued that "alteration [*Veränderung*] is a way of existing which follows upon another way of existing *of the same subject*. Everything which changes [sich *verändert*] persists, and only its *state* [*Zustand*] changes."[17] He added: "Substances, in the field of appearance, are the substrata of all determinations of time. . . . Permanence is thus a necessary condition under which alone appearances are determinable as things or objects in a possible experience."[18]

The problem involved in the situation so briefly characterized by Kant has led Hartmann to his detailed analysis of the "cosmological categories," which are determinative of inorganic nature.[19]

Within the Kantian system, the categories 'substance' and 'causality' are central. But even when we add to them the relationship of 'interaction', we have no complete list of all cosmological categories. This is evident as soon as we consider such basic concepts of physics as mass, force, energy, radiation, electron, and proton. And even when we take substance, causal nexus, lawfulness, and interaction also into consideration, we still have overlooked a category that "stands in the middle between real time and the causal nexus"—the category 'process' (referred to earlier). Although any process moves in the direction of the flow of time, it is (as Hartmann puts it) "this side" of any specific form

17. *Critique of Pure Reason*, A187/B230; Smith, 216.
18. Ibid., A188–89/B231–32; Smith, 217.
19. *Natur*, 251–511. For an evaluation of this analysis, see Hans J. Hoefert, "Kategorialanalyse und physikalische Grundlagenforschung," in Heimsoeth and Heiss, eds., *Nicolai Hartmann, Der Denker*, 186–207.

of determination; for it can be determined causally and in some other way as well. A causal connection already presupposes the categorial form of process (*Natur*, 252).

But if 'process' is a category of what is real, then 'state' or situation (*Zustand*) must also be a category, for in every process there are 'states' that maintain themselves. And since this is so, there is still another category that is more general than either 'process' or 'state' and that encompasses them both—the category 'real relation'.

In addition to these three categories, which are the most general, there are categories of narrower range. In contrast to process we thus encounter in the world 'dynamic structures' (*dynamische Gefüge*). Their basic type includes all the special forms of structure we find at the various strata of reality. Since structures of various types stand in relation and condition one another in various ways, what we encounter here is the categorial structure of stratified nature itself—together with the modes of determination intrinsic to that structure insofar as this is not a matter of mere causality. And in all dynamic structures there is also the categorial aspect of stability—the 'dynamic equilibrium'.

Though the series of categories thus briefly referred to is not complete, we can attempt at least to interpret the various strata of reality and their interrelations in terms of the categories mentioned; and we can augment that list as may be required by the results of our analysis of what we encounter at the various strata of the real.

7. Substance and Substrata

As we have seen already, real space and real time form a system of dimensions within which real relations occur. We know that all 'processes' occur in time and that their antithesis is *Zustand,* or situation. The interdependence of process and situation is the 'dynamic structure' of reality. All realities in nature are in this sense "relational structures" (*Natur*, 261).

However, situations are subject to change, and within these changes the stages in the process stand in manifold real relationships. But only modern science has placed the emphasis upon these interlinked processes—a development that entails "the replacement of substantial forms by laws" (254f.). It means the recognition that '*becoming*' (*Werden*) is the universal form of Being, the "eminent category of reality" for the entire spatiotemporal world (256). It is not something between Being and non-Being, but is in itself pure Being (259).

We must note, however, that the mere succession of states or situations is not yet a process. It is a process only when the states in succession are related by a transition from one into another (261f.).

It is "the belonging together" of the states despite their succession in time that is essential to process. That is, the modal structure of any process has the character of an uninterrupted movement in the flux of time, and of an inexhaustible manifoldness of ever new phases or aspects of the process itself. But despite all changes, there is always 'something' that persists—'something' that survives the changes of its states. This 'something' is *substance* (265f.).

For the unity of a process it is merely necessary that the subject of an alteration survive the change of its states. How long it persists as one and the same 'something' is of no significance. The human body, for example, need not be immortal in order to change. It is sufficient that it remain the same during the individual's lifetime. But no one will confuse this persistence of the human being with substance. Nor will anyone confuse substantiality with structures of a very flighty nature, such as a drop of water; or with highly stable things whose changes are so slow that they cannot be observed, such as rocks. Still, if there is not something that persists, then there is also no process.

What, then, is that which persists? Hartmann speaks of it as *substratum*—that which philosophers in the past have tried to comprehend as "the principle of matter." However, in the ordinary meaning of the term, matter is encountered only at the lower strata of reality; and there it is what is comprehensible with quantitative exactitude. But what Hartmann means by 'substratum' is a fundamental category, in contrast to the equally fundamental category 'relation'. Where there are real relations there must also be real substrata—and they must be there at every level of reality.

The conception of a substratum is thus intrinsic to the traditional view of 'matter' as a substance, but it is not identical with it.[20]

---

20. *Natur*, 274–94. See Eduard May's statement: "It is testimony for the extraordinary philosophical significance that Hartmann's philosophy of nature, although meant to be 'ontological', is most significant for research in basic principles (*Grundlagenforschung*)," Eduard May, "Die Stellung Nicolai Hartmanns," in Heimsoeth and Heiss, eds., *Nicolai Hartmann, Der Denker*, 225.

In the natural sciences 'matter' has always been regarded as the only substance. But there is no reason why substance should be nothing but matter. No decision can here be made *a priori,* but only on the basis of empirical evidence. After all, what do we actually know about matter? We know only its manifestations, and these we experience as forces—impenetrability, inertia, and gravity. What maintains itself in the change of material conditions is energy, and this is substance dynamically understood. As dynamic substratum it persists in all processes but is changed in various appearances. Where the process enters a relatively stable phase, energy maintains itself as "potential energy"; the law of entropy, however, sets a limit to its preservation. Although entropy is not a destruction of energy, it is a "neutralization" which prevents further transformation. But even physicists can make only hypothetical statements concerning the extent to which this 'neutralization' of energy is final and irreversible. What is ontologically significant is the fact that even energy does not in every respect measure up to the postulate of an absolute substance.

In Hartmann's view, substance is a characteristic cosmological category and belongs only to inorganic nature. Moreover, there are only two substrata which can be substances: matter and energy. If one takes substance in the strict sense as a synthesis of substratum and perseverance, then there can be no recurrence of this category at any of the higher strata of Being, for not all perseverance is one of substance.

As far as mere duration is concerned, nothing is comparable to matter and energy. But this does not alter the fact that, from the human point of view, the higher forms of conservation are incomparably more important and richer in content—although (or perhaps because) they lie above the realm of mere matter. What is involved in the higher strata of reality are the creative forces that bring forth structures and forms of a higher order. At the level of organismic existence, for example, we encounter the uninterrupted coming into being and ceasing to be of individual entities of the same kind—a process in which the type is preserved despite the change of individual entities. In place of a substance as unchanging basis, we have here the constancy of form as recurrence in process. What is preserved is a 'form-giving' power that determines individual occurrences. And this is obviously in contrast to the formless matter and energy of the lowest strata of reality.

At the level of organismic existence, matter and energy take on a new mode of reality. There exists no specific matter or specific energy that in itself is life. In the living organism, matter and energy change constantly. What is preserved is the supported whole—the highly complex structure of the organism—as a manifestation of life. And in its organismic reality, life preserves itself through its own activity— through the assimilation of matter as food, through the reproduction of its own kind, and through the transformation of the species, the emergence of new species types.

And there are still higher forms of preservation, the most remarkable one being that of the *self* as the basis of all mental activity.

The 'I' is obviously not a substance, but it does have constancy (self-identity) despite all changes of moods, contents, and acts. As the unity of apperception, it is basic to any and all experiences, and to experience as a whole. Remembrance in particular presupposes the continuing identity of the 'I', and is itself a great riddle. A physiological interpretation is not possible, although physiological conditions are indisputably involved. An entirely new form of 'self-preservation' is here in evidence—one that differs even from the organismic. It is an active holding fast on itself—a self-assertion *as unity* against its own dissolution in the course of time.

The facts of human existence may be difficult to understand at the lower levels of existence. At the higher levels, however, they take on a form of self-affirmation, self-acknowledgment, and self-directed action. As a moral person, the 'I' can even negate itself. That is, it can repudiate accepted duties and can deny its own actions. The very nature of the moral person consists in the power that consciousness has over itself—the power to 'stand up' for itself, to accept responsibility, and to be security for itself.

The question is, What is the substratum of it all—of all the diverse strata of reality?

As Hartmann points out (*Natur*, 278), Aristotle saw the substratum in the principle of 'matter' as that which is "formless, inexpressible, unknowable." It is merely the undifferentiated 'something' that is basic to all physical form-giving. It is the passive principle—form being the active principle.

Since Aristotle and the Greek philosophers in general, substance has been understood as the changeless substratum of all changes. Heated metaphysical discussions about it have been carried on for centuries. Substance was seen as what gives permanency to reality.

Even Kant maintained in the First Analogy of Experience that "in all change of appearances substance is permanent; its quantum in nature is neither increased nor diminished."[21] And at the end of his discussion of the problem, Kant came to the conclusion that in the field of appearances "substances are the substrata of all determinations in time" —that is, they are the substrata of all processes. "Permanence is thus a necessary condition under which alone appearances are determinable as things or objects in a possible experience."[22]

What is crucial in Kant's position—in contrast to traditional metaphysical conceptions of *the permanent*—is that he sees substance not as something beyond the realm of time, but as permanency *in* time. But, surely, what is thus 'permanent' in all processes needs clarification in an analysis of the categories involved.

The Kantian thesis obviously is that what is permanent is precisely that which alone can change. In fact, its permanency reveals itself in and through its changes.[23] This is the thought Hartmann develops in his categorial analysis of substantiality (*Natur*, 280ff.).

Hartmann's basic point is that a requisite for the unity of any process is that there is something that undergoes changes; that there is a relatively stable "bearer of genuine change"—one that remains stable as long as the changes form a closed unity of the process. Within such processes all things, organisms, persons, and even spiral nebulae undergo manifold changes, but they do so only within limits. Beyond these limits they cease to be the same entities, and all further changes are no longer *their* changes.

This is also true in principle of material elements, whether we are dealing with atoms or with electrons, protons, or neutrons. None of these is an absolute entity or substance in the traditional sense.[24]

Does this mean that the process alone is what is permanent in the real world? It cannot be so; for the process, even if it does go on eternally, does not have the character of a substance. "Eternal becoming is but the eternalization of coming into being and ceasing to be; it is not

21. *Critique of Pure Reason*, A182/N224; Smith, 312.
22. Ibid., A188f/B231f; Smith, 217.
23. Ibid., A183/B226; Smith, 214. "In bare succession existence is always vanishing and recommencing. . . . Without the permanent there is therefore no time-relation."
24. For a survey of the development of modern physics, see Werkmeister, *A Philosophy of Science*, 238–66. Detailed footnotes support the argument.

something which subsists" (*Natur*, 283). And this fact again entails the problem of substance.

Hartmann considers five distinct aspects of the problem (284f.):

1. Substance is not something outside the process but is in it. It is not timeless but has the form of duration, as has the process.
2. Substance is not the process itself but something that, though in process, resists it and persists.
3. Such persistence, if it occurs at all, can be found only at the lowest and most elementary strata of reality.
4. Substance is both persistence and the substratum of persistence. What kind of substratum it is cannot be ascertained *a priori*.
5. There is no valid argument in support of an absolutely persisting 'something'. Whatever the substratum may be, it is always only relatively persistent.

The question still is, What is that which thus remains itself? It is, of course, what philosophers have tried to comprehend as *matter*. But as substratum, "matter" is restricted to the lowest strata of reality (288).

Taken in a general sense, the substratum is a fundamental category, in contrast to the category relation. Wherever there are real relations, there must also be some kind of real substratum. This fact is basic to the ancient conception of matter that presumably underlies all changes and measurable quantities.

However, for Hartmann, substance is in its very essence not a singular (290f.). There can be a plurality of different substances. And substance need not be infinite. It is divisible and not absolute. What all of this comes to is that substance has "no Being besides its being as a principle" (292). It is but the strict correlate of its opposite, which is relation. Although substance is *Seiendes*, it is not *Seiendes for itself*.

In the natural sciences, matter alone has been regarded as substance. Actually, however, there is no reason why substance can be nothing but matter (295f.). In fact, there need not be just one substance; there can be many that are interrelated. In this respect, however, a division is not possible *a priori*.

The principle of the preservation of energy comes close to the problem of substance as that which persists in the process, for energy is the dynamic "inner side" of process. It is what persists in the process as the dynamic substratum. Where a process enters a relatively stable condition, energy is preserved as 'potential' energy; but the difference between potential and kinetic energy is only relative. Both are covered by the law of the conservation of energy. This law, however, must not be confused with the law of entropy—i.e., with the law of thermo-dynamics—nor does 'entropy' mean a destruction or annihilation of energy. It merely identifies a kind of neutralization in which no further transformation takes place.

From an ontological point of view it is important to note that even the conception of energy does not in every respect meet the require-ments of the postulate of an absolute substance.

"Substance is a characteristically cosmological category" (297). In-sofar as it exists at all, it belongs exclusively to the realm of inorganic nature. And even there we encounter only two substrata that might be substances: matter and energy. Both persevere, but not absolutely. At very high temperatures, for example, matter is dissolved into radiation; and energy, being subject to entropy, is preserved in processes only con-ditionally. But this means that either we do not as yet know an absolute substance, or the ultimate substratum of processes in nature, although having a high degree of constancy, is not absolutely constant. The fact is that relatively constant substrata suffice for our understanding of the phenomena. It thus makes sense to retain the synthesis of substratum and perseverance, as expressed in the principle of substance, although the perseverance is perhaps not absolute.

8. Grundlagenforschung

Commenting on Hartmann's work, Eduard May wrote: "It can never be emphasized too much that Hartmann's analysis of categories as basic research is of inestimable value."[25] And Hans-Joachim Höfert agrees with Hartmann's thesis that the ontologically most significant fact in mathematics is that its objects are "ideal structures" that are completely determined through a system of postulates, and that it is "quite otherwise" in physics, where the objects are determined by

25. May, "Die Stellung Nicolai Hartmanns," in Heimsoeth and Heiss, eds., *Nicolai Hartmann, Der Denker*, 208–25.

numerous additional categories, and where an analysis of the categories is essential to any possible investigation of the foundations (*Grundlagenforschung*) of physics, categories are not only principles of cognition—as Kant had it—but are also principles of Being: "If this were not so, a true cognition of reality would not be possible."[26]

From a broad historical perspective, the change in the formulation of the categories involved is a steady, progressive development. Even revolutions in the world-picture of the natural sciences are but further developments and not reversals of the process. Old theories merge into new ones as special cases: Newtonian mechanics into relativity mechanics, atomism and molecular mechanics (chemistry) into subatomic dynamics. But, as Werner Heisenberg has put it: No complete or closed theory is invalid. It is merely limited in its range of application when a new theory is developed.[27] The phenomenon of categorial stratification recurs here as separation of the fields of objects that appear coordinated under the more general categories. They appear as separate fields within the network of physical theories.

The category substance, firmly embedded in the old theory of nature and in traditional philosophy, has lost significance but has by no means been eliminated. The independence of the category 'dynamic structures' seems to today's atomic physicists quite obvious.

The infinitely complex context of determinations of the mode of Being of the real world reveals itself as subdivided into occurrences of relatively independent processes. That this context of processes is not an unanalyzable chaos, but that certain spatially and temporally limited occurrences can be discerned and can be further isolated in experiments is an ontic fact that contains within it a condition of the possibility of physics as an exact science. "But as method of the quantitative comprehension of partial possibilities physics can tell us nothing about the necessity of the real process."[28] This fact finds full recognition in the "principle of indeterminacy" and in the statistical interpretation of the function of 'states' within the processes of nature.

26. Hans-Joachim Hoefert, "Kategorialanalyse und physikalische Grundlagenforschung," in Heimsoeth and Heiss, eds., *Nicolai Hartmann, Der Denker* 190f.

27. Werner Heisenberg, "Der Begriff 'abgeschlossene Theorie' in der Modernen Naturwissenschaft," in *Dialectica* 2 (1948): 331–36.

28. Hoefert, "Kategorialanalyses und physikalische Grundlagenforschung," in Heimsoeth and Heiss, *Nicolai Hartmann, Der Denker*, 207.

As a method of quantitative comprehension of partial possibilities in nature, physics can say nothing about the necessity of the processes of reality as such and as a whole.

In view of the developments in modern physics, Hartmann now argues that when we take substance in the strict sense of a synthesis of persistence and substratum, then there is no recurrence of the category 'substance' at the higher strata of reality. We cannot even speak of a change of substance.[29] But there does occur a change of persistence, and not everything that persists is a substance.

The facts transcend the realm of the physical sciences, for the higher and supported strata of reality also persist. At the organismic level, for example, despite the perishing of individuals, the species is preserved. What here persists is not an undifferentiated "something" but a specific form of determinateness of structure of a higher stratum, of what is supported as a conditioned whole. Hartmann sees in this fact the fundamental difference between substance and persistence (*Beharrung*), substance being merely the preservation of the formless and existentially lower mode of Being, whereas what persists (*beharrt*) maintains itself as something highly structured. It is a form-giving factor, a power that determines the specific character of the various strata of reality and is the bearer of values and of meanings in the real world.

The basic difference between substance and persistence is that as substance only the lowest and formless strata of Being are preserved, whereas through persistence the highly formed bearers of values and meaning in the world are preserved. The special forms of persistence are manifold and reveal different traits from stratum to stratum. At the physicochemical level the special forms of persistence are best understood in the laws governing the various processes, for the laws persist (*Natur*, 299).

At the level of inorganic nature—where the idea of substance prevails—laws play a truly determinative role. But a special problem is encountered when we consider the realm of organismic reality; for life is neither matter nor energy nor a special 'life-force', as the vitalists had it. In the living organism, matter and energy change constantly. What is preserved is the organism as a whole—the highly complex structure

29. See also Grete Henry-Hermann, *Die naturphilosophischen Grundlagen der Quantenmechanik* (Berlin, 1935).

that is dependent upon, but not determined by, mere physicochemical processes.[30] Life maintains itself through assimilation and reproduction, and through the modification of lower species into higher forms.

Beyond the strata of organismic existence there are still higher forms of preservation (*Natur*, 304f.). The most remarkable of these is the preservation of the personal 'I' which is basic to all mental life. The 'I' is not a substance but, as mentioned before, has constancy despite the changes of its states, contents, moods, and acts. The identity of this 'I' is the presupposition even of the unity of apperception and is, in fact, its basic condition. But how is it possible that the whole of consciousness remains identical during a person's lifetime while everything in it constantly changes? Memory plays an important role but is not an explanation; for memory itself presupposes the lasting 'I', and in this sense is itself the great riddle.

We are obviously dealing here with an entirely new form of self-preservation—a self that in the stream of experience actively asserts itself as a unity against its dissolution. It is a form of self-affirmation despite all actual changes of it. Of special significance here is the self-identity of the moral person who has the power over himself to be his own bondsman and surety.

Beyond the individual human being there are the unities of man's spiritual life as manifest in history, in law, in life-style, in morals, in language, and knowledge (306ff.). The historical spirit common to individuals is a unity eminently capable of persisting. It is independent of individuals but exerts a specific influence over them, determining the basic directions of attitudes and valuations even of social groups. It is reflected in the amazing constancy with which certain spiritual products are maintained historically long after the living spirit that produced them has ceased to exist, for example, works of art and of literature of every kind. The spirit of Beethoven still lives in his compositions (311ff.).

In order to make sense of all of this, Hartmann (as we have seen)

30. *Natur*, pp. 302f. For specific details see Werkmeister, *A Philosophy of Science*, 318–51; J. B. Haldane, *The Philosophical Basis of Biology* (New York: Macmillan, 1935); Hans Driesch, *The Science and Philosophy of the Organism*, vol. 1 (London: George Allen and Unwin, 1908). H. Spemann, "Über die Determination der ersten Organanlagen des Amphibienembryos" parts 1–4, *Archiv für Entwicklungmecanik* 43 (1918); and other authors of that period.

distinguishes between 'situation' or 'state' (*Zustand*) and 'substance'. A situation or state in the categorial sense is the real relationship of simultaneity of things and events at a specific given time. How stable it is or how long it prevails makes no difference in principle. But only a context of manifold real relationships in some particular *Now* constitutes a situation or state, and every situation is but a stage in a process.

But states and situations can also be very persistent when the process in which they replace one another is a slow one. However, the distinctions of slow and rapid are quite arbitrary and are ontologically insignificant. Although we are inclined to give existential priority to states and situations, it is the process rather than the situation or state that transcends the passing moment; for it consists in the coming into being and the ceasing to be of all situations.

9. Cause and Effect

It is the essence of a real process that continually new states or situations arise in sequential order. But if this order were without internal necessity, no anticipation of the future, no practical attitude, planning, or action would be possible. Fortunately, reality is otherwise. In any real process a linear form of determination prevails whose form is that of causality (*Natur*, 318ff.).

The meaning of causality is simply that the sequence of states or situations in a process is not arbitrary but one of definite sequential order. The earlier state is the *cause,* the later is *effect*. But every cause is already the effect of earlier causes, and every effect is in turn a cause of later effects. This linear form of determination, which corresponds to the advance in time of process, is the simple '*causal nexus*'.

This nexus must not be confused with 'ground' and 'consequence', nor with 'determination' and 'dependence'. Cause and effect are but special forms of these. In the real world we encounter many forms of determination, and not all of them have the lineal form of a sequence in time. As logical determination, for example, ground and consequence do not depend upon the flux of time.

Characteristic of causal determination are linear dependencies, sequential order in time, the constant bringing forth of effects, and the irreversibility of the process.

Hartmann specifically notes that linear causality does not move from thing to thing, as older theories often imply; for causes are neither things nor substances but collocations, situations, states, and stages in process. Depending on the segment of reality taken into consideration, the relationships can be narrowly or broadly defined. We must keep this in mind when we try to analyze causal determination. The only aspect that is essential is that to every phase of the cause there corresponds a phase of the effect. The slightest change in the total cause of an event entails a corresponding change in the total effect.

This relationship between cause and effect is an ultimate and not further analyzable basic fact. And causal necessity is other than the necessity of law; for, like all real necessities, it differs from case to case, whereas laws express universal necessity.

Since the causal nexus is nothing other than the determination involved in the continual bringing forth and being brought forth of something in every process, it is in effect the dynamic inner aspect of the process itself. It is not simply the sequential order of states and situations in time but is the determination of their following each other in specific order.

What is preserved here is the process itself. The effect comes into being only in the ceasing to be of the cause. The disappearance of the cause in the effect and the coming forth of the effect out of the cause are actually one and the same process. And in this sense "the causal relation is indeed an eminently creative process" (326).

But we must keep in mind that in the causal process itself there is neither a first nor a final state. All such distinctions are but arbitrarily fixed points in our contemplation of the process. And we must also note that in real causal relationships there is nothing like preformation. The coming forth of the effect because of the cause is a genuine coming into Being, not simply an unfolding of what is already present. The causal nexus is not an "evolution," because nothing evolves which already exists in involved form.

It is possible to trace causal effectiveness in its manifold forms and to determine special forces and laws governing the process. But forces and laws thus discovered already have causal relationships as their presupposition. Hartmann agrees with Kant when the latter states in the Second Analogy: "How anything can be altered, and how it should be possible that upon one state in a given moment an opposite state may follow in the next moment—of this we have not, *a priori,* the least conception." [31] This means that "the bringing forth" is itself unknowable.

What is unknown and unknowable here in the causal relationship is the nexus itself. All attempts to make comprehensible the incomprehensible have failed. Still, as category of cognition, causality is the most important means of comprehending events in nature. This does not mean, however, that causality itself must be knowable, for all comprehension is possible on the basis of what one presupposes. The first presuppositions are always either assumptions or are in themselves evident. In both cases, however, they remain uncomprehended. As far as the causal nexus is concerned, the bringing forth of an effect *as effect* is not comprehensible, even when nobody can doubt the causal context. How, for example, does gravitational attraction as such come about? All we can say is that material bodies attract one another. The *how* and *why* remain unknown.

10. The Causal Nexus

It is evident from what has been said that causal relations involve metaphysical, i.e., unsolvable, problems (*Natur,* 331ff.). Kant touched upon these problems in his discussion of the antinomy of First Causes, and Hume raised the question of the objective validity of causal efficacy. But, as Hartmann points out, from the time of Aristotle to the philosophy of Hegel there occurs in many variations the idea that behind the relationship of cause and effect lies that of purpose and of means for its realization. Even Leibniz included this idea in his metaphysics. But Hartmann argues at length that the "final *nexus*" is a much more complex mode of determination than is the causal nexus. [32]

The causal nexus is neutral as to the effect that ensues, and this is of greatest importance for the human position and human actions in this world; for it leaves room for decisions about the goals to be attained.

Causality is the lowest and simplest basic form of the real nexus of events in the direction of the flow of time, the nexus that at any specific stage in the process entails only one possibility, namely, that which

31. *Critique of Pure Reason,* A206f/B252; Smith, 230.
32. Nicolai Hartmann, *Ethik,* 3d ed. (Berlin: Walter de Gruyter & Co., 1949), 174–79; *Aufbau* (see chap. 2, n. 5), 313–16, 559–63, 566–75. I shall deal with this problem in detail in chap. 5.

in the continuation of the process is actually realized. This means, however, that all conditions of any real possibility must already be contained in the earlier stages of the process. Otherwise the possibility would not be complete and nothing would actually occur.

The fact that all partial conditions of an event are already contained in the earlier stages of the process constitutes the specific mode of determination in the causal nexus. When all the conditions of the possibility of an event are present, the event cannot fail to occur. This 'cannot fail to occur' is the real necessity intrinsic to the causal nexus.[33] In other words, causality is that form of determination of the real process according to which everything that is really possible is also that which necessarily occurs; and it cannot fail to occur when all the conditions for its occurrence are realized. It is this necessity that connects total cause with total effect and partial cause with partial effect; it also entails that nothing can occur other than what actually does occur (*Natur*, 336).

This, however, is the very minimum of determination. Total determination of a complexus of conditions—that is, a total cause in the strict sense—can be only the whole of world process. Moreover, pure causal determination prevails only in natural processes. In the sphere of human activity, only mixed determination is possible.

The question is, How is causality related to substance?

Both are categorial aspects of one and the same process (430f.), but they characterize different aspects of it. Substance is what persists in the process; causality is what determines the process *as* process. But persistence consists essentially in the continuation of the determination, and determination is itself something that persists in the process. Dynamically understood, substance consists in the irresistible continuation of the process-dynamics. Its persistence is identical with the fusion of cause into effect, and the emergence of the latter out of the former.

The persistence of substance is therefore nothing beside or behind the causal chain of real events. And in this sense the necessity of causal contexts is nothing but the persistence of substance: It is completely identical with it. The very essence of the necessity here encountered is that the dynamics of the process is nowhere interrupted, that upon every A a B necessarily follows.

33. Hartmann, *Möglichkeit und Wirklichkeit*, 161–74, 239–57.

Understood as specific states, cause and effect are thus but boundary stages in a mode of comprehension that selects a specific segment
of the process. The causal process itself is not characterized by actual
stages. "When one views the process as a whole, the sequence of causes
is identical with the sequence of effects" (*Natur*, 431).

What we ordinarily regard as causes are actually but partial causes;
for in reality there are no isolated causes, nor are there isolated causal
sequences. There exists only a highly complex interrelation of
causal sequences and, in the last analysis, only the all-encompassing
causal process involving the world as a whole.

Ordinarily we deal with only partial causes, even in our sciences.
In our most exact experimental sciences we try to isolate causal relations pertaining to specific problems so that they form relatively closed
systems. This is possible because in isolated segments of events, certain partial causes predominate while others can be neglected for purposes of special investigation. The predictability of certain processes
is rooted in this possibility of isolating causal factors, but this predictability has its natural limitation.

Let it be noted also that all conditions that together are effective
are entirely affirmative. There are no negative causal factors, although
there are factors which 'prevent' specific effects. The determinative sequence of the causal nexus shows at every point the total conditions
from the past and those of the future. Through this double aspect the
whole cosmic process is bound into a unity. If by 'accidental' we mean
something uncaused, it just is not encountered in the real world. What
we experience as freedom in our actions is but the superposition of
higher types of determination upon the causal nexus. Our freedom is
a plus, not a deficiency, of determination.

As far as the causal nexus is concerned, the complete determination
of an event never recurs. The collocation of the factors may be similar
to those of an earlier event, but it is never identical with it, because the
later event occurs at another stage in the one real context of events.
That is, in the causal events in nature, similarities, sometimes strik-
ing similarities, may occur; but everything that happens, happens only
once. Insofar as the causal efficaciousness in the world-process is the
equivalent of the dissolution of substance into the dynamics of process,
it is also its dissolution into individuality.

Up to this point we have not even mentioned the epistemological
problem of the 'objective validity' of the conception of causality. In a

somewhat Humean sense we now ask: Is the causal nexus actually a real nexus?

In considering this problem we must keep in mind that causality is one of many forms of determination. It has nothing in common, for example, with logical and mathematical determination, and it cannot be identified with purposive action. Kant pointed out that

the very concept of a cuase so manifestly contains the concept of a necessity of connection with an effect and of the strict universality of the rule, that the concept would be altogether lost if we attempted to derive it, as Hume has done, from a repeated association of that which happens with that which precedes, and from a custom of connecting representations . . . constituting therefore a merely subjective necessity.[34]

It is Kant's thesis, however, that

the *objective relation* of appearances that follow upon one another is not to be determined through mere perception. . . . The relation between the two states must be so thought that it is thereby determined as necessary which of them must be placed before, and which of them after, and that they cannot be placed in reverse relation. . . . Experience itself . . . is thus possible only insofar as we subject the succession of appearances, and therefore of all alteration, to the law of causality.[35]

This is so because "only insofar as our representations are necessitated in a certain order as regards their time-relations do they acquire objective meaning."[36] "Hume was therefore in error in inferring from the contingency of our determination *in accordance with the law* the contingency of the *law* itself."[37]

Hume is right, however—as Hartmann points out—in maintaining that we can never know directly that a cause is a cause, or an effect is an effect, nor what effect a cause will produce. 'Causality' as a cate-

34. *Critique of Pure Reason*, B5; Smith, 44.
35. Ibid., A189/B234; Smith, 219.
36. Ibid., A197/B243; Smith, 224.
37. Ibid., A766/B794; Smith, 610.

gory of cognition is but a schema of possible understanding. It is not the understanding of causal determination itself.

In modern physics a special problem with respect to the principle of causality has arisen. The quantum mechanical transformation of classical physics seems to imply that micromechanical processes are not subject to causal determination. All laws pertain to averages only. Modern wave mechanics relinquishes even the conception of universal determination.[38]

However, all micromechanical processes stand in precise correlation with macromechanical processes, and actually are basic to them. It is therefore not possible to disregard causality at one level and retain it at the other. And let us keep in mind that the famous "principle of indeterminacy" pertains only to an indeterminacy of measurements that itself is causally conditioned.

We must also keep in mind that the laws of classical physics are not identical with causality but presuppose it and lose their significance without it; causality does not presuppose those laws. What creates the problem in the realm of atomic processes is the fact that the determinative laws are not yet understood. But this does not mean that there are here no laws. All it means is that physical objects of the size of atoms are not 'closed systems' that can be understood with exactitude; and from this we cannot infer that the individual processes are not 'effects' or that there are no totality-determinations (*Ganzheitsdeterminationen*). As far as the so-called statistical laws are concerned, we must keep in mind that the expression *statistical* pertains only to the initial data, not to the nature of the laws themselves, for it is not the laws that are statistical, but only the initial approach to them.

This is also true in principle at the higher levels of causality. In the events in our daily life and in world history, we also encounter events that are incalculable. But this is no reason to doubt causal determinations; rather, it enhances our belief in causes.

11. Epistemological Problems

Causality is generally regarded as a law of nature. The laws of nature, however, are not propositions or mathematical equations, for these are

38. Werkmeister, *A Philosophy of Science*, 263–77. See also P. A. Dirac, "Relativity Quantum Mechanics," in *Proceedings of the Royal Society* A36 (London, 1932).

but formulations of the laws. Still, there is something real in the events of nature that corresponds to these formulations, and this is intrinsically related to any process. In Hartmann's view, "The lawfulness of nature is, first of all, nothing but the homogeneity of the processes" (*Natur*, 383). This homogeneity consists in the fact that within the progress of the total process of nature there are partial processes of specific types—processes that recur and whose recurrence reveals a strict but not necessarily simple form-type or consistency in development.

What maintains itself in process is, first of all, the process itself. But the laws of nature show that something else also maintains itself in the process, namely, the recurrence of particular partial processes. Although this recurrence is not identical in every detail, it is so in certain basic respects; and these are the constant laws within the process.

In its mode of being, a law of nature is thus similar to the categories of Being. The laws are merely more specific and have the character of principles. They determine the real course of processes and bring certain uniformities into them. In this sense they are laws of what is real. Scientific formulations of laws are but attempts to comprehend them.

However, it is important to note that a law of nature is a universal in the strict sense of that term. Its universality consists in the fact that it includes all relevant facts and allows no exception. But this universality is not an ideal or logical conception, for the formulations of our sciences are not themselves the laws of nature. We must clearly distinguish between the laws that are intrinsic to the real process and scientific formulations of these laws—even where we have reason to believe that the scientific formulations are adequate (384).

Still, our comprehension of relationships in nature is rooted in the comprehension of their laws. This means that the aspect of the *a priori* in our cognition of nature is bound to the aspect of nature's laws, for only the universal is *a priori* comprehensible. In the procedures of science we encounter a crucial synthesis of *a posteriori* and *a priori* elements of cognition. Induction can yield really universal propositions only when this universality is presupposed in the major premise. A real 'generalization' is not possible in induction alone; and our sciences do not begin with induction pure and simple, but always also with the presupposition that in the real processes strict lawfulness prevails. One simply does not know in advance what the laws are. About this only a controlled observation can inform us, for a universal law must prevail in any particular instance. An experiment isolates the conditions of a

specific partial process and gives us information about the specifics of
a law.

John Stuart Mill referred to the general presupposition of induction
as the "Law of the Uniformity of Nature," and Kant stated in "the principle of analogies": "All appearances are, as regards their existence,
subject *a priori* to rules determined by their relation to one another in
one time."[39] And in the Second Analogy he specifically stated: "Everything that happens, that is, begins to be, presupposes something upon
which it follows according to a law."[40]

Both thinkers, Mill and Kant, presuppose a uniformity of nature
that is not obtained by generalization but is presumed as inherent in
nature itself. The laws manifesting this uniformity need not be mathematical nor causal, but in the world in which we live they are obviously
both. And there may be still other modes of determination. The important fact is that laws of some type determine the nature of the
world-process as a whole.

The laws of nature are strict: They entail necessity and permit no
exceptions. But necessity and lawfulness in nature are not limited to
the causal nexus, for causality is the necessity of a sequence of occurrences only on the basis of specific and unique collocations. Causality
is not identical with the necessity inherent in the temporal flux of processes, but is a necessity grounded in the specific nature of individual
cases based on a principle. Only the two together—the specific nature
of individual cases and a principle—entail real necessity in nature.

This double relationship Hartmann characterizes in four propositions (*Natur*, 393):

1. Everything that occurs in nature depends upon a coincidence
   of conditions which is not predetermined, and in this sense is
   'fortuitous'.
2. But everything which in this sense occurs 'fortuitously' can be
   no other than it is. It occurs necessarily.
3. Everything which occurs necessarily happens only once in its
   completeness, and is thus qualitatively unique. It possesses this
   uniqueness not on the basis of a principle but because of the
   real context within which it occurs.

39. *Critique of Pure Reason*, A177; Smith, 208.
40. Ibid., A189; Smith, 218.

4. Everything which occurs only once stands nevertheless in its individual characteristics under universal principles, and thus contains within itself the necessity which is of the essence of the strictly universal. This strict universal within the particular is the determinative law of nature.

That the process itself is not the 'effect' of the laws and that only the *causa transiens* can justifiably be called cause, that it disappears in its effect and thus is but a stage in the process, and that the law does not disappear because it is the form of the process itself—all of this is an insight that careful analysis gives us.

The really remarkable aspect of the laws of nature is their mathematical structure, upon which the apriorism of our knowledge of nature depends. But the exactitude of this knowledge is limited to the realm of the quantitative, which plays a dominating role only in the lowest regions of the world.

We must also take into consideration the fact that any individual law is always taken out of context and exists only in abstraction. There are neither isolated causes nor isolated causal sequences in nature. Only the complex total cause and the complex total process are real. And this total process is subject to a complexus of laws that can as little be torn apart as can the causal structure itself.

To be sure, the laws are the rational side of the events in nature. But even they are by no means completely rational.

With the advance of physics from molar mechanics to molecular and subatomic processes, the whole picture has changed. Nevertheless, one basic fact remains; for if the subatomic processes are building up to observable molar mechanical events that are under strict causal laws, then the former cannot be entirely lawless, and the unknown laws of the subatomic processes must stand in some determinative ontic relation to the laws of classical physics. How far this relationship can be scientifically clarified is a different question and depends on epistemological considerations.[41]

41. For discussions of this problem, see Werner Heisenberg, *The Physical Principles of Quantum Theory* (Chicago: University of Chicago Press, 1930); Henry Margenau, "Causality and Modern Physics," *The Monist* 41 (1931); Richard von Mises, "Über kausale und statistische Gesetzmässigkeit in der Physik," *Die Naturwissenschaften* 18 (1930); Hoefert, "Kategorialanalyse und Physikalische Grund-

What in quantum mechanical considerations is radically changed is the conception of the process itself. The process of nature is no longer conceived as the steady transition postulated by classical physics. The continuum is suspended. The process advances in the smallest but finite and determinable leaps of quanta of energy. How these leaps can fuse into the process as a continuum is a problem for statistical interpretations and a calculation of probabilities. We must keep in mind, however, that such probabilities are not laws of the individual micromechanical events but are only laws of averages.

Still, even these statistical laws could not be discerned if the micromechanical processes themselves were not such as to result in determinative averages. The replacement of classical laws by statistical laws thus merely places the actual laws of nature into a greater depth of reality—into the "inner depths of nature" no longer available for direct observation or experimentation. What happens here is the dissolution of all macroprocesses into an immense number of microprocesses. The result is that the classical laws of the macroprocesses, hitherto regarded as fundamental, do not pertain to the ultimate elements of reality. This does not mean, however, that the stratum of the elementary processes is not determined by laws. The limit of our cognition is not a limit of Being, not a limit of law in nature.

12. Central Determination

So far we have considered actual structures in nature: bodies and things. They are formations having limits and forms, which coexist but do not fuse into one another either spatially or temporally, and which thus provide distinctions within the process of events. The peculiarity of the physical world is that all formations of which it consists are basically *discreta,* whereas the continuities are but the categorial conditions of these structures, be these conditions dimensions, substrata, forms of determination, or universal laws: the specific characteristic of the higher particularities of the discretion (*Natur,* 442).

Far from being itself a substratum, every structure of relative constancy is basically a combination of manifold temporary states of lim-

---

lagenforschung," in Heimsoeth and Heiss, eds., *Nicolai Hartmann, Der Denker,* 186–225.

ited efficaciousness. This includes everything that in its compactness persists in the cosmic process, even if it is not limited by strict spatial boundaries. The planetary system as a whole, for example, is no less a dynamic structure than is our earth.

A structure is 'dynamic' insofar as it is the result, not of a mere collection of parts, but of the interplay of forces and processes (445f.). That is, the limits of a dynamic structure are the function of its inner forces insofar as these oppose any dissolving influence from the outside. The external form of such structures is thus internally determined.

This fact is obvious in the case of structures such as planetary systems and spiral nebulae. But the full extent of the principle of inner determination is realized only when we see that it is valid even in the regions of the smallest structural elements in nature. In the case of atoms this has been demonstrated to be the case, for we deal here with a dynamic structure involving a nucleus and electrons moving in surrounding orbits. The immense forces released in nuclear explosions are but proof of the dynamic inner structure of the elementary particles of matter.

The stability of any structure in nature can be understood only as the manifestation of a relatively stable equilibrium of internal processes. This is true in the case of atoms no less than in the case of the solar system, in which the gravitational attraction of the sun is balanced by the tangential inertia of the moving planets. Such dynamic structures maintain themselves through oscillations around a median state of equilibration, and in this respect they already resemble the form of self-active regulation.

When we consider all the facts, it seems highly probable that in the cosmos as a whole, the structures of minor dimensions are the *stronger,* and that nature in general is built up "from below"; that the structures which support everything are the smallest, and that the universe as a whole is stratified from within in levels corresponding to the order of magnitude of the structures—from elementary particles and forces to cosmic entities.

Kant had argued that the world is "entitled nature when it is viewed as a dynamic whole";[42] but he had added in B that "by nature . . . taken *materialiter* is meant the sum of appearances insofar as they stand, in virtue of an inner principle of causality, in thorough-going

42. *Critique of Pure Reason*, A418; Smith, 392.

interconnection." [43] Hartmann certainly would agree that the world is a dynamic whole. But the Kantian restriction of the whole to "an inner principle of causality" is too simple. The dynamic structure is the basic category of all that in nature has the character of a 'thing'—of the thing in contrast to process as well as to an ephemeral state. Discretion of the continua, spatial limitations, internal coherence, structural form, and physical totality—where these occur with relative independence— are functions of the dynamic aspects of reality (*Natur*, 449). The external aspects of these formations appear as persisting form-totalities, whereas their inner reality is the dynamic structure that maintains the specific form. To this inner aspect belongs the dynamic interaction of forces, in many cases that of the process itself with its characteristic states. The outer aspect, as an integrated persistent whole, depends upon that interaction.

As Hartmann puts it: "The dynamic structure is that natural formation which is a unity developed and maintained by its own internal forces, and therefore has dynamic centrality" (468). And this is indeed a new type of determination. It is supported by causality and reciprocal action, but it is more than these in the sense that it is a special "*Überformung*" or higher form-giving of them. The *novum* here is that to the earlier forms of determination there is now added the characteristic preservation of the whole structure without there being a permanent substratum underlying the structure.

For this type of determination we have no traditional term. Hartmann calls it "central determination" (*Zentraldetermination*) and limits its meaning to purely physicochemical realities (470). The conception is not adequate for the interpretation of organismic or still higher totalities, such as communities at the human level.

It is important to understand what Hartmann means by the "centrality" within central determination. It is not a spatial center but a context of dynamic factors that determine the unity and external form of a thing from within. According to traditional interpretations, the principle of form was taken to be 'preformation'; explanations in terms of determinative form remained tautological. But, in Hartmann's view, form comes into being only as the result of an inner determination whose dynamic components are heterogeneous. Their unity comes about only in the balance of opposing forces.

43. Ibid., B446; Smith, 392.

Central determination in this sense—not to be confused with simple reciprocal action—is a categorial basic factor. It is the form of determination of all natural unities that show a degree of independence. This does not preclude the possibility, however, that at the higher strata of reality—at the organismic level, for example—still other modes of determination prevail.

13. Stratification of Nature

"Nature as a whole is not only articulated (*gegliedert*) but is also stratified" (*Natur*, 474). There exist not only structures as systems of parts, processes, and forms—structures that are merely dynamic wholes—but also structures of structures—totalities whose parts are themselves dynamic wholes. That is, every structure is a possible element of larger structures, and every element can in turn be the structure of smaller elements. However, dynamically speaking, this series of interrelated structures has its limit, both at the highest as well as at the lowest level.

Every structure has its special relationship of inner and outer, its unique central determination, its own limits, and its own wholeness. And not just any larger structure is built up out of just any smaller ones. Specific kinds of structures are built up only out of specific smaller ones. The elements, which themselves are whole systems, are being built into encompassing dynamic forms. That is, they are being built into a larger and more complex relationship of forces and motions. They retain, however, their own central determination, and it is by virtue of this fact that they are constitutive elements within the larger structure (479).

Every order of structure is internally an equilibrium of forces that, at the same time, is for its environment a center of externally effective forces that transcend the limits of the structure.[44] And every dynamic structure also has some external forces that in definite ways form a sphere of influence around it, and that, in accordance with specific laws, form a particular "field of forces" that corresponds to the specific internal character of the structure. Insofar as structures of different magnitudes include one another spatially, they form unique relationships of their respective fields of forces. The external forces of the

44. For a brief discussion, see Paul Hossfeld, "Nicolai Hartmanns Kategorien des Naturprozesses," in *Philosophia Naturalis* 6 (1960/61): 377–417.

smaller structures are at the same time internal forces of the larger structures. In this sense they are positive and constructive forces. But this means that, given certain elementary structures, only such larger structures can emerge in which the external forces of the elements are at the same time the internal forces of the larger structures.

This does not mean, however, that all internal forces of the larger structures are merely the external forces of the smaller structures. In the larger structures there also occur unique forces that come into being through the special dynamics of the encompassing whole, and that by no means belong to the component elements (*Natur*, 481). The ellipsoidal paths of the planets, for example, presuppose the gravitational attraction of all material particles; but they also involve more than this, for they involve the counteracting centrifugal forces of motion.

More important is the fact that there are two closed series of dynamic structures. One is that of the microsystems of atoms. Whether their 'building materials' are to be regarded as ultimate and are not further dissoluble can not as yet be decided. But it cannot well be denied that above the stratum of atoms the molecules of chemical compounds are genuine dynamic structures.

The other closed series is that of the macrosystems. It begins with the condensation of matter that forms stars and planets, and ends with the large spiral systems of galaxies. This series includes structures of clearly discernible magnitudes, although transitional forms may not be lacking.

Between these two series, the molecules and the galaxies, is a large gap—the absence, namely, of dynamically independent structures that might form a transition between them. What we face here is not a 'stratification', in the sense that the external forces of the molecules are the inner forces of the galaxies. Planetary systems are thus but forms of spatiodynamical inclusion as far as the various systems are concerned. The strongest structures are probably the smallest ones.

The highest natural structures are actually found in the large gap between molecules and galaxies; for here we find the stratum of organic beings, which, while still dynamic entities, are more than merely dynamic structures. Their structure and form of determination transcend the merely dynamic.

Dynamic structures pure and simple reveal a special type of determination that has serial order and univocal direction. It is the determination of the whole by the parts, or of the structure by the elements.

If this were the only relationship in nature, the forces of the smallest structures would actually account for everything in the world. But that this is not so is already evident from the occurrence of a dynamic *novum* at every stratum of reality. Not only do larger formations depend upon lower ones, but lower ones may also depend upon larger ones. Since the larger structure as the encompassing one is superordinated to the smaller ones and includes them as parts, there is here also a determination on the part of the whole—a *Ganzheitsdetermination* ("wholeness-determination"), as Hartmann calls it (487). This form of determination is a categorial *novum*. Its specific characteristics cannot be described generally but must be determined empirically in specific cases.

Although the external forces of the smaller structures are also internal forces of larger structures, it is not necessarily true that *all* internal forces of the larger structures are merely external forces of the smaller ones. The most obvious case of *Ganzheitsdetermination* is found at the organismic level of existence, and beyond this at the still higher strata of reality.

Should it now be argued that in such cases the individual processes and their forces are but elements out of which the higher structures are built up, we must note, first, that the larger structures consist not merely of individual processes but also of small structures that themselves are already dynamically built up; and, second, that the special form of the processes within the structure do not occur prior to the existence of the larger structure but come into existence only with that structure itself. Assimilative changes of materials, for example, do not occur prior to the existence of an organism.

What all this comes to is that nature is not built up completely 'from below'. Large structures in their specific wholeness determine just as much 'from above' as the small structures determine from below. But this fact must not be interpreted teleologically. There is here no reference to goals or purposes. The fact that the processes involved *tend necessarily* toward an equilibrium does not mean that they *strive* to achieve it, but merely that the processes cease after an equilibrium has been reached, and that no state other than that of an equilibrium can maintain itself dynamically. The basic form of all processes of nature is and remains that of causality (508).

The facts are such that they have constantly given rise to teleological interpretations of reality. But what, precisely, is involved here? Hartmann has dealt with the problem in a book entitled *Teleologisches Denken*,[45] whose central part is a categorial analysis of purposiveness or finalistic determination.

Hartmann begins:

> In the beginning of human thinking was the purpose. Gods cre-
> ated the world, as man creates his human works, simply in order
> to create something. They planned, arranged, combined and sepa-
> rated according to their wisdom and within the limits of their
> ability, just as men do within the limits of their ability. What the
> forces of nature bring about in human life was intended for man.
> . . . This is teleological thinking. It is no longer a merely naive
> view of the world, but one of the means to the end of nature in
> its manifoldness. That is, nature is represented by this concept
> as if an understanding contained the ground of the unity of the
> manifold of its empirical laws. The suitableness of the means to
> an end in nature is, therefore, a particular concept, which has its
> origin solely in the reflective faculty of judgment; for we cannot
> ascribe to the products of nature anything in them like a rela-
> tion of nature to purposes. We can make use of this concept only
> to reflect upon the *nexus* of the phenomena in nature—a *nexus*
> given according to empirical law. (*Teleologisches Denken*, 1)

And Kant distinguished strictly between thinking of a thing's 'suitableness' for existence and regarding it as a 'purpose of nature'.[46] The
problem involved here is, of course, at the center of the mechanism-
vitalism controversy.[47]

The positive aspect of the vitalistic interpretation is to have rec-
ognized the uniqueness of the self-active and form-building processes
characteristic of organismic existence and development. The oppo-

45. Berlin: Walter de Gruyter & Co., 1951. The book was written in 1944.
Its publication was withheld at the author's request until after the publication of
Philosophie der Natur.

46. Immanuel Kant, *Kritik der Urteilskraft*, vol. 5 Akademie Ausgabe, Akademie der Wissenschafter zu Göttingen (Berlin: Walter de Gruyter & Co.: 1966),
181f. Translated by James Creed Meredith under the title *The Critique of Judgment* (Oxford: The Clarendon Press, 1952), 180f; and by J. H. Bernard under the
title *Critique of Judgment* (New York and London: Hafner Publishing Co., 1969),
17. My own translation differs in some respects from both of these translations.

47. See Werkmeister (n. 3 above), chap. 10: "Interpretations of Life," 317–65.

nents of vitalism can show that many aspects of existence and development may yet be explainable in terms of mere causal relations. But the categorial *novum* of the forms of life cannot be explained in terms of causality as can events at the purely physical stratum of reality. If the vitalists were to do nothing but emphasize this fact, they would have the best of the argument. But when vitalists try to account for the facts of organismic existence by introducing special 'metaphysical agencies', such as "entelechies" (Hans Driesch) or an "*élan vital*" (Henri Bergson), they confuse rather than clarify the problem.

When we disregard all metaphysical hypotheses we find that mechanists and vitalists are really not radical antagonists; for the mechanists merely insist on pursuing causal interrelations as far as possible in our understanding of organismic existence; and the vitalists merely seek for a positive expression of what is beyond mere causal determination in an organism. The antagonism of mechanists and vitalists is but a failure to acknowledge the affirmative aspects of the position taken by their respective opponents. Only a careful categorial analysis of the involved stratum of reality can lead to a defensible solution of the problem, and this analysis Hartmann provides.

14. Categorial Dependence

In the realm of organismic existence we encounter the strongest temptation to teleological thinking and interpretation (*Natur*, 512f.). Four groups of phenomena in particular must be considered here.

1. The organic structure and the categories it involves: (a) the individual, (b) the form-building process, (c) the interplay of processes, (d) the form-structure and the process-structure, and (e) self-regulation.
2. The superindividual life and its categories: (a) the life of the species, (b) restitution and heredity, (c) death and generation, (d) variability, and (e) regulative factors in the life of a species.
3. Phylogenesis and its categories: (a) variation, (b) purposiveness, (c) selection, (d) mutation, and (e) descendence.
4. Organic determination: (a) the organic equilibrium, (b) vivacity, (c) the vital nexus, and (d) the law of species.

Consider the items mentioned in the first group.

In a closed unity every structure has its own form. This is true of atoms and molecules no less than of organisms. In the case of organisms, however, the form is a closed unity whose parts are organs within the articulated whole of interacting processes (517). The life of an organism consists in the interrelations of the partial organic processes. What we call 'life' is not something added from the outside to the organismic form, but is the developed unity of manifold processes that, from the very beginning, are characteristic parts such that in the whole, as in the parts, the form comes into being together with the function, and the function with the form. In other words, from the first coming into being of an organism to the time when it ceases to be a living reality, form and function are inseparably united. This 'life' of the organism cannot be understood in terms of physicochemical dynamics, but it is not the manifestation of a mysterious "principle of life."

Life is a special form of process that differs from all mere physical processes by its specific kind of limitation, both as to its beginning and its end (519). In organic nature the continuation of a process is automatic and unstoppable, but the life of an individual does not continue after death unless first a new individual has been formed. In ceasing to be, the living organism does not become another living being but returns to the realm of the nonliving—to molecules and atoms.

In a sense the process of living can be understood as a persistent although temporally limited structure of interrelated processes. The conditions of this structure change *from within* as specific changes in the partial processes affect the whole. In brief, the organism changes itself, elevates itself to a certain height, remains at this height for a determined period, and then declines. We recognize this fact in the distinctions we make of youth, maturity, old age, and the death of the organism. These phases of existence form a temporal whole of a typical character.

And here a new categorial aspect of what is essential in the organic process is in evidence: the closed temporal wholeness of the articulated process of living as given between its beginning and its end. A process-totality of this type is not found at strata of reality below that of organismic existence. At the level of life, the autonomous structure of the process itself determines the rhythm of its articulations, its periods, and its limits.

But these facts involve a new riddle, namely this: If the process as a whole determines the individual stages, then the later stages, just like the earlier ones, must affect what is given in the present. A simple causal explanation is not possible here because causality never runs backwards in time. We face here the difficult problem of a nexus of determination that is unique: the *nexus organicus,* or *vital nexus.*[48]

In living, the organism is in manifold ways interrelated with the surrounding world. This is especially true in the case of animals. Breathing, search for food, metabolism, and self-preservation illustrate the point. The organism is simply not confined to its epidermis. It is an 'expansive unity' that from the beginning lives in and into its surroundings and makes itself the center of a 'sphere of life'.

What is essential here is the "character of self-activity," a special form of "organismic central determination" (*Natur,* 529), which is in evidence already in the relationship of stimulus and response. Although a stimulus may be followed by a reaction, it is not the *sufficient cause* of the reaction. The organic-functional wholeness of the organism is also involved, and the reaction to the stimulus is already a form of organismic spontaneity. The question is, How did the wholeness of the reacting organism come into existence?

The living organism is not a static structure but one that builds and maintains itself in a morphogenetic process. Its basic character is clearly in evidence in all processes of assimilation in which matter (food) is transformed to fill 'the needs' of the organism.

In contrast to merely dynamic structures, the organism is a structure that builds itself. Seen from the outside, this 'morphogenetic process' —this univocal unfolding of an organism—gives one the impression of a "finalistically determined process" in which the final state was determined by a predetermined goal (532ff.).

Every interpretation of organismic forms that does not take into consideration the form-building process remains an abstraction. And every contemplation of the process that does not concern itself with its direction-giving form misses the very essence of that process. "The form is basically [*von Hause aus*] merely a functional form; the process, however, is a form-building process. . . . The mutual conditionedness [*Wechselbedingtheit*] of the two is a complex one" (534f.).

---

48. *Natur,* 522ff. For a critical evaluation of this thesis, see Max Hartmann, "Die Philosophie des Organischen im Werke von Nicolai Hartmann," in Heimsoeth and Heiss, eds., *Nicolai Hartmann, Der Denker,* 226–48.

The form-building process dominates the organism in details as well as a whole. It forms the colloidal protoplasm, the individual cells, and the structures of the multicellular organisms. The process itself involves chemical syntheses, but syntheses of a kind that, in nature, only the organism achieves.

From the physicochemical point of view, the process of life consists in metabolism. But what is important here is not the taking of "food" and the elimination of "waste material," but the highly differentiated partial processes that go on within the organism—processes ranging from diffusions through osmosis to the formation of special secreta of the various glands. Even the functions of the nervous system have metabolism and assimilation as their basis.

Assimilation is a "forming upwards" of what has been taken in. In this process the organism builds the matter taken in "up to itself." "The enigmatical aspect of this process is the way in which the living 'form' brings it about to 'assimilate' matter which is dissimilar to it" (537). The truly basic aspect of this assimilation has so far remained inaccessible to analysis. This is understandable when we consider the immense number of partial processes involved in the life process as a whole. Every kind of cell not only functions differently but also assimilates in a different way. In every cell the form-giving process is different and builds up different forms. Specific aspects of assimilation correspond to these differences. And, surely, "the preservation of the form of the organism as a whole through continuing assimilation is the result of a coherent system of differentiated morphogenetic processes within one central whole" (541). In this total process each individual subordinated process is the condition for every other, and is conditioned by others.

The organismic structure is thus a reactive system of a unique kind. It reacts not only to external influences but also, and especially, to influences of its own internal processes, for it simply is the system of these processes (546f.)—of complementary processes that together regulate the development and maintenance of the whole.

15. Productive Morphogenesis

Seen in the perspective of a living species, the individual is not an independent structure but a link within a structure. That is, within a given time dimension, each individual organism is a link in a large chain connecting ancestors and descendants. In its own time it is the actual bearer of the life of the species.

The living species is in principle bound to the living individual, as the individual is bound to the species, being not only a limited stage of transition but also a necessary link in the chain of events between past and future.

The secret of the life of the species is the reproduction of individuals. Hartmann formulates the basic 'law' that prevails here in this way: "The reproduction of the lower unity of life is preservation of the higher" (*Natur*, 553). In its direction, the process is one of self-abandonment and self-transcendence.

But there is also development—genuine morphogenesis—in this process. Behind the formation of new individuals lies the 'germinal' system of *genes* that determines the building of new forms (561ff.). But such a system is itself already a living whole, an organic structure in miniature; for each chromosome is already a whole system of determinative factors. In a sense, therefore, the morphogenetic process is predetermined. But this predeterminateness is not total. It is effective only under preexisting conditions that in part are purely external, such as warmth, water, proper soil, and light in the case of plants. When these conditions are given, then every blastomere has a specific "prospective significance" for the rest of the process.

This new type of determination is not indifferent to the result, as is the causal nexus. But it is also not identifiable with the finalistic determination of teleological thinking. Hartmann speaks of this special form of determination, which is neither causal nor finalistic, as "descendence" (*Deszendenz*).

It is in this perspective that Hartmann now considers the phenomena of phylogenesis (611ff.).

Darwin's theory of evolution opened up the range of problems involved here. Research in the field revealed more difficulties. "The great idea was soon obfuscated because it was applied too hastily. On the basis of little evidence 'genealogical trees' were constructed and were not without some sensationalism dwelt upon when it came to the problem of human existence" (611). A conflict with religious interpretations was inevitable.

As far as the unity of all life on earth is concerned, the living species are related to it as individuals, and yet also not as individuals. They come into existence and disappear; they do not reproduce themselves.

Although particular species may continue for some time, they do not form a simple continuum. There occur not only variations, which indicate merely an instability of a species, but also changes of the species type itself. What is important here is that the acquisition of new organic traits is at the same time a development of higher forms of life. In brief, we face here a "process of ascending new creations (*Prozess aufsteigender Neuschöpfung*)" (614). That is, descendence is form-building in the original sense—a form-creating process without pregiven form or plan. Of all the organic form-building processes, only phylogenesis is purely productive—"*productive morphogenesis*" (615).

As far as the origin of life in general is concerned we are as much in the dark as before. But this does not change the fact of the further origination of manifold species. Although comparative anatomy has revealed the essential similarity of the inner structure of externally quite different living beings—a similarity that remains incomprehensible if it is not taken to be evidence of the common origin of diverse species—the facts themselves are no explanation of the process.

It is true that the morphogenesis of the individual follows in basic respects the original and unique morphogenesis of the species. Nature embarks, as it were, upon a specific way of form-building, and sticks to it in all secondary rebuilding of the original form. But the unique original production and the continuous reproduction are meshed like the wheels of gears. The life of a species can maintain itself only through the reproduction of what once was produced. Understood categorially, the two stages of the form-building process, origination and reproduction, are reciprocally condition and conditioned. Only together and firmly intertwined can they exist.

But here we face once more the problem of purposiveness, for purposiveness is basically the constitutive character of all living forms. The question is, What is the basis of this purposiveness? Is there an origination of purposiveness out of the purposiveless? And if there is, how are we to understand it?

Life can maintain itself only where all forms and functions are "purposive" for its existence. In every structure, form and function are mutually supportive of each other. This relationship is one of suitableness as means to an end—to the maintenance and development of the organism. Moreover, the inherent purposiveness in the morphogenetic process has an upward-directed trend. "The process of a lower order is always suitable [*zweckmässig*] for the process of a higher order. And the crucial problem is: Must not a purposive action correspond to this suitableness? Here we face the strongest temptation to teleological thinking (629ff.).

But let us remember that the forms and structures of all living beings are essentially products of adaptation—adaptation not only to the environment but of various species to one another. Plants, for example, are dependent upon insects for their fertilization; insects, in turn, are dependent upon plants for nourishment. A "purpose" is clearly in evidence here. What is questionable is whether it is really a preset purpose (617).

In the Introduction to his *Kritik der Urteilskraft* Kant had maintained that

> the transcendental concept of a purposiveness of nature is neither a concept of nature nor a concept of freedom because it ascribes nothing to the object, *i.e.*, to nature, but only represents the unique way in which we must proceed in our reflection upon the objects of nature with a view of getting a thoroughly interconnected experience, and so to a subjective principle, *i.e.*, a maxim of judgment.[49]

In other words, to regard a thing as purposive "because of its *inner form*" is something quite different from "regarding the *existence* of this thing as a purpose of nature." Kant here quite clearly rejects a teleological interpretation of nature. But he still sees everything under the simple alternative of either causal or finalistic determination, and this leaves the problem of the origin of life unresolved. How can what is inherently purposive come into being out of the purposeless?

In his *Origin of Species* (1859) Charles Darwin has given us the first useful beginning to an understanding of the origin of purposiveness. The "struggle for existence," with its "selection of the fittest," implies a direction toward what is useful or suitable for organismic existence, and thus shows how what is suitable can arise out of what is not purposive (*Natur*, 642). It gives us exactly what Kant spoke of when he referred to living organisms as "purposive" without being a

49. *Kritik der Urteilskraft*, 20; Meredith, 23; Bernard, 20.

"purpose of nature." The survival of the suitable in the struggle for existence plays a role in the life of a species "as if" an understanding were guiding it.

But selection can isolate only what already exists as deviation from a form-type. It thus presupposes deviations and does not explain them.

Granted that ontogeny is the effect of an initial system of determining factors—the genes. Phylogenesis, however, is pure, original production, without a pregiven form-type, and is in some way basic to all ontogeny. The reference to genes is misleading here rather than illuminating. To attempt to explain phylogenesis in terms of "predispositions" or "*Anlagen*" is but an evasion of the crucial problem of origin. And the concept of 'mutation' may be descriptive but itself lacks explanation. Since mutation may also be of a kind that leads to results incapable of survival, it alone does not account for phylogenetic development of higher forms of life. Even selection and mutation together are by no means sufficient to solve the riddle of the phylogenetic origin of new forms of life (663f.).

What is really important in phylogenesis is not the descendence but the change of form and the mode of Being—the morphogenesis of new species, their epigenetic new creation (665). What is crucial here is the *ascension* of life. Everything that in some sense is important and decisive here cannot be seen in the beginnings but only in the progress of the process and in the special way in which it proceeds. Spontaneous generation (*Urzeugung*) as the original starting point of phylogenesis explains little, for phylogenesis itself is a single long sequence of new formations out of lower forms. At every stage in the process the problem of the first occurrence of new organic forms recurs.

As far as the whole process is concerned, it is evident that as soon as purely physicochemical structures rose to a level at which an "inner self-rebuilding of the form" occurred, they came under new principles that from this point on determine what happens. These new principles are the categories of the organic. They share with the range of facts for which they are effective an aspect of the irrational that cannot be abrogated. What alone is clear is that "processes of selection" precede the beginnings of life, and that they become organic selections when the structures begin to reproduce themselves in some way. With this self-reproduction a "hereditary preservation" of characteristic qualities begins. It is in principle what in all subsequent elevations of forms is the driving force behind the process of rising organismic forms. But here, as everywhere else, the first form-renewal remains obscure. The deviation within the germ is "a matter of that *contingentia* whose lawfulness and necessity we do not understand" (*Natur*, 667).

Taken as a whole, life is not adjusted to mere maintenance but is a forming of the new. In the last analysis, the creative aspect of form-building (the original morphogenesis) superposes itself upon form-maintenance. Life maintains itself on the whole in its manifoldness of forms by replacing old forms through new ones.

It is evident that real life does not have the categorial form of a substratum but that of a process, and this process must be understood as the basic essence of organismic existence itself. "Vivacity (*Lebendigkeit*) is the specific process-form of the organic and is indeed its categorial basic form" (677).

This process-form, however, is an extremely complex one, and it is not possible to reduce all of its specific aspects to one basic type. The process is different at every level, and at each level there are aspects of purely causal determination. But there are also aspects that are startlingly similar to finalistic occurrences. The riddle here is not the decay of organismic forms but their genesis. The stages of this ontogenesis are related to the end result "as if" they were carefully selected as means for the purpose of realizing the final product. It is so in the process of assimilation, but it is so also in an eminent sense in the reproduction of individuals and therefore in the whole of phylogenetic development. It is here that we encounter the opposition of vitalistic and mechanistic interpretations. What is crucial is the contrast of teleological and causal conceptualizations. Hartmann maintains, however, that "the whole alternative 'either finality or causality' is wrong, for it depends upon an incomplete disjunction" (689f.).

Even below the stratum of organismic existence, though, some types of determination can be found in which the causal nexus constitutes the basis but not the uniqueness of the processes. The form of reciprocal actions is of this type. And beyond them are the special forms of internal connections—the central determinations of the structures of atoms and molecules, of solar systems and living organisms. In the phylogenetic process it is already possible in principle to understand the apparent purposiveness in terms of a unique category of determination, that of 'natural selection'. This process is the coming into being of the purposive out of the purposeless. It is a process that stands between simple causality and the highly complex finalistic nexus. But the crux of the matter is that in this process of natural selection there is no guiding principle, no goal setting as we know it in human activity. Purposiveness is replaced by the survival of the fittest in the struggle for existence. The rest is a complex and, in many respects, unclear but essentially causal determination.

All categories of the purely physicochemical strata of reality are here insufficient, for the germ plasm determining the development of the organism is precisely the great riddle. It is here that the difference between ontogenesis and phylogenesis is of special importance. Ontogenesis is a process of genuine development that has a precise beginning and, generally, a precise end. It is determined and guided toward a development of form quite dissimilar to the initial configuration of elements that give rise to it. But this process is reproduction, not production. The astonishing fact, however, is that reproduction is the more puzzling because the mode of determination must be sought for it, not for the original production of the initial configuration of elements. And this is the problem of the *nexus organicus* in the strict sense (693f.)

The problems here are the interdependencies of various states of articulation in the process of morphogenesis, for not one of them exists for itself. Assimilation, reproduction, and the development of a species presuppose one another; not one of them can be isolated except in abstraction. When we view this stratified process as a whole—i.e., when we view it as a combination of production and reproduction—then the crux of the matter is the reproduction. It is here that we encounter the essential *novum* or organic determination. Only because of the basic hereditary rebuilding of individuals does natural selection in phylogenesis attain so high a significance that it can throw light upon the miracle of the origin of what is organically suitable out of the merely physical. In the mode of determination found in organismic reproduction all the aspects of the organological problematic are concentrated.

Considered individually, the processes of ontogenesis are causally determined. But this does not mean that they are simply mechanical, for the arrangement of the causal factors is here a specific one. And this initial arrangement and its effectiveness in ontogenesis are the problem. How can a complexus of causal factors determine the development of intricate organic structures?

To be sure, causal factors do determine structures and functions of the cells that come into being through the continuous division of the initial 'egg cells'. But the position and arrangement of the visible form of a multicellular organism—that which constitutes the visible form of the organism—is not determined by mere causal factors. It depends on "the function of their place within the whole." And this means that at every stage in the development, the structure achieved has an effect upon its parts. We can speak here of "wholeness-determination." [50] We must keep in mind, however, that the determining wholeness is not that toward which the process moves, for this does not yet exist. What is essential here is the wholeness of each transition stage, and this means a specific new kind of energetic central determination. The germ cell does indeed play the role of a determining center whose function is the division and differentiation of cells—a process through which, in the end, the whole organism is unfolded. But this process actually involves both an original central determination and, at every stage, a specific wholeness-determination. Since in ontogenesis the wholeness comes into existence epigenetically at every stage, the main factor in the development is obviously the central determination on the part of the germ cell. And since the 'germ plasm' of the cell has come into being phylogenetically, it must be the result of selective processes in which its suitableness was formed (*Natur*, 696).

Reference to a "prospective potency" of the germ cell as the determining factor of organismic development—as some vitalists have it —is rather meaningless; for the result to be developed is as yet only 'prospective' and therefore cannot be an actual factor in the process of organismic development. What is involved here is a very specific and new type of central determination: determination by a germinal predisposition which, in the course of development, plays the part of a determinative center whose function is gradually transmitted through the division and differentiation of the organic cells until the complete organism is actualized. The prospective potency and function of the place of cells in the developing organism are nothing less than an interaction of the original germinal determination and a determination by that whole which has been attained at every stage in the development. This means that, despite everything else, the main factor in the devel-

50. *Natur*, 694ff. Hans Driesch called it "wholeness causality." For a discussion of the experimental work that led Driesch to the formulation of this concept, see Werkmeister, *A Philosophy of Science*, 334–51.

opment is the central determination by the germinal system, which is a closed complexus of causal relations.

But this initial germinal system itself has come into existence phylogenetically and therefore has behind it processes of selection in and through which its purposiveness has been derived. This means that the internal arrangement of the elements within the germinal whole and the "prospective potencies" of the whole can at least be understood as the product of selection within the species-forming process. This selection, however, in which the germ plasm builds up to higher species is not a second process in addition to the species-forming one, but is identical with it; for the selection of individuals already involves many selective processes in the modification and development of individual parts, organs, and functions that are reproduced in every individual and therefore must have their appropriate 'determination' within the germ plasm.

We must note, however, that the complexus of causes contained in the germ plasm is not the totality of the conditions necessary for the development of organic forms. It is only one of three basic factors. The function of place within the whole and external conditions also play important roles. Together they have the character of a new type of determination that involves two aspects. One of these is "the categorial form of wholeness-determination; the other is simple reciprocal action" (*Natur*, 678).

However, both modes of determination depend for their effectiveness upon still other factors, such as environmental conditions, which at every stage in the development are supplementary to the basic process. To put it differently: The central determination, which the genes provide, continuously conditions the selection of those external causal factors that at any given stage in the individual development may play a part in the wholeness-forming process in its interactions with the surrounding world. The genes thus also provide a selective principle for the developmental conditions which they themselves do not contain. The process they guide is determined by them in such a way as to include, at specific stages, certain external factors in the course of development. The genes thus constitute the selective principle. But this means that the genes are a system of causal relations of astonishingly complete integration for all of the individual aspects involved in the developmental process as a whole. In its completeness, this determination is in many respects superior to the teleologically determined actions of human beings.

In the *Critique of Judgment*, Kant pointed out that

> the organized natural product is one in which every part is recip-
> rocally both end and means. In such a product nothing is in vain,
> without an end (purpose, *Zweck*), or to be ascribed to a blind
> mechanism of nature.

And he added that

> the principle is no doubt . . . derived from experience . . . but
> cannot rest solely on empirical grounds. . . . The cause which
> brings together the required matter, modifies it, and puts it in its
> proper place, must always be judged teleologically.[51]

But teleological judgments are "judgments of reflective reason" only and lack the *a priori* basis of the categories for understanding what is involved here. Such judgments can give us only an "as if" interpreta-tion—"as if" all processes were purposively arranged for the function they have in organismic development.

16. Suitableness and the Nexus Organicus

Hartmann puts it this way: "The basic phenomenon is here the pro-found suitability of relationships of the inner functions and forms of the organism, as well as their relations to the environmental world."[52]

Three aspects must be noted:

1. The 'purpose' to which forms and functions are here related
   is always life itself—its preservation and self-maintenance in
   the form of individuals no less than in that of the species. In
   this sense practically everything pertaining to an organism is
   purposive, from the external protective colors and markings to
   the most subtle regulations, reactions, and instincts.

51. Kant, *Kritik der Urteilskraft*, 376; Meredith, 24ff.
52. Hartmann, *Teleologisches Denken*, 23.

2. This suitableness is an obvious empirical phenomenon, and is not debatable.

3. This suitableness is not only empirically given, it is also *a priori* understandable as a category of the organic; for it is obvious that an organism with unsuitable organs, limbs, forms, and functions cannot be capable of living. This basic proposition remains unchallengeable so long as one relates it only to what is essential and therefore really relevant to life.

Once we have understood these facts, they reveal that there is an essential suitableness outside of human intentions and actions. But we must be clear on one point: Suitableness is something quite other than suitable or purposive action. An analysis of the categories involved proves this.

The most important processes in an organism are the form-building ones. It is characteristic of them that via a series of form-differentiated stages they move unerringly to a final state, i.e., to a completely developed integrated form capable of living. This integrated whole, the living organism, appears to be the determining purpose of the whole complex process. But, as we have seen, Kant already regarded "this transcendental concept of purposiveness" as neither a "concept of nature" nor a "concept of freedom" because "it merely represents the unique mode in which we must proceed in our reflection upon the objects of nature in order to get a thoroughly interconnected whole of experience." In other words, Kant regarded this "transcendental concept of purposiveness" as merely a subjective principle or "maxim of judgment."

However, Kant's view did not prevail. The mechanism–vitalism controversy is proof of this. Neither one of these approaches really comes to terms with the issue, but rather each tries to capitalize on the weakness of its opponent. It is Hartmann's contention that we must take seriously the differentiating uniqueness in nature of self-active and form-building processes; for it is here that we encounter a categorial *novum* of reality, one that transcends mere causality.

The mechanists and the vitalists quite obviously agree on one point, namely, that there is no third possibility besides causal and finalistic determination. Kant had maintained in effect that the development of an organism goes on "as if" a purposive determination were involved;

but he meant the "as if" as a merely "regulative" idea for the purpose of investigating organismic processes.

After a detailed analysis of various interpretations of the problem of organismic reality (*Teleologisches Denken*, 91), Hartmann points out that life is observable in two completely different aspects—although in the last analysis both pertain to the same reality. On the one hand there is given to us the inner aspect of life in our feeling and experiencing ourselves:

> In our own self, life 'experiences' itself. The inner givenness presses on to a comprehension of the organic in terms of an analogy to the mental; the *external* givenness presses on to a comprehension in analogy to the physico-material. (91)

Because of these two forms of the givenness of life, the alternative "finalistic-causal" is inescapable. But both interpretations do violence to the phenomena, for they judge life in terms of categories that have not been obtained from the phenomena of organismic existence but have been carried over from other strata of Being—the causal nexus being that of a lower stratum. Finalistic determination in the realm of the organic would presuppose a consciousness of purpose, for which the presuppositions are lacking. The category of causality, although insufficient to account for the riddle of life as a whole, makes at least careful research in the realm of the organic possible.

That there is a "suitableness" in organismic existence and development cannot well be doubted, but how can we account for it? Why do we regard the origin of suitableness out of the unsuitable as *a priori* impossible? Perhaps organismic existence has a mode of determination all its own.

Where "immanent purposes" determine a process, they must have been present from the very beginning. But in that case the process is a *development*, i.e., it is the unfolding of what was "involved" at its very beginning.

Two specific cases may illustrate the point.

The first case is that of the transformation of the aquatic naiad into the airborne damselfly. When the naiad reaches maturity, some inner urges compel it to crawl up the stump of a plant or whatever is available that projects above the water. And now the naiad's skin splits along the back; legs are withdrawn; the gills peel off; and wings are unpacked. When all this has been accomplished, the new insect—the damselfly—is ready for its maiden flight. How can we account for this? A mere causal explanation is obviously impossible.

And consider the case of a butterfly. From its eggs emerge small caterpillars instead of miniature butterflies. Their actions appear to defy the laws of genetics, for the caterpillars are vegetarians and cannot fly. The collection of genes that the butterfly passes on in its eggs must program the structure and behavior of the caterpillar but must also "carry in trust," as it were, the traits of the butterfly which the caterpillar will one day become. At some point an intermission in growth must occur during which the determining genes are reset. This is the pupal stage. The animal that was the caterpillar seems to be in a dormant stage, but fundamental changes occur in the gene pattern. As caterpillar organs are dismantled, their raw materials are building organs of the butterfly. When we consider the biochemical and physiological changes that have to be coordinated to complete the transformation from caterpillar into butterfly, the process seems quite magical indeed. The category of causality is utterly inadequate to account for it.[53]

Beyond such startling examples as these, it cannot be denied that in organismic nature many processes occur that *look deceptively like finalistic processes*—"as if" some mind were guiding them. However, in finalistic or purposive actions consciousness plays the decisive role, and there is no evidence that this is the case in organismic nature as such. We encounter it only when a spiritual being posits and pursues specific goals.

There have been various reactions to Hartmann's interpretation of organismic existence.[54] Most of them are essentially supportive of Hartmann's position, pointing out in particular that, next to the

53. The problem has been extensively analyzed in *Metamorphosis: A Problem of Developmental Biology*, ed. William Etkin and Lawrence I. Gilbert (Appleton: Century Crofts, 1968). The two examples I have given are discussed by Vincent G. Dethier in "The Magic of Metamorphoses: Nature's Own Sleight of Hand," *The Smithsonian*, vol. 17, no. 2 (May 1986): 123–30.

54. I mention only four: (1) Willibald Baumann, *Das Problem der Finalität im Organischen bei Nicolai Hartmann* (Meisenheim/Glen 1955); (2) Max Hartmann, "Die Philosophie des Organischen im Werke von Nicolai Hartmann," in *Der Denker*, 226–47; (3) Hans-Joachim Hoefert, "Nicolai Hartmanns Ontologie und die Naturphilosophie," *Philosophia Naturalis* 1 (1950/51): 36–55; (4) Paul Hossfeld, "Nicolai Hartmanns Kategorien des Naturprozesses," 377–90.

analysis of the categories of assimilation, his conception of the *nexus organicus* is for the biologist the most important insight; and that the latest findings in biological research have largely confirmed Hartmann's thesis that we are dealing here with a unique type of determination that transcends mere causality but is also not finalistically directed.

Does evolution explain the phenomena of organismic reality? Strictly speaking, evolution means *evolvement*—a mere unfolding of an initial predisposition. Concepts like 'creative evolution' (Bergson) and 'emergent evolution' (Morgan), although perhaps descriptive of basic aspects of organismic existence, are self-contradictory terms and provide no explanation. I find that Goethe was right when he wrote, "Denn eben wo Begriffe fehlen, da stellt zur rechten Zeit ein Wort sich ein" (Precisely where we lack true understanding, there, at the proper time, a word pops up).

5

The Realm of Spiritual Being

IN THE PREFACE TO his book *Das Problem des geistigen Seins* Hart-mann states that the many years of coming to terms with the Hegelian 'philosophy of spirit' opened up for him the approach to the problems with which he deals here.[1] This intensive study of Hegel is reflected in Hartmann's *Philosophie des deutschen Idealismus*, vol. 2: *Hegel*.[2] At the end of this book Hartmann states:

> It is always tempting to see Hegel as a phenomenon under his own categories. One sees him then as a stage in a long road to completion. . . . His system is not only complete in its categories; it is also imprisoned in them. . . . One sees him as a stage in a long road to completion, but also as a first step upon a new path. (*Hegel*, 389)

Hartmann's study of Hegel convinced him that the problem of spiritual Being is not simply a problem for the philosophy of history; for "history is not a history of spirit only, nor is spirit a matter of history" (*Das Problem*, 1). Granted that the only spiritual being we know is

---

1. Nicolai Hartmann, *Das Problem des geistigen Seins* (Berlin and Leipzig: Walter de Gruyter & Co., 1933), iv.
2. Berlin and Leipzig: Walter de Gruyter & Co., 1929.

man, but he is certainly not "only" a spiritual being. He is at best "also" a spiritual Being. History discloses both aspects.

Opposed to the Hegelian thesis that history is the dramatic disclosure of Objective Spirit is, of course, the Marxian 'materialistic' interpretation of history. Since there is some truth in both these interpretations, Hartmann finds that the error of both lies in the one-sidedness of their respective initial assumptions (10f.).

Both theses attempt to understand the whole of historical reality in terms of a single principle. Hegel leaves no space for the fact that, besides the self-realization of spirit, economic factors independently affect the historical process; and Marx sees no original effectiveness of spiritual tendencies in addition to the effects of the forms of production. Both accept as valid only one-sided and irreversible dependence and exclude from the very beginning the interdependencies of determining factors of different strata of reality. Their interpretations of history are purely monistic. Both are victims of the ancient prejudice that an explanation in terms of one principle is the best account of reality; that "simplicity is the seal of truth" (13).

We have seen in Chapter 3, however, that reality is stratified; that each stratum has its own categories; that the higher strata are supported by the lower but have their own autonomy. Each lower stratum is only a *conditio sine qua non* for a higher one; and the *novum* of each higher stratum is the independence or "freedom" of the higher categories over the lower. The world as a whole is a stratified reality; and so is history. It is

> just as much an economic as a spiritual process; just as much the vital as the cultural life of peoples. Geographic and climatic conditions are no less influential than are ideas, valuations, errors and prejudices; technical means no less than mass-psychological suggestions; "accidental" encounters no less than planned meetings, spontaneous applications of energies no less than projections of goals. (17)

The structure or form of the historical process is thus an extremely complex one, and the fundamental problem of the philosophy of history is no more solvable than are other fundamental problems. An irrational element always remains. Is history a blind happening like the process of nature, or is it guided teleologically? Does man determine the course of history? Does he have the freedom to do so? Or is there some other determining factor in history? Is history value-accentuated and the realization of a goal, or is it all a merely senseless happening? Is it at least an ascending process? Is there a simple answer to all of these questions?

Our prescientific awareness of history is supported by what out of the past is actually effective in the present. Paradoxical as it may seem, in our experience the past is actually present; and this fact is a basic element in the structure of historical Being (29). We realize that history is a context of events, and that it is part of this basic context that the past is not absolutely gone but somehow remains effective in the present. If the historical process were merely a *causally* determined process, such effectiveness of the past could not be possible, for a cause ceases to be in its effects. But the effectiveness of the past in the present is obvious.

There is the past experienced as tradition—as customs, good manners, forms of speaking, valuations, prejudices and superstitions, of viewing things and events. And there is also the remembrance of personal experiences and of what one has been told, what 'lives on' in family and regional traditions, in legends and anecdotes, in monuments, art, buildings, and ruins. A special mode of the past's being in the present is found in written records and in literature. Moreover, in the course of history there are periods of fidelity to tradition, and times of rebellion against tradition. This varying attitude toward tradition characterizes the basic modes of the "spirit of the times"—of the *Zeitgeist*. Religious orientation generally means a positive attitude toward the past—toward 'revelations' and the absolute authority of *The Book*. In an age of science and technology, on the other hand, the orientation is primarily toward the present and future. But "between these extremes there is a long chain of gradations" (57).

It is Hartmann's contention that, "without doubt, all spirit has history" (57). But there are also aspects of the historical process—conditions of its structure—that are not themselves historical conditions but are rooted in the very essence of spiritual Being, in specific aspects of its existence, and in the interrelations of those aspects. Strictly speaking, 'history' is not partial processes as manifest in specific areas of human activity but is the interrelation and interaction in a given time and in concrete unity of all partial processes involved. This fact is basic to any interpretation of history, and for a philosophy of history the analysis of the structural conditions of events is only a preliminary task. For the philosophy of history itself we must know first what is meant by that aspect of reality within which the partial processes occur. Beyond this we must attempt to clarify what is meant by, and involved in, the objectification of spirit. And for this it is necessary, first of all, to try to understand what spirit is. What is the individual or personal spirit involved in history?

The problems with which Hartmann now deals are thus indicated.

1. Preliminary Problems

In the so-called philosophy of life (*Lebensphilosophie*) spirit was characterized as 'life'. But, of course, the term 'life' was here taken to mean 'spiritual life' and was not meant to refer to organismic existence. The definition was obviously circular.

A rather common view, frequently associated with idealistic metaphysical theories, has been that spirit is consciousness. Although it is true that consciousness is somehow involved in spirit, there exists very unspiritual consciousness of which even a certain degree of intelligence cannot be denied. It is readily observable in the case of higher animals. But it is also true that not all actions of spirit are conscious, as is evident in certain aspects of artistic creation. This, however, does not preclude the fact that the unconscious is the background of spirit as well as of consciousness. As Hartmann sees it, spirit is the *specifically human* in human beings—in contrast to the material, the organic, and the mental aspects of their existence (47). But what *is* 'specifically human'?

Man is quite generally defined as a 'rational being'. But when we limit the essence of man to his rationality, we overlook the active side of spiritual life. That there is this active side is unquestionable: It manifests itself in willing, acting, reacting, refusing, loving, hating. Even cognizing, reflecting, and thinking are modes of acting. "An inactive spirit is dead" (50f.).

When Hartmann speaks of spirit he means:

1. Spirit within the limits of our experience—the "empirical spirit."
2. All spirit that we encounter in our experience is limited in time; for what lives comes to an end in death.
3. As far as our experience is concerned there is no "hovering

spirit" (*schwebender Geist*). We know of no spiritual Being that is unsupported by mental Being. This relationship of being supported by a lower stratum—this ontic dependency—is characteristic of the world we know and live in. There is no exception.

But it would be a misconception to believe that because the existence of spirit is conditioned by lower strata of reality it must be 'explainable' in terms of them. Materialism reduces itself to an absurdity.

We have seen in Chapter 4 that organisms are more than merely spatiomaterial conglomerations of atoms and molecules, that the categories and laws of purely physical reality remain in effect, but are superseded by the *novum* of organismic developments, structures, and actions. Mental existence is based in a similar way upon organismic reality and has its own mode of Being, its own categories, laws, and determinants. And human existence is based upon but transcends the merely organismic and mental stratum, and reaches its completion only at the level of spiritual reality.

The characteristic aspect of spiritual reality is that individuals do not exist by and for themselves; that they do not have an isolated existence outside a common sphere of spiritual life. The individual human being grows into a common sphere and is rooted in the richness of its content. This sphere—"a historically given spiritual *niveau*"—does not consist of mere individuals and is something quite other than purely mental existence. "It is a spirit-phenomenon of a different rank and magnitude; it is historical or objective spirit. . . . And insofar as the individual person as a spiritual being is co-conditioned by the objective spirit his characteristic mode of being is exempt [*enthoben*] from the categories of the merely mental" (60f.).

Every individual has his mental existence all by himself, and it is not transferable. But the thought an individual thinks can be thought also by other persons who understand it, for a thought is intrinsically objective. It is expansive and connects where mental processes isolate—just as beliefs, convictions, valuations, and ways of viewing things can be shared. "All of them belong to the sphere of spirit. Consciousness isolates, but spirit unites" (61).

Hartmann distinguishes three forms of the modes of spirit:

1. Only *personal spirit* can love and hate; only personal spirit has an ethos, has responsibility, is accountable for its actions, is

guilty or deserves praise; only personal spirit has consciousness, will, and self-consciousness.

2. Only the *objective spirit* is in the strict and primary sense the spirit that "has history." It is superindividual but at the same time is also a real and living spirit. Its modifications are historical changes. Its fate is historical fate. Although this objective spirit shares temporality and perishableness with all living beings, its life moves in dimensions other than that of individual persons. Its time-dimensions are historical periods.

3. Only the *objectified spirit* transcends temporal limits. Its fate lies in the realm of ideas—in what is timeless in the historical process (63).

All three modes of Being of spirit are coordinated; none is preeminent. As inseparable and concrete unity they belong to the same stratum of reality and, despite their differences, have the same relation to the mental, the organismic, and the material modes of Being (65f.).

As far as individual human beings are concerned, no one can doubt that we encounter *the spiritual in man* never otherwise than in connection with body-mind existence. *Objective spirit,* however, is always the spirit of a living group, a community or a nation. It exists and vanishes with the group that is its supportive base. *Objectifications of the spirit* are possible only in some 'matter' in which the spiritual content is made manifest, as in the arts and in literature.

This reality of spirit in three forms is possible only when all three have the same ontic basis. That such a basis exists is the presupposition of Hartmann's discussions of "the realm of spiritual Being" (68).

The reference to the "reality" of spirit needs clarification; for spirit can obviously not be real if by reality we mean the material mode of Being of things. But we have seen already in Chapter 4 that even organismic existence is not reducible to the mere matter of things. As far as man is concerned, a reduction of his existence to the merely material would mean that his awareness of things, his moods and actions, his loving and hating are unreal, as would be historical events, crises, and developments. Surely, a simple materialistic conception of reality does violence to all of these facts.

It is obviously an error to think that matter has a priority in the mode of Being, just as it would be an error to attribute this priority to mind or spirit. Although spirit does not have a higher mode of Being than has matter, it does have a preeminence as reality of a higher stratum. Only a concept of reality that includes all—the material and the immaterial and spiritual—is adequate for an interpretation of what we encounter in the world. "The stratum of the spirit is the highest form of reality only insofar as content and categorial form-giving are concerned" (70f.).

In this perspective the life of human beings and of historical events can be understood as real processes—*Realprozesse*—in the full sense of that term. They presuppose a real context of *Dasein*, a context that includes the living and the lifeless, the mental and the nonmental, the spiritual and the spiritless—a context, in brief, involving the unity and the wholeness of the world we live in.

In this world spirit is something unique, with its own essential characteristics, and in this sense it is individual. The individuality of the human person is obvious, but so also is the individuality of situations in our lives and in history. All are qualitatively distinct.

Two basic aspects, reality and individuality, thus characterize the mode of 'existence' of all spirit. *Ontologically understood*, existence is common to the material, the organismic, the mental, and the spiritual strata of reality; so is temporality. "Everything temporal is real, even that which is not spatial; and everything real is temporal" (73). And there is only *one time*. It is identical for all strata of reality, for it is their fundamental category (75).

Related to time is the very essence of process. What we regard as the constancy of things depends on the mode of our viewing them. What we call a thing, for example, is in reality but a relatively stable stage in a process. We now know that even matter is process: The spontaneous deterioration of the higher forms of atoms proves it. Life is certainly process; so is what is mental. And spirit is no exception. It exists only in its accomplishments. What we call mobility and liveliness has its roots here—roots spirit has in common with all that is real in the world. The life of the spirit, however—whether that of the private and personal, or that of the historical, spirit—is not merely movement nor a mere form-building process as in organismic existence. It is rather a spontaneous inner change, a continuous seeking and finding new ways of forming and expressing itself. It never forms itself as that which it was, and perseveres neither mechanically through inertia nor organically through reproduction. Its perseverance is a spontaneous remaining true to itself, of being its own surety (78f.).

When a person promises something, he commits himself in the present as the one he is going to be in the future. The power to make such a commitment is grounded in his freedom as a person. What is astonishing here is that he can actually maintain himself as identical despite changes in his existence. The unity of personal reality is and remains always a problem of the power to preserve an inner synthesis despite changes in one's own existence. What we call 'personality', 'moral character', and the 'ethos' of man is rooted entirely in this power.

Something similar can be observed in the life of the historical spirit; for this spirit, too, is self-identical only to the extent to which it identifies itself in relation to past and future.

Another aspect rooted in temporality is the fact that all spirit is finite. This is a characteristic that spirit shares with things, with organisms, and with the mental. Finitude is simply an essential attribute of everything that is real, the whole world included.

Spirit comes into being and ceases to be. In every human being, for example, it has its awakening and its fading away. The beginning and end of the personal spirit are quite obviously bound to organic life, to birth and death. The basis of personal spirit is consciousness. In these respects the objective spirit is different. But even here we find inner limitations. Objective spirit grows when facing specific tasks and rises to a certain height. But then its creative power slackens, and the objective spirit rests upon what has been achieved. Its real life ebbs away.

But nothing characterizes the living spirit more, or more basically, than its being embedded in a real world. It belongs to this world as much as does spiritless Being. "Its Being is a Being of this world. It is a Being that can be experienced, and experienced in itself" (85). The world is homogeneous to spirit because it is as much a world of individuals and of historical life as it is the world of things and thing-relations. The one world we live in is the complete structure of interrelated strata—the world of spiritual as well as of spiritless Being.

2. Personal Spirit

After these general observations we must now turn to more specific analyses of what is involved in the complex spectrum of spiritual reality.

Hartmann turns first to a discussion of *personal spirit,* for "as object of contemplation the spiritual individual occupies a unique position. . . . The advantage is obvious; for, as an individual, spirit can see itself inside. . . . The proof of this is the self-consciousness of the person" (*Das Problem des geistigen Seins,* 87–150).

The spiritual individual develops itself, as an organism does; but the development is quite different in the two cases. The organism unfolds what is given in the determinative DNA molecule. Spirit, on the other hand, "must always make itself what it is." An organism reproduces itself in new individuals. Its new form is determined by the old form. Any variation of it is merely accidental. The mental is, of course, not continuous; it awakens to consciousness in each individual anew. But this awakening is nevertheless part of the whole process of development of an individual.

It is entirely different in the case of spirit. Like consciousness, spirit comes into existence anew in every individual; but it is not inherited together with life. And it is not a mere unfolding of initially given factors. A child learns to see and walk with the development of its organs and limbs, but it does not learn to speak in the same way. It must learn to combine and comprehend. In association with mutes only the child would never learn to speak. The situation is similar with respect to man's practical orientation in the world, with the sphere of his attitudes. Each individual must develop his or her own experience—must make mistakes, must try and try again. Even the most brilliant endowments alone are not sufficient. Practical wisdom (*Lebensweisheit*) is acquired only through the individual's own efforts.

Spiritual consciousness begins only with a liberation from instincts and the achievement of an objective relationship to the surrounding world.[3] Man's understanding of this relationship makes all the difference between the merely subjective world of animal existence and the objectified world of contemplation. "It is a radical re-orientation of consciousness" (*Das Problem,* 86), which entails the possibility of seeing the world not simply as related to me, but seeing it as a "world in itself."

To be sure, man never completely outgrows the stratum of animal

    3. For an illuminating discussion of this fact, see Helmuth Plessner, *Die Stufen des Organischen und der Mensch* (Berlin: Walter de Gruyter, 1928), chap. 6, "Die Sphäre des Tieres," and chap. 7, "Die Sphäre des Menschen."

consciousness. But rising above it, he 'objectifies' things and events, seeing them as something "in themselves," not merely as related to him.

But this reorientation with respect to the world is only one side of human development. The other side pertains to the very essence of spirit itself insofar, namely, as this objectification of the world entails a recognition of our position in that world. For a beast of prey, other animals are but prey. The human spirit, however, recognizes even the beast of prey for what it is in itself: an objective reality, "a living work of art of nature." In this objectification of what is experienced, human spirit attains a unique position in the world. One here transcends the mere 'being-for-me' of things and comes to see what they are in themselves. This fact is basic for spiritual consciousness. The subject-object relationship is the characteristic creation of spirit (130f.).

This very same reorientation of consciousness that makes the world into an object also transforms consciousness into a subject; and as subject it separates itself inwardly from the world as an object, and thus becomes fully aware of itself as 'I'. In this 'knowing itself as subject', spirit is indeed what it is in itself and for itself. And this implies that from the very beginning, in its objectification of things and events, it is spirit that gives meaning to the world.

However, spirit is not only reflective. The human being is also interrelated with the actualities of the context of life. "He acts and suffers, expects and fears, worries and hopes, creates and struggles."[4] Despite the manifoldness of these acts and relations he remains identical with himself, and it is precisely this that is characteristic of spirit. What spirit thus accomplishes is not only a surpassing of the level of mere instincts but also an objectification of the whole richness of relationships in the world, and his mastery over them. He emerges not only as a subject but also as a person. And as a person he meets other human beings also as persons. He is an object for them as they are objects for him; and in this relationship the world is disclosed not only as object for him, but also as a reality for which he himself is something. His relationship to the world is thus twofold: a forming and a being formed. He not only exists in the world and depends on it, he also is a

4. *Das Próblem des geistigen Seins*, 107. For a comment on this fact, see Gerhard Hennemann, "Welt und Mensch in der Sicht Nicolai Hartmanns," *Zeitschrift für Philosophische Forschung* 4 (1950): 269–78.

creative factor in the world. Within the limits of his abilities he creates forms and structures of a new stratum of Being. He creates "a world of spirit within a spiritless world" (*Das Problem*, 109). And as this creative being, man himself emerges as a "person."

"Personality" is thus the basic characteristic of the spiritual individual. But to define spirit in terms of personality is impossible. Analysis fails here because we know personality only as a whole. All attempts at derivation are futile because there is nothing from which it can be derived. The characteristic of spirit, the categorial *novum* that separates it from everything else in the world, is precisely the transintelligible and alogical.

The mode in which we know about persons is in living with them. We feel affected by them in special ways—by their actions, their intentions, their dispositions, even by the way they look at us. This givenness of the other person is immediate but is not an objective comprehension of what is essential to being a person. A person knows another person simply as "something like himself," but he cannot really say what that 'something' is. And this knowledge of the other person is by no means a knowledge of individual characteristics of a specific personality. It is, rather, a knowledge about personality as such, about the general character of personality. An individual person we come to know gradually through actions, attitudes, and positions taken.

Although a person is given as an individual whole, its wholeness is not present in any particular *Now*. It is extended in living, in duration and change. Its identity is not something permanent, but something the person himself must achieve despite all changes in time. The wholeness of the person, which appears in intuition as immediately given, is actually a synthesis of what in reality is never given together. It is temporally extended. Each individual person must carry on this synthesis for himself.

The "constituting himself" (*dies Sich-Selbst-Konstituieren*) is a first positive aspect of the essence of personality as a category of reality (*Realkategorie*) of spiritual Being (114f.). But the realm of the personal spirit is also a field of actions and reactions that are neither mechanical nor organismic. And it is a field much narrower in scope than is the field of objects for a subject. The life of the personal is a singular and uninterrupted chain of situations in and through which the person must find his way.

The relationship between situation and person is unique and, despite all actual manifoldness, basically the same. A person does not select the situations but "happens to get into them." He may see some situations arise and, within limits, may be able to avoid them; but he cannot prevent new situations from arising. It is a characteristic fact of life that situations in which man finds himself come 'fate-like' upon him, although not always without his contributing to their approach. But once man finds himself in a specific situation, he cannot reverse its coming nor avoid it. He can only deal with it the best he can. The situation forces him to a decision but does not tell him specifically what to do. That is up to him, and he has the freedom to make the decision.[5]

It is now clear what the very essence of a personality is. Hartmann puts it this way: "A person is that being which in ever new situations is forced to make free decisions" (*Das Problem*, 116). In this sense, the world exists for a person in a much more profound way than as mere object for a subject. The person experiences events not only cognitively. He is involved in them, although he retains his spontaneity of action. He is a being that contributes to his own formation and development by his actions, and he does so in the midst of real forces that support and affect him. The human being 'experiences' not only as observer and theoretician but also as affected by events and as affecting them. He "experiences" situations, "suffers" his fate and must "bear" it. In the fact that events are inescapable he experiences them in the hardness of their reality; and in dealing with that reality he 'experiences' also the consequences of his own actions. In fact, "the life of the person consists in his emotional-transcendent acts—be they spontaneous or receptive. The person is that being which lives its life in these acts" (120).

But the person is not merely the sum total of the acts. He is not the experiencing, not volition and action. He is rather the one who experiences, who wills and acts. His identity is not pregiven but must be achieved. In other words, a person is a being that has strength to maintain itself despite the manifoldness of his sensory responses, feel-

5. For a detailed analysis of the problem of this freedom, see Nicolai Hartmann, *Ethik*, part 3 (Berlin and Leipzig: Walter de Gruyter & Co., 1926), 565–746: "Das Problem der Willensfreiheit." Translated by Stanton Coit under the title *Ethics*, vol. 3: *Moral Freedom* (London: Allen, 1932). I shall deal with the problem in chap. 6.

ings, and actions. Only in this self-maintained unity is the person an individual. No one else can enter into him and see him from the inside.

But the individual person identifies himself not only with himself as one integral whole; he also identifies himself with a specific aspect of the world—with the events to which he feels connected as if by fate. Part of these events is his encounter with other persons, and this encounter opens up a new dimension of existence. The individual now identifies himself not only as himself but also as a segment of the surrounding world. As subject he is merely the counterpart of objects; but as a person related to other persons he transcends mere subjectivity. As Hartmann puts it: "Consciousness separates human beings. Spirit combines them" (121). The person remains an individual but extends himself into a sphere of reality in which he exists with other persons and shares with them the events of the times.

The "sphere of life" (*Lebenskreis*) of the person is a fundamental characteristic of personality as a category. It structures reality and forms a world far beyond a merely conscious activity of the person's transcendent acts. In these acts he transcends the mere inwardness of his own consciousness and enters into a relationship to the world, a relationship through which part of that world belongs to him as his own. This fact is already observable at the lowest level of his dealing with things—with 'his' things. At this level, ownership is not a matter of law but of mastery. We observe it in the use of *tools* that would be *nothing but things* in the hands of individuals who do not know how to use them. It is similar with everything that really belongs to man: his home, his land, his domesticated animals—in brief, his daily surroundings. All of this bears some imprint of his spirit, just as he himself is affected by it all. The degree of this interrelation varies, of course, from person to person. It is different for the farmer on his land and for the craftsman in his workshop, and it is perhaps least stable in the uprooted persons in our large cities. But the sphere and the unity of the person in it are not absent anywhere.

This interrelation of person and environment is most important when one person is related to another. Each person involved in this mutual relationship is affected by it. It is as much a relationship of shared experiences and joined actions, of solidarity in given situations, and of common responsibility. But even in this complex relationship it is the individual person who gives his sphere its special characteristics.

What we call a great or strong personality is one whose influence has creative force and gives even other persons a richer life.

A person is thus a being who transcends himself not only in his actions but who in his whole mode of being lives basically in self-transcendence and is intimately related to the whole sphere of existence. He exists in that sphere as much as within himself. He is basically the expansive being who, despite growing into the world, never loses himself but develops and realizes himself by living beyond himself (123).

A person seldom knows in full consciousness what he really is. Measured against the whole spiritual being of a person, his self-consciousness is secondary. Self-knowledge is actually a matter of the *ethos* of the person—a late insight seldom achieved even in its maturity. A person forms himself in experience, in suffering and action, in becoming guilty and bearing the burden. He lives in his transcendent acts, especially in the emotional acts. In his relation to others, in their reactions and evaluations of him, his awareness awakens to what is in his attitudes. This new knowledge of himself is his conscience (125). It is not a spontaneous insight nor simply a reflection upon himself. It is acquired in at times painful reactions to the consequences of his actions upon others. And

> man experiences the greatest surprises in himself as he learns to see himself in his actions. The image of himself, growing luxuriantly out of an empty self-consciousness, is broken by the harshness of moral self-experience. Man is taught by life what he is in life. . . . Only the situation in which I find myself reveals—to myself and to others—who I am. (126)

It is in this sense that we must understand the Socratic challenge "know thyself." And this self-knowledge is essential to personal spirit, to developing moral maturity and, in general, to man's position as a person. All of his activity—all initiative, intervention, and creativity—depends upon it. The minimum of anticipatory insight that man has opens up for him a perspective of possible activity and raises him above spiritless consciousness and its limitation to the present. This anticipatory insight is "the Archimedean point" from which spirit begins to move the world (131). It is basic to man and to his actions. His position in the world depends on it.

The superiority of the spirit consists in the exploitation of forces which without man would be blindly effective. Man dominates by using the forces in nature for his own purposes. This is possible to the extent that he knows the effect of the forces and anticipates them. The superiority of spirit thus lies in its ability to set goals and select means for their realization. Contemporary man, always looking with astonishment on the latest wonders of technological achievements, has forgotten what really is astounding. He accepts as self-evident that water and wind, fire and steam, chemical processes and electricity work for him; that he himself merely guides and regulates them, and thinks of new ways of using them. What is no longer considered is the basic phenomenon of spirit. The forces of nature cannot oppose spirit so long as man understands them and respects their unique character-istics. This is so because the forces of nature have no will of their own and are neutral with respect to man's intentions. This is man's advan-tage in the world, and he exploits it. He dominates ever new forces of nature and makes them serve as the basis for his own existence. But the power of man's spirit over spiritless Being is dominance over "foreign" powers—a dominance possible only through foresight and anticipa-tory actions. Where man loses this control he is even more powerless than animals.

As far as man is concerned, everything in the world that affects him appears to be value-related. It is either valuable or inimical, friendly or hostile. This valuation is apparent in acknowledgment, approval, respect, sympathy, and admiration; but also in their counterparts: re-jection, disapproval, contempt, antipathy, indignation, and rebellion. The person reacts with specific attitudes toward whatever enters the sphere of his experience, and these attitudes are responses to the values or disvalues encountered. They are 'reactive acts' and show that man's reactions to the world are from the very beginning directed toward what appears to be value-related. Only pure cognition, as we find it in the sciences and as distinguished from our reactions to the world in general, transcends this elementary fact; but science itself is in this respect a secondary matter.

To believe that the valuable is what one desires or strives for, and is valuable because of one's desire and striving, is a *circulus vitiosis* (135). Were it not so, man would first be able to desire and strive for what is not valuable; but he is not capable of doing this. In desiring and striving he is from the very beginning bound to felt values. And it is this value-feeling that gives him his freedom of choice and of action.[6]

It is obvious that something can be valuable for man without his being aware of this fact. The progress in man's consciousness of values is "his opening up to the manifoldness of values that surround him" (*Das Problem*, 136).

It is in this perspective that Hartmann sees all activity of a person as conditioned by values in a twofold way: by the existence of values in what is desired and by one's own value-feeling (*Wertgefühl*) that gives one's actions their direction. It is not purposive actions as such but the value-feeling behind them that decides what goals man sets for himself. The action itself is completely value-indifferent, and is but the form in which a being capable of action manifests itself. The essential character of a person is, however, that he or she can will only what in some respect appears to him or her as valuable. "Man is not a satanic being," not a being that in principle wills what is contrary to values. What evil he does he does only because he sees some good to be realized. One does not deceive, for example, because one simply wants the disadvantage of the person being deceived, but because one wants one's own advantage. "Man is in principle turned towards values, and is in principle turned away from disvalue. . . . But he is not predestined towards the good. He has a choice between value and disvalue" (137). He feels value as an 'ought to be' in contrast to what actually is the case.

In this feeling for values lies man's relationship to a world other than that of mere things. It gives him his unique position in the world as a whole; for he alone, as personal-spiritual being, is capable of pursuing and realizing values. He alone is a moral being, the 'mediator of values' in the real world. Only in him do 'real determination' (*Realdetermination*) and 'ideal determination' (*Idealdetermination*) collide. It is man's task to resolve the conflict. The ability to do so is his freedom (139f.). And this freedom, understood as the power to make decisions, is the essential but irrational inner being of a person.

6. Hartmann commits himself here to the position on values developed by Max Scheler in *Der Formalismus in der Ethik und die Materiale Wertethik*, 4th ed., in Max Scheler, *Gesammelte Werke*. I shall deal with this problem more specifically in chap. 6.

To be sure, man is not the only being for whom the valuable in the world has value. But he is the only one for whom values have meaning. In the personal spirit an awareness of the world rises to the level of an awareness of values. And by virtue of this fact man becomes in a new sense the center of this world. The world becomes *his* world, for it is he who in his activities realizes the values inherent in what is given. "When and where in the world a spirit arises that understands values, the richness of values [*Wertfülle*] of the world belongs to it as noetic property; and besides this spirit there is nothing in the world nor outside it 'for whom' the world would be meaningful" (147). The world 'belongs' to spirit as the being that is 'opened up' to it and is axiologically sensitive. And it is a moral demand upon man to measure up to this 'openness' and to realize values.

3. The Objective Spirit

When we now turn to a discussion of the objective spirit[7] we must keep in mind that Hartmann developed his position during "twenty years of struggle" with Hegel (*Hegel*, v), years that convinced him that "the more critically we view Hegel the more we learn from him (vi). But in Hegel's system itself "one will not find the key to going beyond him. His system is not only complete in its categories, it is imprisoned in them" (*Das Problem*, 389).

What characterizes Hartmann's interpretation of objective spirit is that he begins not with metaphysical speculation but with an analysis of relevant phenomena. He does so because he is convinced that "modes of Being (*Seinsweisen*) cannot be defined but only described" (226; 161). What, then, are relevant phenomena?

In interactions with others the individual human being lives in a sphere of reality that transcends his own existence. That is, he lives in an interpersonal sphere that itself has the character of a superpersonal spiritual context. "This sphere of spiritual communality [*Gemeinsamkeit*], this common life of the spirit which transcends the individuals, relates and supports them, and thus provides the basis for their growth

7. *Das Problem*, 151–347. For an analysis of this discussion, see Hilda Diana Oakeley, "Professor Nicolai Hartmann's Concept of Objective Spirit," *Mind* 64 (1935): 39–57. See also Karl Gross, "Nicolai Hartmanns Lehre vom Objektivierten und Objektiven Geist," *Zeitschrift für Deutsche Kulturphilosophie* 3 (1937): 266–85.

and differentiation and this growth and differentiation is the life of the objective spirit" (152). It is "the great self-evident fact of our human existence which we generally do not notice because we completely live in it" (153).

The task now is to analyze this fact without indulging in metaphysical speculations.

In considering the human being,—i.e., in considering personal spirit —we have found that the individual's experience includes an interrelation with other persons, and that this interrelation is part of a living community. It is, in effect, part of a living common spirit. The task now is to understand this phenomenon in its full extent and manifoldness. In order to accomplish this, we must consider all regions of the historically real and changing spirit: custom, law, language, and the political life no less than beliefs, morals, knowledge, and the arts. All of these are contents of the historical spirit; and it is precisely their historical character which shows that they have a coming-into-being and a ceasing-to-be like any living being (161). They exemplify objective spirit.

We readily speak of the 'spirit' of Hellenism, of the Renaissance and Rococo, and, more specifically, of the Ciceronian and the Augustinian Roman periods. Such terms are quite clear to the person who understands part of human history. What we call the 'spirit of the time' consists of the characteristic ideas that prevail at the time: the goals aimed at, the general tendencies and achievements, the events and the common fate of the people living at those times (163).

In the same way we speak of 'the spirit of the people'—meaning the specific characteristics that distinguish the communal life of various groups of people. This spirit is something quite concrete and comprehensible. It can be observed without any reference to history. We experience it as a power that affects and engulfs us, and makes demands upon us. We encounter it in our everyday experience. But it is identical neither with a plurality of human beings nor with a particular selection of them. It is in everything, but is completely present in nothing. It connects the most heterogeneous things—from the minimal forms of politeness to the forms of political passions, to prevailing views of the world, to valuations and prejudices. But this manifoldness does not prevent that it is precisely the interrelation of various aspects that impresses us. Despite all divergencies in detail, we experience the spirit of a people as a whole. As far as history is concerned, the spirit of the times superposes itself upon the spirit of a people. It is differentiated in the contemporaneously existing people who, in turn, are sequentially changing forms of the spirit of the times.

What we must avoid in our interpretation of the facts is accepting a mechanically genetic point of view—attempting to explain a whole in terms of its parts. As far as history reaches back, we find that the individual human being always finds a definitely formed common spirit already in existence and "grows into" it. He finds and accepts customs, language, prevailing valuations, and ideas (165). The objective spirit is obviously many-sided and complex. But it is part of the real world and not something transcendent "hovering over" it (168).

Hartmann regards Hegel as "the discoverer of the objective spirit," but finds that this discovery got lost in Hegel's "highly speculative metaphysics of spirit" (170–76). What, then, is Hartmann's own position?[8]

In Hartmann's view,

> objective spirit is neither a substance behind the spiritual life of a human community nor a mere sum of the individuals; it is also neither a mere type of what is spiritually common [to individuals] nor a mere product of spirit. It is spiritual life in its totality as it forms and develops itself historically in an existing group of human beings; it attains a certain height and then declines. (*Das Problem*, 177)

This historical life of the spirit is a phenomenon that must be examined in its manifestations.

Since the objective spirit exists only in collective groups of individuals, the form it gives each group is basic to all higher developments of them. It is the modus vivendi of a tribe, of a people, and of a group of peoples. The "material" of such formations is the mere coexistence and interaction of persons. And it is evident that, "ontologically understood, the herd as a form of life is the harbinger of the human community" (180). The stratification of reality implies that, because of its being a higher mode of Being, spirit presupposes and rests upon

8. For an appreciative but critical reaction to Hartmann's interpretation see Eduard Spranger, "Das Echte im objektiven Geist," in Heimsoeth and Heiss, eds., *Nicolai Hartmann, Der Denker*, 29–46.

all lower strata: that it exists only where it is supported by "a living group of people." Spirit does not conceive and then create the collective whole, but takes it over from the sphere of organismic life and transforms it. As a mere collectivity the common sphere of existence is a category of life and not of the spirit. Spirit, however, "takes over" the unity of life, and does so in a twofold way: (1) simply as mere unity of the species, and (2) as a form of living together collectively (181). The unity of the species remains in the background as supportive basis for spirit, but spirit transforms it into something not known at the level of mere animal existence. But this transformation must not be understood in terms of a "contract," as some theories have it. It occurs rather in "a progressive self-transformation of the living community" for which the initiative of the individual personal spirit is not sufficient. It is a process that advances in historical time-segments in which much personal initiative is involved. But a contract, as such, is never entered into. The collective whole exists as modus vivendi prior to any ability of the individuals to enter into a formal contract.

Neither is the theory of *bellum omnium contra omnia* a key to an understanding of the structure of a community. That theory is as unnecessary as it is improbable—unless it be modified to account merely for the historical development of larger units out of smaller ones for the purpose of eliminating conflicts.

In any case, a state is not nothing but spirit, nor is spirit nothing but state. To be sure, the state is a *collectivum* of people; but it is also a geographical-spatial entity, and is spirit only in the sense of self-formation and of the policies it pursues (182).

We can comprehend the essence of the objective spirit only when we consider its unique manifestations: language, prevailing mores, valuations, laws and morals, forms of production, typical attitudes, artistic developments and understanding, the status of the sciences, and predominant worldviews in every form, be they mythology, religion, or philosophy.

Consider language as a manifestation of spirit. It is obviously not the individual who creates his language. The individual finds it as it is spoken in the community into which he is born. He "grows into it" as the common sphere of communication. And with the language the individual also accepts the spiritual heritage of the group into which he is born, for language is part of the formed and living communal spirit.

What is evident even here is that objective spirit itself is not inherited but is a matter of tradition (185). Growing into it is a matter of learning and acquiring, and depends on the capacity of the individual to rise up to it.

We have seen earlier that consciousness separates individuals. Now we see that, and in what sense, spirit establishes a new unity—the unity of tradition. An individual consciousness cannot transmit itself directly to others; but it can transmit its thoughts, opinions, insights, and point of view. What is thus capable of transcending the individuals—that which in this sense is objective—is "the life of the objective spirit" (187).

If language were nothing but a convention of communication, acquiring it would be nothing more than the ability of the individual to communicate with others. Even animals possess a minimum of this ability. But language cannot be separated from its giving form to the manifold content to which it gives expression. The word, the structure of the sentence, the "turn of phrase," the manner of speaking, even the cadence connected with it—all of these have a unique power to mold the content being communicated. They emphasize certain aspects and minimize others. They are effectively selective not only in the communication itself but in the comprehension of what is being communicated; for seen in their true essence, words are concepts representing preformed generalities that are imposed upon experiential content. Words and phrases are thus an abundance of "vehicles of spiritual form-giving"—categories of thinking and comprehension. In forming the vocabulary and the mode of speaking, the objective spirit forms itself also. Even what the individual person creates in this respect is at once subject to the law of projectivity and may become part of the tradition. "What is expressed becomes public property of the living spirit" (189) and is carried on historically with the development of the objective spirit.

What can thus be demonstrated in the case of language can be found, *mutatis mutandis,* in all fields of the objective spirit, for the relationship of the objective spirit and an individual person is the same everywhere. That this is so is quite obvious in the fields of education and knowledge. The individual always begins as a learner and must exert himself to grow into the prevailing level of achievement before he can properly evaluate what has already been achieved and can contribute to further advancement.

This educational process is not merely a matter of acquiring information, but is "nothing less than the individual's becoming a human being" (192); for the individual is a human being in the full meaning of his historical times only when he can actively participate in the common spiritual life of his community. But only insofar as he himself contributes to that life does he transcend what he himself has received. It is the prevailing situation into which he has grown—a situation he himself has not created—that presents him with the tasks still to be accomplished.

The facts are especially clear in the field of the sciences but are much more complicated in the realm of evaluations and value consciousness —in ethics and aesthetics.[9] In no field of experience, however, is "the close unity and wholeness of the objective spirit" as powerful and acknowledged as in the field of religion and the closely related mythos" (*Das Problem*, 209). There exists no "spirit of the time" (*Zeitgeist*) that does not have its definite and dominant view of the world and that does not assign to humankind a definite place in that world. It is a unified picture of the world that satisfies the metaphysical needs of the times.

A worldview in this sense is never the product of an individual thinker. It is a historically grown common property (*Gemeingut*) of spirit, which the individual takes over and into which he grows.

The most impressive form of this spiritual manifestation is religion. Its traditional form is consciously and carefully preserved. Its origins are historical, even where faith accepts its doctrine as above history.

In the case of the objective spirit the problem is not so much a matter of truth or error as it is of morals and 'the' law. For faith it is the relationship of the individual to the tradition: his growing into and accepting it, his devoted surrender to it as the "higher truth." The primary and essential respect here is the profound and undisturbed feeling in the individual of security in the living spirit that thinks and cares for him and solves the tormenting problems he himself cannot solve. As a religious person the individual feels that he is supported by a living common spirit.

To be sure, each individual must determine for himself his relation to this higher power. In this respect the religious spirit preserves the

---

9. *Das Problem*, 195–209. Hartmann deals here with the relevant problems quite briefly. I shall discuss them specifically in chap. 6.

individual's freedom. But with respect to how the individual understands the higher power and what attitude toward it he has to take,
the individual is a child of the religious spirit within which he finds
himself. The individual does not determine his conception of God, of
the world, and of his own fate by and for himself. The sanctification
of what is believed through the faith of his contemporaries—and even
more through a living tradition—is felt as the power that supports his
personal conviction (211).

For the historian the political life of a community is more central
and more comprehensible than all other fields. He deals with a manifestation of objective spirit that transcends the original community
by building a new form above it. With this new form, the life of an
individual as a 'citizen' begins (213).

Although in the state the initiative is always taken by an individual
who points out goals to be achieved, the specifically directed 'policy'
is always a matter of community and not of the individual. What is
involved is a matter of concern for all. And political situations arise
whether intended or not: needs, population growth, economic situations, rivalry of nations. Such situations are always communal, but
they are not spiritual situations. Still, the attitudes a community takes
with respect to them, as well as the attempts to deal with the problems, may well be manifestations of the spirit of the community—of
its objective spirit.

Of special interest here is the prevailing and slowly developing basic
orientation in the political life of a people and of its institutions. We
can thus find a uniform tendency in the political aspects of the Roman
Republic of old that remained basic through all changes. The same is
true in the case of the Papacy, which, despite all vacillations, declines,
and revivals in nearly two thousand years, has persevered. Something
analogous can be observed in the development of the form of parlia-
mentary government. In all of these cases a certain "spirit" maintained
itself in changing situations. A spirit that can change, but not arbitrarily in conformity with the will of an individual, is here manifest as
the historical spirit of a community. Individual statesman must act out
of this objective spirit. "Only as one inspired by the historical spirit of
his people, and taking the leadership in the direction of that spirit, is
he at all a statesman" (214).

4. The Historical Spirit

Education of course plays an important role in the development of the objective spirit; and "education is the individual's way of becoming human [*Menschwerdung des Einzelnen*]" (*Das Problem des geistigen Seins*, 216), of rising to the level of the objective spirit. In educational institutions of various kinds the objective spirit fosters the individual's rising above the merely personal level of existence. There is no education toward the merely personal.

But it is also not the case that the development of the individual as individual, as a unique personality, is merely the effect of the objective or communal spirit of the time. Personal individuality grows spontaneously in accordance with its own law within the communal whole. The living community encompasses within its unity an immense variety of personal originality (219), for the objective spirit is not a straitjacket for the personal spirit. It is merely the basis for individual development. The uniqueness of the individual grows along with what is common within the communal whole; it is both personal and communal. The characteristic aspect of this dual process is that all formal education involves only what the living objective spirit represents and does not pertain to what is uniquely individual in spiritual endowments. The relationship of the personal and the objective spirit is thus one of reciprocal supporting and being supported, and within this basic relationship the various realms of the life of the spirit are but different aspects.

Every *Zeitgeist*—the prevailing spirit of any given time—has its specific social and legal aspects, its political tendencies, its morality, its general view of the world, its faith, its arts, its literature, and its techniques. And all of these together constitute a unique totality from which the individual aspects can be separated only by abstraction—a totality into which the individual grows and within which he develops his own personality.

The historical development of this objective spirit cannot be doubted. But neither can it be doubted that the objective spirit is present only fragmentarily in each individual representative. In its entirety the objective spirit is present only within the collective whole of all contemporary individuals (223). And even then we can comprehend its unity only in terms of its content as that content is manifest in individuals. But neither is the individual exclusively a representative of the objective spirit, nor is the objective spirit in its totality embodied in the individual. This fact is perhaps most evident in the sciences. In the beginning it may have been possible for an individual to master all knowledge, but with the advance of the various sciences such mastery is simply impossible. Does this mean that there is not a whole range of scientific knowledge? The actual 'status of science'—especially the status of each particular science—is far from being a mere abstraction. It is perfectly real in the cooperation of the scientists in their respective fields. The particular problems individual scientists face at any given time, and to whose solution they contribute, represent a progressive and uniquely developing manifestation of the objective spirit.

Although it may not be equally obvious, the same is true when we consider "life-styles," artistic tastes, or moral sensitivity, or the social and political life of a community. In all manifestations of the objective spirit, we find the moving forces that emanate from individuals and that in their total effect determine the historical movement of the objective spirit (233). There is no action or intention of individuals that, in its origin and coming to consciousness, does not show in its content and direction some common basic tendencies. This initial and basic orientation is nothing other than a phenomenon of the objective spirit (238).

Wherever this spirit is manifest in the unique totality, it can be seen as a real force in all forms and degrees of realization, and can be felt by any individual in a given community and by foreign communities; for the objective spirit itself is unique in all its forms (246), but it is not a life 'behind' the individuals. It is rather that which 'in' the individuals develops as a constantly changing and growing manifoldness. It is a reality that maintains and develops itself despite the change of individuals and that manifests itself by following laws other than those of the personal spirit. It grows only historically. We can observe the changes of typical periods in history, although we do not know the laws governing those changes. In every case, however, we are here confronted by an "inner dynamic of the historical-spiritual life; for the mere manifoldness of external circumstances alone can not make the sequence of the phenomena understandable" (251).

It is true, however, that ideas are an eminently moving force in the developmental process of the objective spirit. They are the exponent of the spirit's reality and life in the consciousness of the individuals. They are shared by individuals. Their force is not a blind pushing but an anticipating and, within limits, a creatively predetermining force. Upon them depends the element of teleological directedness in the historical process. But this directedness is not all-powerful in history, for it is only one force among many. It is therefore not possible to construe a teleological image of history solely in terms of ideas. But the presence of ideas as historicospiritual reality within the total process cannot be doubted (257f.); neither can the spiritual conflicts manifest in the clash of ideas. Ideas are those powers in the life of the objective spirit in which the autonomy and spontaneity of that spirit become comprehensible.

The objective spirit is thus a reality in the full sense of that term. Like anything real it is temporal, destructible, individual, and empirically given. It is historically real in the same sense in which visible things are real as part of nature, and it has its own autonomous dynamic (260). But the objective spirit is neither consciousness nor a person. It is spirit in another mode of Being. Here we must radically reorient ourselves.

Either the phenomena described are misunderstood or the traditional concept of spirit is false, and its categories must be revised; for the phenomena reveal a spiritual reality that has neither consciousness nor a personality of its own.

It is obvious that the stratification of spiritual Being is highly complex. Consciousness, for example, which is an essential characteristic of personal spirit, is not found in the objective spirit. The historical spirit is something radically other than consciousness and person. It is not simply a higher form, but is something "built over" (*überbaut*) the lower forms and their categories. Just as in the case of consciousness the spatiomaterial aspects of reality were *überbaut*, so in the case of the objective spirit consciousness and personality are "left behind," and the realm of the objective spirit has its own mode of Being, its own essential categories.

To regard the objective spirit as a conscious personal spirit of a higher order may be a metaphysico-speculative possibility, but the phenomena do not justify it. We do not know a general consciousness above our human consciousness, nor do we know a personality above the human. Human consciousness and human personality are exclusively characteristics of individuals and not of communities. The facts indicate quite clearly that the objective spirit exists without a supportive total consciousness and without a supportive total person, and is itself neither consciousness nor person (203). The whole metaphysic of personalism is speculative construction without real contact with the actualities of the phenomena. Only the individual human being is a person. The objective spirit is neither simple nor individual. Man is spirit, to be sure; but he is subjective (and not objective) spirit (266).

Still, without some knowledge of itself no spirit can exist, not even the objective spirit. But just as the objective spirit rises above the spirit of individuals as a supported superexistence, so it finds only in personal spirit what it needs for its own completion. It must 'borrow' consciousness from the personal spirit. This fact is ontologically of greatest importance; for it shows that the objective spirit, taken by itself, is by no means in every respect the higher form of Being. In fact, only the individual is a responsible being. Only the individual has will, has the freedom to make decisions and to take initiatives. And all of this presupposes consciousness (244).

But a compensatory aspect is the fact that the modes of Being of both forms of spirit, the individual and the objective, never exist in isolation. What is essential here is that, ontologically, each form of spirit has its special kind of superiority. Personal spirit without the objective would be empty, for its content is acquired by growing into a community. And objective spirit without the personal would be unconscious and blind. The subjective spirit finds in the objective spirit the power that raises him to the *niveau* of human existence and provides the surroundings within which he lives and works. But the objective spirit finds in the personal one not only an ephemeral 'bearer', but also knowledge of itself, its being in itself, and its completion.

Still, the individual human being cannot fully replace the missing communal consciousness (the *Gemeinbewusstsein*). This fact is especially clear when we consider the relationship of the individual to the state as a human community. For all regions of spiritual life except for this one, the existential form of the objective spirit is sufficient. In the individual's relation to the state, however, the *modus deficiens* becomes apparent. The state depends upon the personal spirit in a sense quite different from that in which the arts and sciences depend upon it. The individual human being is no adequate substitute for the lacking common consciousness. He may be able to act as a representative of the state but he can never be a sufficient consciousness for the state as such. All political activity, insofar as it consists in deliberate decisions and the pursuit of goals, remains the work of human beings. It is *Menschenwerk* and reflects all the characteristics of human action:

one-sidedness, shortsightedness, and subjective conditionedness. The personal spirit is in principle incapable of meeting the requirements of the objective spirit. Its power is not superhuman (279). No individual has the power to identify himself inwardly and completely with the objective spirit, as the idea of political leadership implies. He would have to cease to be a private person—a human being (281). Neither the human personal spirit nor the objective historical spirit can take over the guiding political leadership (*Führertum*). The realities of political life are only a mutual supplementation; and this supplementation is not a synthesis, not a real fusion of one into the other, but only a compromise. It is, nevertheless, sufficient for a limited political consciousness and temporary leadership.

But we note also that masses of human beings as such are not the objective spirit (292). They do not initiate realistic political action, and they present no plans. They can only agree or oppose when something is suggested. The initiative, the plan, and the vision belong to an individual who projects them; what is left for the masses is approval or disapproval. But this is important; for with the decision, the masses take over the responsibility for what they approve.

Such decisions, however, are made only by a majority of the members of a community, not by all of them. This 'principle of majority rule' presupposes ideally that all individual members of a community are capable of making sound political judgments. But how is that possible in view of the pressures of political parties and the news media the parties control? Every individual is a captive of the party of which he is a member. Indeed, "the individual sees only what he comprehends, and he comprehends only what in his opinion affects him" (297). The result is very simple but serious: Where parties prevail, the spirit of genuine and proper political life is dormant. And it is precisely when a people attains political maturity that it is threatened by the gravest internal danger: the danger of remaining completely without conscious leadership. It is at this time that majority parties become determinative. But as a rule they are not genuine "majorities of opinion" (*Meinungsmajoritäten*), but majorities artificially brought about by propaganda and suggestion. In order to attain their support, the demagogues of all times have told the masses what they wanted to hear but then have done what even they themselves would reject.

The ideal would be that every individual be politically mature and capable of sound judgment. This ideal cannot be achieved, but as an approximation to it there is education of human beings in citizenship. And since, in the last analysis, all forms of education are an education through the objective spirit, there is here no other way than that of "growing into citizenship"—a process identical with the mode of development of the objective spirit.

But the greatest danger for a state—the influence upon, and the misleading of, the masses—also offers an escape from the blind alley of the principle of majority rule. "The superior statesman who really sees more than do the masses will always seek and find means for moving the masses towards goals which the masses do not see or understand, but which in the higher understanding are precisely their own."[10]

This raises the question of whether or not there is a unique and entirely positive morality of the statesman that must be evaluated in terms of a special standard, because in the will and the action of the statesman something much greater than individual interests are at stake. After all, public opinion is not simply the opinion of individuals, and it is also something other than a political majority. It is the background for conscious and responsible decisions. We find in it both truth and error: truth in the sense of a feeling for what is right and genuine, and error in the sense of an unlimited possibility of falsification. It is the embodiment of a people that is at issue in public affairs (*Das Problem*, 301). And if this is so, then we must ask, What is the criterion of the genuine in public affairs? A close examination will then show that public opinion in itself provides no criterion of what is or is not genuine. The decision is a matter for personal spirit. But it is of the essence of personality, and therefore of the personal spirit, to be limited.

The difficulty is encountered not only in political life, but in all other areas of the objective spirit. It is perhaps most obvious in art, in 'good taste', and in 'life-style', but it is discernible also in matters of a general philosophy of life (*Weltanschauung*), in valuations, and morals. Here the falsification lies in the objective spirit itself (304). Wherever something new arises, there also arise the slogans that dispose of it. But the truth is that behind the ready and apparently superior negative judgments we find confusion and profound ignorance. This is especially

10. *Das Problem des geistigen Seins*, 299. One can see this statement as a commentary on the political conditions in Germany that gave rise to the Hitler years. But let me state on the basis of my personal contacts with Hartmann that he was not in sympathy with the Hitler regime.

true in the region of the arts, where the striving for novelty readily entails a falsification of standards that affect the artistic experience of a whole generation of contemporaries.[11]

The question obviously is, What is genuine? What is the criterion of genuineness (*Das Problem*, 316ff.)?

Hartmann maintains that at all times a feeling prevails that somewhere in the background of public opinion and sensationalism there is something that is genuine and that in reality is the concern of the community; and that there is also a dim awareness of what is falsification of the genuine. The latter is the mode in which what is genuine makes itself known.

In reflecting upon the historical past it is rather easy to distinguish between the genuine and the spurious in the spirit of some particular historical past; for the historical process itself has separated them. The genuine alone is capable of historical transformation. In that transformation the spurious is condemned through nonpreservation. In this sense Hartmann accepts Hegel's famous thesis that history is indeed "*das Weltgericht*"—the Supreme Court of the world. But if there exists a criterion of the genuine in objective spirit, it does not lie in the extremes (322).

There is one area of human activity where what is genuine is readily recognizable: the area of the sciences. In their modifications, the earlier insights are preserved and new insights are based upon them. In the process, the errors of the past are discarded, and only what proves to be tenable is preserved. Seen as a whole, the history of science reveals an immense growth of knowledge and gives to the sciences a special place in the realm of the objective spirit (323–47), a realm not subject to what is spurious.

What is of special importance here is the fact that practical knowledge and science have in principle the same structure. In this mutuality of scientific and nonscientific cognition, human knowledge is subject to historical change—a change in which what is genuine prevails. Where this contact with reality is lost, man's thinking deteriorates into the infinite relativity of what is thinkable but not necessarily true (335).

However, in science nothing is a free gift, and the spiritual content of science cannot be passed on to persons incapable of comprehending

11. The problems of art and of morals as well I shall discuss in chapters 6 and 7.

it. It excludes individuals from its community. This is not envy, nor arbitrariness. It is rooted in differences in human abilities, and these cannot be changed. Here the facts of existence limit indeed the freedom of the individual. At the same time, however, they also bring forth the objective in its purity. The exclusiveness of science pertaining to personal insufficiency is nothing other than the radical exclusion of the spurious from the life of science. "It is hardness for the sake of salvation" (341). Here it is evident that the objective spirit is not a mere collection of subjective spirits but is something which at all times exists in a certain indifference to the mere sum of individuals. Yet its spiritual content is in its very essence common property—even though it cannot be shared by all at any given time. In a true sense it is the education of human beings to factuality (*zur Sachlichkeit*).

5. The Objectified Spirit

The living historical spirit is not only objective in itself, it also brings forth structures and patterns of a special kind in which it 'objectifies' itself. These formations are not the spirit itself but are results of its creative activity (348). In them the objective spirit remains recognizable even long after it itself no longer prevails but is part of the historical past. The most obvious of these creations of the objective spirit are literature and the arts, and they are indeed the most central and most perfect forms of the objectification. They represent 'objectified spirit' at its best.

   This third mode of Being of the spirit is *real* only as objectification of both the personal and the objective spirit. Its mode of Being is not that of a developing reality but is instead the totality of a spirit that has become historically stable in its configurations or patterns. In its persistence in time, it reflects something of what the living spirit was that objectified itself in it. And "all living spirit objectifies itself— the personal as well as the communal—and does so in all its spheres" (350).

   The living spirit, whether personal or communal, is subject to the law of all living things: it dies. But what spirit creates survives the creator. It is subject to another law. To be sure, a literary work can get lost, and a work of art—a picture or a statue in marble or bronze— can be destroyed. They are conditioned by temporalities and reality, and yet their mode of Being is other than that of the living spirit. As

Hartmann maintains, once created as product, the objectified spirit attains independence from the creative spirit and has a *Dasein* of its own in history, its own mode of Being aside from the continuing life of the objective spirit. Although bound to the living spirit generally, the objectified spirit is not restricted to the particular spirit which has created it, and is always something other than the living spirit (352). Although objectifications occur in all regions of the living spirit, they have an independent mode of Being only when they are embodied in some lasting material.

The purest representations of the objectified spirit are found in literature, in architecture, in sculpture, in paintings, and in music; and within limits in tools, in weapons, and in industrial products. In brief, all works of man reveal his inventive and creative spirit (356f.).

In the broadest sense this includes the thoughts contained in literature, especially in scientific, philosophical, and religious literature; for here we encounter the specifically historical forms and ideas: the symbols and dogmas, the gods and heroes of the past. Of all these it is characteristic that they are basic manifestations of the specific historical spirit that has created them.

But there are two clearly discernible modes in which the spirit of the past can enter the present. Both frequently occur together in the historical process. They pertain to the same spiritual content but are largely independent with respect to each other. A language, for example, develops over centuries. But despite its development it contains, even if only in modified form, elements of its past: its vocabulary, structure, and concept formation. Despite these changes, however, the continuity is not disrupted. And with the language broad aspects of the spiritual goods of the past are preserved. This is manifest in the case of written records and in the literature of the past, as well as in science, in philosophy, and in religions based upon "the sacred Book." "Objectification thus reveals itself as a power which, once it is again actualized, moves the living spirit" (360).

But what precisely is that which is preserved in objectified spirit? Is it but linguistic marks on parchment or cut into a rock? Is it the marble or bronze of a statue? There is unquestionably much more preserved than these purely material things. When we read ancient manuscripts, for example, we 'recognize' the spirit behind them. In the term 'recognize' is disclosed the whole riddle of the mode of Being of the objectified spirit, for 'recognition' is an achievement of the objective spirit. It shows that the objectified spirit does not continue as real spirit, that only the living spirit is historically real. And where living spirit does not accept with understanding the objectifications of the past, the objectified spirit has no historical existence. Dependency upon the living spirit is thus essential to the objectified spirit (362).

All objectified spirit involves two strata of heterogeneous modes of Being. Its sensorially real stratum exists independently of spirit; but the spiritual content embodied in the material exists only "for" a comprehending living spirit. It is not itself in the material, but is only "for us" (365).

Hartmann elaborates and illustrates this stratification of the objectifications of spirit with special reference to the arts (367–83). As we shall see in Chapter 7, the resolution of a work of art into a plurality of strata is decisive for aesthetics. It must be noted, however, that despite the heterogeneity of their modes of Being, even the two basic strata (*Grundschichten*) are not sufficient to account for the reality of the objectified spirit. It is necessary that there be a specific living spirit that responds to what is preserved historically.

The complex mode of Being of the objectified spirit is thus threefold: In addition to the physical realities and the spiritual content embodied in them, there necessarily must be a living spirit—both personal and communal—that responds to what is transmitted in the course of history. This means that the objectified spirit has no Being-in-itself, but only a Being-for-us (*ein Für-uns-Sein*) (387). It thus seems that we face here an antinomy: On the one hand, the basic phenomenon seems to be that the objectified spirit exists 'detached' from the living spirit. On the other hand, however, we have just seen that the objectified spirit always remains dependent upon the living spirit and does not exist without it. The antinomy, however, can readily be seen to be a merely superficial difficulty. It is true, of course, that the objectified spirit exists separated from the living spirit that brought it forth as its own achievement and that embodied it in its material form; but what is thus embodied is not separated from living spirit as such. It is related to, and dependent upon, the living spirit in two ways. "It is originally dependent upon the creative spirit, and is then bound to the spirit that again finds it" (398). When the latter is lacking, the objectified spirit is lost.

But the question still is, What precisely is preserved in the objectified spirit? When we deal with literature, for example, are we to say that nothing but the writing is preserved? If so, then nothing is preserved but the ink on paper, or whatever the material is. Or are we to say that what is preserved are the characters and situations described? To put it differently: Is there something in the objectification that transcends the material modes of existence and is preserved despite the change of the living spirit? Everything the historian regards as a source is objectification, and this objectification is precisely what requires interpretation. Does this not entail a *circulus in probandum*? One has presupposed what is to be shown: that the material items are indeed objectifications of the spirit (398).

As a matter of fact, however, some types of spiritual goods have an obvious transtemporal meaning. This is true especially in the case of literature and the arts. But how is it to be understood? What, precisely, is transtemporal in a work of art? It is obviously not the real object as such. Nor is it its transparency for the spiritual content of the background. And, surely, it is not the appearance of this content for the observer. Transtemporality pertains in truth exclusively to the spiritual background of which the work of art is a manifestation (401). The actions, passions, and fates of the characters in a literary work appear to the observer elevated into the timeless—"the hero in eternal youth, the intriguer in eternal envy, the fate in eternal tragedy: all characters, relations and situations 'appear' elevated into an ideal Being" (403). They are in a way taken out of time and are 'eternalized'. But this eternity is only an apparent one. It is not real in itself, just as the characters and situations are not real. The transtemporality inseparably associated with the nature of a work of art is nothing other than the appearing nontemporality of the background. It is only because the background has a merely apparent Being that it appears elevated into ideality.

The question was, How can the transtemporality of a work of art be reconciled with its limited duration? The answer is that a work of art has historical existence only as long as it exists and is viewed with artistic understanding by living spirit. It is obviously one thing for something timeless and eternal to appear, and quite another for its appearance to be an eternal appearance.

We must note, however, that what is obvious in the case of a work of art is true of all modes of objectification of spirit. All records of events and reports of the results of investigation—everything formulated in judgments or expressed in concepts, especially convictions

and insights, viewed purely as to content, is timeless and appears to
the comprehending spirit as timeless. But it does not appear at all
times. It does so only under specific circumstances. "The preservation
of the writing and the historical presence of a comprehending spirit
are always conditions of appearing" (405). But the formed content can
appear at any time to anyone capable of understanding it. In the content something is preserved that outlasts time, but is available only to
a living spirit capable of comprehending it.

The historicity of the objectified spirit is thus more or less an epi-
phenomenon of the historicity of the living spirit (413), and as such
it has its own historical fate in the changes of the living spirit. The
independence of the objectified spirit is that of a supported autonomy.
The objectified spiritual content has its Being in history only where the
living spirit becomes "adequate" to it. Its actualization depends on the
coincidence of challenge and attitude—the challenge emanating from
the embodiment, the attitude from the living spirit. All cultures of some
degree of development enjoy manifold objectified spiritual goods that,
once created, remain always available. But where the living spirit lacks
an appropriate attitude toward what is preserved of the past, the past
is felt to be an intrusion. Still, in the encounter of the living spirit with
an actualized spirit of the past, something of the latter may become
an influence in the present; and the living spirit may experience it as a
'rebirth', for the living spirit is not simply receptive. It also makes use
of the creations of the past. This is especially clear in the field of the
arts. But it is also evident in the case of the history of concepts (426–
34). The basic concepts of Aristotelian philosophy, for example, have
become a common heritage of Western education and are in modified
form so much a part of our culture that their original meaning is hardly
recognizable. When the living spirit no longer knows the total context
of thoughts that is basic to them, it regards the concepts as fixed in-
gredients of its own thinking for which the concept-forming thoughts
appear strange when they are encountered again in new studies of Aristotle's writings. Scientific thinking is, in this respect, no less naive than
is popular tradition. The demand for logical identity of concepts is an
ideal that has its proper place within a given system of thoughts but
finds no confirmation beyond that system. As far as the meaning of
concepts is concerned, it is at all times only what is actually understood by the concept; and what is understood is conditioned by the
context within which the concepts are used. That context changes in

the course of time. Retaining the traditional concepts is thus not necessarily a retention of their original content. Hartmann speaks here of
a "decline" (*Absinken*) of the concepts, and adds: "Most of the traditional concepts of philosophy, as also many concepts of the positive
sciences, are "declined (*abgesunkene*) concepts" (428). But it is hazardous to work with them and to rely upon them. Where 'declined'
concepts dominate the thinking of the times, the spirit of science is
dead. Thinking deteriorates into hairsplitting.

It is evident that concepts themselves are not independent entities
but are always rooted in, and dependent on, a context of compre-
hensions. Taken out of that context their meaning is subject to the
arbitrariness of the living spirit and, therefore, to misunderstanding
and distortion.

What is true in the case of concepts is true also in the case of whole
systems of thought and integrative theories. The history of philosophy is itself ample proof of this. Wherever a system develops into a
"school" (*wo es Schule macht*), it is already brought down to the level
of a broad discipleship (*Nachtreterschaft*). The germinal meaning of a
theory can be ascertained only in connection with the broader context
within which it was developed.

To be sure, in the history of concepts and theories we can also note
an advancement. But this advancement is the achievement of the objective, not of the objectified, spirit (432). It is the result of progress
in research. It continues as long as direct contact with problems persists and cognition progresses. In all research, concept formation is an
uninterrupted and continuing process. Every new insight is elevated
to the logical form of a proposition, and every proposition adds a
new characteristic to the meaning of the concepts. The changes in the
conception of time in the development from Newtonian absolutism to
Einsteinian relativism illustrate the point. This progressive modification constitutes the life of a concept, its enrichment in meaning in the
progress of cognition.

But from a single line of progressive development numerous lines of
decline are historically also possible. Every advance in the history of a
concept can also become the point at which a progressive trivialization
begins. "In the case of philosophical concepts this danger increases
into the unmeasurable [*ins Ungemessene*]" (434).

The basic categorial form of spiritual Being in history is the living
objective spirit. The objectified spirit is only spiritual possession or

property, not spiritual life. As spiritual possession it is created and formed by living spirit and remains always related to it as being for it. Any change in the objectified spirit is always the work of the living spirit. Despite its dependence, however, the objectified spirit has its own categorial independence, its own laws. This entails that the living spirit not only supports the objectified spirit but is also affected by it. Spiritual possession, insofar as it convinces, is also a power within the living spirit—both personal and communal. If such power maintains itself in history, the objectified spirit of the past manifests itself as a determinative power in the present life of the spirit. "The historical process of spirit is one; and seen as a whole it is first of all the living process of the objective spirit. Embedded in this is the limited historicity of individuals, and supported by it are production, preservation, fate and the return of the objectified spirit" (443).

In the unitary process of the life of the spirit, the objectified spirit is but one factor among many. But it is a most unique one, for the living spirit becomes comprehensible only in its objectifications. That is, it becomes comprehensible only in what it itself is not. The history of spirit is thus first of all a science concerned with the objectified spirit. The objectifications in art, in literature, in science, and in architecture are materially what remains of the spirit of the past. The living spirit retains only what is needed for its own purposes, and rejects the rest of past achievement. It responds only to what it regards as valuable and important, and only this does it embody in its own objectifications.

This characteristic interrelation of the objective and the objectified spirit is obvious in the matter of law. The feeling for law objectifies itself in the written law, and in the law objective spirit submits itself to the authority of its own creation. It can 'break its chains' only by creating new laws (446ff.).

Similarly, in the regions of faith, the interrelation of the objective and the objectified spirit is recognizable as the conflict between religious feeling and dogma. But dogma itself is originally nothing but the objectification of a felt relationship to the world that requires a formulation. The spiritual content of religion cannot be preserved without a formulation acceptable to a whole community. As a matter of feeling, the religious attitude is much too ephemeral, too much subject to the arbitrariness of human subjectivity to persist for any length of time. But by expressing itself in dogmas, the religious sentiment finds itself progressively pitted against itself.

As far as the historical life of the sciences is concerned, the situation is similar, for that life consists not in concepts and theories but in progressive research. Because the advance is a common achievement on a broad front of problems, every result of the investigations must be objectified in concepts and theories. But, in so objectifying the new discoveries, cognition imposes upon itself certain limitations that in the progress of discoveries must be broken again, if progress is not to come to a halt. It is of the nature of objectifications that the changing spirit manifesting itself in them must either transcend any particular objectification or must accept it as standing against itself. The life of the spirit thus consists in forming and transforming itself. Only the living spirit, therefore, is properly spirit. Its creations, separated from their creator, are not only lifeless, but their mode of Being is that of limitations to the creative spirit itself. The history of man's achievements is thus one of creativity and of self-imposed limitations. Both aspects are exemplified in the character of the objectified spirit.

6

Ethics

HARTMANN'S CONCEPTION OF ETHICS IS developed in great detail in his formidable (746 pages) *Ethik*.[1] His argument is presented in three sections: (1) Phenomenology of Morals, (2) The Realm of Moral Values, and (3) The Problem of Free Will. Of these the second section deserves special attention, for here Hartmann develops his own position.

Despite the readily available translation by Stanton Coit,[2] Hartmann's *Ethik* has been much neglected. The only significant discussion in English that I know of is Eva H. Cadwallader's *Searchlight on Values: Nicolai Hartmann's Twentieth-Century Value Platonism.*[3] But even German-language discussions of Hartmann's *Ethik* are scarce. The most important ones are Mayer, Emanuel, *Die Objektivität der Werterkenntnis bei Nicolai Hartmann,*[4] Meisenheim/Glan: Westkulturverlag Anton Hain, 1952. Walter Blumenthal, "Die Grundlagen der Ethik Nicolai Hartmanns"[5] is an article in *Kant-Studien*, as given in the bibliography. Otto F. Bellow, "Die Behandlung der Tugenden bei

1. Berlin and Leipzig: Walter de Gruyter & Co., 1926.
2. *Ethics* (London: Allen, 1932/33). In this translation the three sections are published in separate volumes.
3. Washington, D.C.: University Press of America, 1984.
4. *Monographien zur philosophischen Forschung* 8 (1952): 173 pp.
5. *Kant-Studien* 53 (1961/62): 3–28.

Nicolai Hartmann"[6] is a chapter in *Nicolai Hartmann, Der Denker und sein Werk*, Heinz Heimsoeth and Robert Heiss, editors.

In the *Vorwort* to his *Ethik* Hartmann states that "philosophical ethics of the 19th century has exhausted itself in analyses of moral consciousness and acts" (*Ethik*, v). It was not concerned with the objective content of moral demands, commandments, and values. A sole warning was Nietzsche's contention that we do not as yet know what good and evil are. This was the first call for a new view about values. However, it was Max Scheler who, in his conception of a "material value-ethics,"[7] argued specifically for a new approach. But, as Hartmann has pointed out, "it is one thing to show a new way, it is another to follow it through"; and it is the latter which Hartmann undertakes in his *Ethik*. He actually sees his task as a synthesis of ancient and modern ethics. But he adds, "The work of an individual can be only a beginning" (*Ethik*, vii).

Our first task must be to clarify what is meant by ethics. What are its special concerns? The answer to this question seems obvious: Ethics is concerned with norms—with the justification of moral commandments and moral valuations. Its basic questions are, What are moral principles? And can we justify their *a priori validity*? (27f.). Of these questions the second one is the really crucial one.

In the realm of knowledge all *a priori* cognition has a corrective in the testimony of our senses. In the case of the moral *a priori*, no such criterion is available. Here apriorism is completely autonomous. But what if this autonomy were merely a disguised despotism, a deceptive play of the imagination conjuring up a 'higher authority'? Ethics is not, nor should it be, mere casuistry. The least that we ought to expect of it is that it provide a dependable criterion of what the good is which it commands us to pursue (32).

Once we agree that this is indeed the least we ought to expect of ethics, various questions arise. If ethics is to deal with the moral

6. Heimsoeth and Heiss, eds., *Nicolai Hartmann, Der Denker*, 81–96.

7. Max Scheler, *Der Formalismus in der Ethik und die Materiale Wertethik*, in *Jahrbuch für Philosophie*, 1913/14. For a summary of Scheler's position, see W. H. Werkmeister, *Historical Spectrum of Value Theories*, vol. 1: *The German Language Group* (Lincoln, Neb.: Johnson Publishing Co., 1970), chap. 11: "The 'Emotional Intuitionism' of Max Scheler," 287–313. See also W. H. Werkmeister, "Value Theory and the Problem of Moral Obligation," in *Proceedings of the Inter-American Congress of Philosophy*, Buenos Aires (1958).

a priori, then which morality is to provide the standard? Is the morality of our times, of our country the standard? Or must we consider also the morality of other times and other countries? Is there a morality that is binding for all times and all places? Which is valid: "Love thy neighbor" or "An eye for an eye"? What about Spinoza's ethics? Or that of Kant or Nietzsche? What about the wisdom of the Stoics or of the Epicureans? What about the otherworldliness of Plotinus and of the Patristic period, and the moralities of India and China—whether of the present or of the past?

Despite all the differences in the moralities thus disclosed, *ethics* must be unitary. Its answer must be the same with respect to all moralities. It must rise categorially above the plurality of morals. The question is, How can philosophical ethics prevail over the undeniable plurality of morals? How is the unity of ethics possible?

Hartmann's answer to this question is: Ethics presupposes a theory of values—an axiology (39). This is so because not only the purpose of human actions, but also the oughtness of moral demands and the character of norms, have their basis in *values*. We do not and cannot set as our goal, or acknowledge as a demand upon us, what we do not regard as "valuable." Only when we regard it as valuable does it become a determinative factor in our moral life.

But have we done more here than give the problem a new name? After all, the realm of values reveals the same confusing manifoldness we find in the realm of moral commandments. In fact, the crucial differences between the various moral attitudes are the direct result of differences in the conception of what is good; and, as Nietzsche put it pointedly, we do not yet know what good and evil are. Although his own attempt at a solution of the problem—his dream of the Superman and of the "transvaluation of all values"—carried Nietzsche beyond any rational goal, he at least inaugurated a new and profound concern for values. And it is this concern that is basic to Hartmann's *Ethik*.

But if values play a crucial role in man's moral life, what is their ontic status? And how do we come to know them? In particular, how do we discover *moral* values? Various answers to this question coincide with the historical changes in the moral content of commandments and norms of actual living; for "the primary value-consciousness grows with the enhancement of the moral life" (43), with its intensifications and elevations. By comparison with this actual development of value-consciousness, any philosophical concern with values is only secondary.

However, philosophical comprehension is more than a sentimental contact with values. It is research for principles upon which all valuations depend (49). But these principles are not laws that are necessarily valid for all of reality, and one can never know empirically whether or not they have been realized. In order to know this, one must already have a standard as to what is good and what is evil. And this obviously must be a form of *a priori* knowledge. Ethical reality is thus richer than is the theoretical, for "it includes the reality of moral consciousness" (53), a consciousness of values.

In the light of this perspective Hartmann examines various ethical theories of the past, including those of Aristippus and Epicurus, of Stoicism, Christianity, Neoplatonism and utilitarianism, Kantian ethics and Scheler's critique of ethical formalism.[8] He agrees with Scheler in arguing that neither is all *a priori* purely formal, nor is all material content merely *a posteriori*.[9] And the subsuming function of judgment is found in moral matters just as little as it is in our natural everyday knowledge of things. Taking a moral attitude is immediate and essentially intuitive. It is from the very beginning permeated by valuations—by attitudes that are emotionally based. There is a pure value-*apriori*, which immediately, intuitively, and with a feeling-accent (*gefühlsmässig*) characterizes our practical consciousness and our whole attitude toward life, and which gives to everything that enters into the range of our experience a value-disvalue accent (*Ethik*, 104f.). As Scheler put it: "The emotional aspect of spirit—the feeling, preferring, loving, hating, willing—has an original *a priori* content which is not borrowed from thinking and which ethics has to disclose independently of logic. As Blaise Pascal said so pertinently: There is an *a priori ordre du cœur*, a *logique du cœur*" (Scheler, *Formalismus*, 59)—which is a cognitive value-feeling that rejects and accepts, that condemns and justifies.

But this priority of feeling must not be confused with empiricism. The value-accents are not abstracted from things but are imposed upon

8. *Ethik*, 64–99: "Aberrations of Philosophical Ethics" (vol. 1 of the Coit translation).

9. Scheler, *Der Formalismus 2* (*Gesammelte Werke*), vol. 2, 48ff.

them by the value-feeling. This fact is basic to the *a priori* determinateness of feeling-based acts and to the immediate apriority of the value-accents that whatever is real has for practical consciousness. "The apriorism of the emotional acts is just as much a 'pure', original, autonomous and—if you want to put it this way—'transcendental' lawfulness as is the logical and categorical apriorism in the theoretical fields of knowledge" (*Ethik*, 105). The primary location of the value–*a priori* is and remains the value-feeling that interpenetrates with our comprehension of reality and our attitudes toward life. Only within this value-feeling can any "moral cognition" be found—any genuine knowledge of good and evil. Even the Kantian moral law is, in truth, nothing other than a secondary formulation of a value that was primarily felt and emotionally seen *a priori*.

1. The Realm of Moral Values

Although moral behavior is always an attitude toward persons, it is also an attitude toward anything that is valuable or that is worthless. That is, in the perspective of ethics everything is either valuable or valueless. The same world that is basic to the ontological phenomena is in the same sense basic to the ethical phenomena. It is just as primary in the one case as it is in the other.[10]

To be sure, moral values pertain only to persons, not to things. Only the acts of persons can be good or evil. Still, the material content of moral values presupposes the value of goods. This is evident even in as simple a case as that of the difference between an honest person and a thief. The value of the act of a person is here completely other than the value of the goods involved, and is quite obviously the higher value. Still, the value of goods is a presupposition without which there would be no moral value.[11]

Hartmann speaks here of a "founding-relation" (*Fundierungsverhältnis*) between the two spheres of values. The lower value becomes 'matter' for the higher values, being only the *conditio sine qua non*

---

10. *Ethik*, 228. Hartmann deals with this fact in part 2 of the *Ethik*, 227–564; vol. 2 of the Coit translation.

11. Hartmann here reverses Scheler's thesis (*Formalismus*, 92ff.), according to which the lower values find their meaning and justification in being based upon the higher values. See Cadwallader, *Searchlight*, and Alois Müller, "Die Ontologie der Werte," in *Philosophisches Jahrbuch der Görres-Gesellschaft* 54 (1941): 321–56.

of the latter. In every other sense the higher value is independent of it. "Where moral values and disvalues appear in real persons, there a world of actual goods is already at hand—a world of value-objects to which the acts of the person pertain" (*Ethik*, 229). And this relationship cannot be reversed. The existence of a world of goods does not in itself entail the emergence of moral values or moral disvalues.

It is also true that the simple foundational relationship just indicated cannot be universalized for the value realm as a whole. The structuralization of that realm is much more complex. In fact, the dependence of moral values on goods has no bearing on the order of rank of the moral values themselves. While the purpose of an action pertains to goods, the moral quality of an action characterizes the person.

In the broadest perspective, the idea of a realm of higher and lower values is the unstated presupposition of all further analysis (154). In such an analysis, however, man's value-feeling can be a guide only if it is at the same time a "feeling for the order of rank" (*Gefühl der Rankordnung*) of values (246f.). And this feeling for the order of rank must be as primary as is the feeling for values generally.

It is the profound and enduring insight of Socrates that no one does what is evil for the sake of evil, but always has something good or valuable in mind—although one may be mistaken as to its true value. And here Christian ethics has added the recognition of an element of human weakness: being entranced by lower powers. As Hartmann sees it, "Even the affect-determined will is directed towards values; it is merely directed towards lower values." The solution to the problem must therefore be found in the order of rank of values.

Behind the moral conflict, as encountered in many forms in life's situations, lies always a conflict of values, not one of value and disvalue. But it is impossible for a person actually to decide in favor of both sides of the conflict. In making a decision, a person cannot avoid regarding the axiologically contrary opposition as contradictory. Here we encounter an absolute limit to all human decisions. Everything that man can do is limited to the tendency to give preference to one value over another—a preference to which the value is objectively entitled. All positive decisions depend on the question of value-preference, which itself is a function of man's awareness of an order of rank of values (248).

What is 'higher' and what is 'lower' in this order of rank of values is readily discerned by our feeling for values, but it can hardly be expressed in strict conceptual form. The scale of the value-height constitutes a dimension sui generis and is undefinable.

It is a common mistake to believe that the most general values are the highest, and that the values of individuality and uniqueness are the lowest. Many forms of philosophical ethics involve this mistake and regard the material relationship of subsumption as indicating a relation of value-height. All theories that seek a highest value from which all lower values can be 'deduced' commit this error. We encounter it in Kant's theory of the 'categorical imperative' and—in continuation of the Kantian thesis—in Fichte's suggestion of a "subsumption under a principle" (249).

Still another prejudice is represented in the assumption of one simple linear scale of values. Such dimensionality would indeed simplify a survey over the realm of values, but the facts of experience do not support it. The variety of values is too great. In what sense, for example, could economic, moral, and aesthetic values be put into one linear scale? The qualitative differences of values are obviously not just a matter of higher and lower. The realm of values is clearly multidimensional, and only one of its dimensions is that of higher-lower.

The question of the order of rank of values entails, of course, the problem of a criterion of the height of values. Scheler dealt with this problem at some length (*Formalismus*, 88ff.), but so did Aristotle (*Ethik*, 256ff.). In fact, as Hartmann has pointed out, "Every living feeling for values stands already under laws of preference which, on their part, are anchored in the order of height of the value-essences themselves" (260).

If all positive morality depends upon a genuine intuition of values (*Wertschau*), and if all such intuition is an *a priori* apprehension of value-essences (*Wertwesenheiten*), then the historical relativity of values is not one of the values themselves but depends solely on the relativity of value intuition. Every prevailing morality acknowledges only a few values, perhaps even only one, to which everything else is related. But no matter how one-sided a prevailing morality may be, it does contain an aspect of truth. A fraction of true value knowledge is contained in all moralities, no matter how mutually contradictory they may be. It is the task of ethics to bridge the contradictions in prevailing moralities. This implies, however, that from the very beginning, concern with values must be directed toward the relationships of values—toward subsumptions and foundational relations, and toward the intersections of value realms; and the unity looked for must not be assumed as a "postulate of harmony." What is decisive is not a monism of value but the plurality of morals. The "monism of ethics" must retain that plurality (266).

Since all prevailing moralities are ultimately grounded in value situations, the first task of ethics must be to clarify the value relations and to deal with the entailed problem of a value scale.

The basic difficulty of all analyses of value is the fact that the characteristic qualities of values cannot be adequately described. We can proceed only by beginning with the objects or situations that entice or the value-feeling concerned with them. If our value-feeling is not aroused, every effort to account for values is in vain. The lowest group of values consists, therefore, of aspects of experience whose value character is barely perceptible. And what is important here is that the basic relation is not that of value-disvalue, but of value as opposed to value. It is "a sphere of positive value contrasts" (268).

The lowest disvalues form a corresponding disvalue-dimension.

The sphere of the basic values thus has an antinomic character— a fact important for ethics. Wherever in a given situation a positive value is opposed to another positive value, no guiltless resolution of the conflict is possible. One of the conflicting values must be violated. Unfortunately, man constantly finds himself in such situations. It is his fate, therefore, that he cannot escape becoming guilty of a violation of some values.

Parallel to this value antinomy, but not coincident with it, is a second and equally fundamental antinomy (273). It is this: In the actualities of moral life, values are always real only in part. Their place is "between Being and non-Being," and this entails a double relationship of values. It is obvious that the reality of a value—whenever and wherever it occurs—is itself a value, and that it is so irrespective of how it has come about. But it is equally obvious that the unreality of a value is itself a disvalue (ein Unwert). Together, these facts imply that the realization of a value is itself valuable; and that the destruction of a value, or the realization of a disvalue, is itself a disvalue.

This is so not only in the completed act of realization or destruction of values, but even in the very tendency (Ansatz) toward them. This fact is especially significant in connection with the realization of values; for "as an act of a person such a tendency is at the same time bearer [Träger] of a value that is higher than the one intended, i.e., it is bearer of a moral value." Fundamental to it all is "the basic value of the reality of values generally" (274).

We must realize, however, that there is also a "value of the non-reality of values." If all things were in themselves valuable, there would be no sense in any attempt to *give* them value; and this would entail the impossibility of the higher values that pertain to giving things their values. To put it pointedly: *The irreality of values that can be intended is itself a fundamental value for the moral Being of a person.*

That this is an antinomy cannot be doubted. Its dissolution is impossible because it is rooted in the very essence of metaphysical reality. However, the antithetic involved here is essential to all ethical phenomena. Seen from the point of view of the reality of values, the realization of values is only a subordinate aspect of experience. But seen from the point of view of the nonreality of values, the process of realizing them —the determination to realize them, regardless of its success—is itself valuable. In the complex situation in which a person assigns value to things, two values are thus actually involved: the value to be assigned, and the value of assigning it. But we must note that the reality of one of these values excludes the reality of the other: If the value to be assigned is already real, there is no need for, and no specific value in, assigning it; and if there is value in assigning value to things, then the things can have no value without such an assignment. This fact, however, does not diminish the value-character of either aspect, for the intended value has a 'bearer' other than has the value of the intention. The antinomic character of this relationship is evident in what traditionally has been regarded as a distinction between values of goods and values of virtue (278). Of these, the former are the lower values, the latter are the higher; and this relation is irreversible.

In this perspective the lower values are the *conditio sine qua non* of the higher values, and become 'matter' for them. In every other respect the higher values are independent of the lower.

Where moral values and disvalues appear in real persons, there a world of goods is already at hand—a world of value-objects to which the acts of persons pertain. This relationship cannot be reversed. That is, the existence of a world of goods does not in itself entail the emergence of moral values or moral disvalues. But we must note that everything valuable—even the morally valuable—is a value-object for consciousness and that every morally selective consciousness of values is necessarily also a consciousness of the order of rank of values. Reflective analysis clearly discloses this fact.

Since the highest values are those of the personal subject, they, too, must be experienced as object-values and must be values of the acts of the particular person to whom the acts pertain. In this sense the subject, the person, is itself a value-object and, specifically, the object of all eminently moral acts.

Granted that no one does evil for evil's sake; it is always something valuable that entices him. The inevitable result is a value conflict that must be resolved, and, maintains Hartmann, resolved in favor of the higher value. The order of rank of values thus takes on a crucial significance for all morality.[12]

But the order of rank of values is not a simple or one-dimensional scale. One basic aspect of the diversity is the difference between the 'strength' and the 'height' of values. What is significant here is the fact that the lower value is the stronger and the higher value the weaker. To violate the lower value is, in general, more grievous than to sin against the higher. But the fulfillment of a higher value is morally more valuable than is that of the lower.

2. Foundational Values

The most elementary values pertaining to the active person are vitality, consciousness, activity, strength, freedom of the will, purposiveness, and the like.

The unfolding of man's moral potencies is conditioned by the supportive life of the individual. The vigor of that life is itself felt as a value. And this value is the ethical affirmative of what is natural and instinct-conditioned in man's life. But the individual is capable of developing to greater heights, and such tendency transforms the natural in life into what is moral (*Ethik*, 311).

Man's consciousness confronts the animality within him, and only what "enters into the light of consciousness" can become a spiritual property of man. In man's cognition, reality becomes a *reality-for-him*. Consciousness is thus the basis and the fundamental value (*Grundwert*)

---

12. Compare Jonas Cohn, "Zu Nicolai Hartmanns Ethik. Ein Versuch kritischer Mitarbeit," in *Logos* 16 (1927): 211–40.

of all spiritual values (313). But the first aspect of personal existence upon which moral values and disvalues depend is activity. It is the most obvious characteristic of a moral being. But there remains the great variety of moral values that cannot be dissolved into mere activity. Examples of such values are love, truthfulness, and loyalty (315).

Freedom of the will means freedom to make a decision. Its value lies in the entailed self-determination of the human person in pursuing intended moral acts (320).

Once one has taken on the moral responsibility for one's own acts, one cannot allow oneself to be deprived of it without being negated. The preservation of one's own person is the preservation and acknowledgment of one's own freedom (321).

But beyond freedom, the measure of personality lies in the purposive activity (*Zwecktätigkeit*) of man. In this is grounded his qualitative superiority over every other manifestation of reality in the world, and because of it he becomes a "bearer of moral values" (326).

A second group consists of the values of 'goods'. These include the general basic values of existence (*Dasein*), of the individual situation, of power, and of happiness.

It is evident that the universal situation of *Dasein* in which man finds himself, including what is needed for his existence, is already a value (329). To the material aspects of the situation belong the natural conditions that make life at all possible, such as soil, water, air, and light, and the specific sources of nourishment and general welfare.

The manifoldness of the individual situations in which human beings find themselves provides a key to their value-feeling; with feeling-conditioned participation in given situations, man grows morally—even when not creatively responding to them (331).

Power, in the sense of being able to do and to dominate, is surely a value desired for its own sake and not merely as a means for the realization of other values (332). But the most popular of the values of goods is 'good fortune' (*Glück*), which very often is regarded as the value of all values. But the term 'good fortune' has a double meaning. Seen objectively, it is the favor of circumstances. Seen subjectively, it is the feeling of a favor received. In the first sense it is a value purely of facts and circumstances. In the second sense it is an 'inner value', and in this sense comes closer to being a moral value (333).

But not all of the values in these two groups, important though they are in human affairs, are moral values.

3. Basic Moral Values

The moral values proper Hartmann divides into four groups. As he sees it, there are, first of all, the "foundational moral values": the Good, the Noble, Richness of Experience, and Purity (336–73).

There are, secondly, the ancient virtues: justice, wisdom, courage, and self-control (379–408). And there are the predominantly Christian virtues of brotherly love, of truthfulness and uprightness, of trust and faith, of modesty, humility, aloofness, and the values of social intercourse (408–39). But in addition to all these, Hartmann recognizes the more 'philosophical virtues': Love of the remote, radiant virtue, personality, and personal love (440–95).

All of these values are related to the freedom of action and entailed responsibility of the individual human being; for only the person who is free in his actions is capable of doing what is good or what is evil (337).

That the 'good' is the basic moral value is hardly subject to dispute. 'Good' and 'morally valuable' are one and the same (339). Unfortunately, 'the Good' is not definable. But, then, strictly speaking, all values are indefinable.

The ancient metaphysical conception of the Good was that of a primordial power in the life of man—as was also the dynamic conception of evil. Religious thinking has personified the conceptions (342). However, in Hartmann's view, the Good is neither the ideal Being of the values nor the mere Being of what is valuable. It is exclusively the teleology of values in the real world—the purposive action for the realization of values (345).

But there is no force that compels man to do the good. The possibility of the good is at the same time and in the same sense also the possibility of evil. In fact, the highest potentiality for the good is at the same time also the greatest danger. It is part of the essence of man to find himself in this danger. But the danger is also the basis for his ethos. Because of it he is a moral being (346).

Although this confrontation of good and evil is highly significant for ethics, even more important is the manifoldness of the values themselves that confront man (350). It is a multidimensional manifoldness, encompassing universality and specificity, simplicity and complexity, strength and weakness of the determinative power; and involving individuals and whole groups of human beings, not to mention relation-

ships of material dependence and foundations. With respect to all of
these distinctions the idea of the Good is indifferent, but the Good is in
essence related to differences in the height of values. The Good always
lies in the direction of higher values; Evil lies in the direction of lower
values. As a value of the intention of an act, the Good always consists in the preference of the higher value, and Evil in the preference of
the lower value. In typical situations of human experience value thus
always stands over against value. The Good is, therefore, the selection of values in accordance with the principle of the height of values;
and this is always faced anew in every experiential situation. Only an
actual feeling for values can serve here initially as a guide, for no fixed
'table of values' as a whole is ever given (352).

4. Special Moral Values

Hartmann is perhaps at his best when he discusses the three strata
of specifically moral values (*Ethik*, 379–495), but it is impossible to
present here his analysis and reflections in all their richness of detail.

The first stratum includes the values of justness (*Gerechtigkeit*), wisdom, courage, self-mastery, and the Aristotelian virtues. The second
stratum consists of the specifically moral values: charity or brotherly
love (*Nächstenliebe*), veracity and sincerity, dependability and faithfulness, trust and faith, modesty, humility, and values of external deportment. The third stratum includes the specifically moral values of love
of the remote (*Fernstenliebe*), bestowing virtue (*schenkende Tugend*),
personality, and personal love.

What governs Hartmann in his discussion of these values is the fact
that it is not the task of ethics to moralize but to reveal the moral
values within the limits of a given view of values (*Wertschau*)—a task
that is strictly "this side of all practical tendencies" (380).

As Hartmann sees it, justness, although based upon the value of
a prevailing order of law, is the value of a personal disposition. The
will to do what is right is in itself valuable; and it is so irrespective of
the value height of what it promotes, protects, or makes secure. It is
valuable even when it fails to accomplish what it intends (385).

For Plato, *sophia* was a virtue, although not the highest. And the
Stoics placed practically the whole content of ethics under the "ideal
of the wise" (388). But it is Hartmann's contention that the genuine
ethical ideal of *sophia* is a moral value of a unique kind. It has nothing

to do with the theoretical value of insight, truth, or knowledge; these are but subordinate values. The true value of wisdom lies in a special mode of man's attitude toward the world, toward life in general—his own and that of others. It is an affirmative and valuing attitude toward anything that is valuable. The wise man has the rare virtue of wanting to understand before he understands, and of letting prevail what he does not understand. His secret is the value-guided sense of reality (393).

While wisdom is a value of the guiding factor in man, courage is a value of the executive aspect of that same factor. It is characteristic of this value that it is independent of the value of the goals to be pursued. One can morally condemn the value of the goals and yet morally admire the high courage exemplified in the pursuit of them. But the distortion of courage—frivolous foolhardiness, the toying with danger—has nothing in common with genuine courage as an independent moral value. Courage has the morally deeper significance of a will to be responsible. Every actual conflict requires the courage to make a decision. In this sense the moral life requires courage in every respect: not only courage to act, but also to face the truth, one's own self, and one's true feelings; courage to love and, yes, even to face life itself (396).

All genuine *ought* is positive. It demands not destruction but construction—the creation of the higher out of the lower. But out of nothing no value can be realized. For the inner development of the person, "the world of emotions is the material." Development is "the unfolding of the affective life itself," its development into harmony. It is the positive form-giving of the life of the emotions that culminates in the well-adjusted inner beauty of the person of noble character. A serious danger of education lies there in the purely external training to mere obedience (399).

The transformation of the *ethos* of antiquity through Christianity entailed a new stratum of moral values. The first of these that Hartmann discusses is charity—love for one's fellowmen (*Nächstenliebe*). Although its value is well known, to delimit its essential characteristics is not an easy task; but a comparison with righteousness may be helpful, for righteousness is also an attitude toward one's fellowmen. But there is a difference here. Love for one's fellowmen is directly concerned with the other person and is "for the sake of the other" (409). What is crucial here is the inner nearness to the other, the being concerned with and for the other. The modern (but much misused) term 'altruism' expresses this basic tendency as being the counterpart to egoism. What is involved here is the morally spontaneous being-for-each-other of persons. The value sphere of 'the other' fuses with one's own. But for the Christian, only the good done out of love is morally good. The motive is crucial. And it is not *Mitleid* or compassion—(*Mitleid* being no *Leiden* at all)—but an affirmative feeling and striving that is of the essence of love for one's fellowmen. We can suffer along with the poor, the weak, and the sick; but "love is essentially directed towards what is valuable" (413). Love of one's fellowmen is thus an active feeling for the other person and his full humanity—for all in him that is worthy of living. Here, and in this sense, an individual transcends his own emotional sphere. The "miracle" is the actual transcending of the ethos from person to person—a relation quite different from the transcendency in the cognitive relation. The loving intention penetrates to where cognition does not reach, namely, into the hidden inner life of the other person: into his experiencing, his feeling, his struggling and failing, and his happiness and suffering. All of this is rooted in the *a priori* attitude of one's own feelings toward the feelings of others (415).

The value of this "loving intention" is not only higher than is the value of goals, it is also independent of the latter. Its moral value grows not with the magnitude of gifts for the other, but with the greatness of love, with the overcoming of one's own self (417).

Both truth and truthfulness are values, but only the latter is a moral value; and credibility is what completes man morally (420). One who lies cannot be accepted as fully worthy. His value as a witness has been destroyed. Truthfulness implies the 'courage to truth' and is an eternal ideal of moral life that, in history, always encounters resistance. But no purpose can sanctify deliberate deception—sanctify in the sense that it ceases to be a moral fault.

And yet, there is a serious moral problem that is not solved by simply rejecting each and every lie. A strict rigorism of any one value at the cost of all others contradicts the sense of our genuine moral feeling. There are borderline cases in which the conflict of conscience is severe; for here value stands against value and it is impossible not to become guilty of violating one. To be sure, it is not the values as such that are in conflict. They are in conflict only in the situation in which they are encountered. And it is part of man's genuine freedom that he must make decisions in situations in which values are in irresolvable conflict. Man's inescapable guilt in such situations is precisely what alone can save him from "lazy morality" (422).

That trustworthiness and loyalty are moral values is obvious. The moral strength of a person to be his own surety, to pledge his own future deportment, is a specific moral power in man and makes him a dependable member of the human community. If sympathy, friendship, and love were only passing sentiments, they would not be worthy of their name (425). Faithfulness is therefore the criterion of a genuine disposition. The faithful person is one who proves his moral identity in the constancy of his sentiments, for the ethos of loyalty is rooted in that constancy. In the last analysis that constancy is the person's loyalty to himself.

Trust and faith depend on specific attitudes of other persons, and therefore involve an element of risk and moral courage. Where trust is far-reaching and faith as solid as a rock, a person's commitment can rise to an unlimited height—and with it the moral value of trust (427). But faith remains always a venture, for, basically, it is always a 'blind faith'. He who sees and knows no longer can merely believe. Knowledge has made faith superfluous.

That "faith can move mountains"—that it is an eminently creative power in life—is well known in the field of religion but is not understood in the full sense of ethics. But, surely, all strength through unity consists in mutual faith in one another. Faith is the positive, binding force that unites persons by transcending the interests of individuals. It is more basic than are justice and neighborly love. It provides a type of solidarity in the unity of a conviction and in the consciousness of mutual trust.

And faith is a creative power in the sense that it actually brings forth in the other person that in which it is placed (429). In this fact is rooted the education of children and young people. Faith can transform a person toward the good or the evil, depending on what kind of faith it is. In any case, however, there is an element of optimism in the ethos of faith, an optimism that differs from the optimism of wisdom but is nevertheless a purely moral value.

The remaining values of the second stratum—modesty, humility, and deportment—need not detain us, for they are well known. We therefore turn now to the values of the third stratum, to the specifically moral values: love of the remote, bestowing virtue, personality, and personal love.

The term 'love of the remote' (*Fernstenliebe*) is obviously conceived in contrast to 'love of one's neighbor' (*Nächstenliebe*); but the 're-mote' pertains here strictly to the future, not to remoteness in space. This is so because all morally active life is anticipatory in character. It is "life into the future and for the future" (440). Only the future is open for man's striving, and his ability to anticipate entails a profound responsibility for the future.

To be sure, man generally tends to limit himself to the concerns of the present. It is already an achievement when he rises to a perspective of his own future, even when this perspective involves merely material or eudaemonistic goals. There exist, of course, laudable exceptions— human beings with high ideals. But this lofty idealism is all too fre-quently an impractical dream that is just as valueless as is the complete absorption in the present. The synthesis of a life seen in the perspec-tive of ideals with a sober view of the present and its possibilities is an ethos that already transcends the average, and bestows upon its bearer a dignity that grows with the magnitude of the goals and the practical results. But precisely this fact shows that even the perspective of an individual person is too narrow for the realization of an ideal humanity.

It is the lasting merit of Plato's philosophy to have seen clearly the unique value of a striving that transcends the immediate sphere of living and of contemporary companions. From the point of view of ethics alone, the *Eros* of the *Symposium* is "the great passion for an idea" that moves man. It is the potency sui generis in and through which man transcends himself. The direction of this transcendence pertains to the future—envisioning what is as yet unreal in order to realize it (443).

Here is the field of human providence and activity that is unlimited in the manifoldness of tasks and limited only subjectively by the limits of human vision and human power to achieve what is envisioned. The realization of the envisioned ideals is man's great historical respon-sibility that every age has for future ages. This love of the remote is an ethos of love other than man's love for his contemporaries. It is a solidarity of a new and greater kind, and it is always one-sided only (445). Its form is process, not coexistence. It is an ethos of love, but a love other than that pertaining to our contemporaries. There is no return of the love of the remote. But the ethos of progress intrinsic to the love of the remote must favor the morally strong and the upward-striving. Still, love of one's fellowmen has its own value and right that must not be minimized. To regard one's fellowmen as mere means only is a dangerous principle; and Kant's categorical imperative rightly demands that we regard every person as an end in itself, and never as a mere means only. But our responsibility for the future appears side by side with our responsibility for our contemporaries, and this conflict entails a limitation of both. Love for our fellowmen is one of sympathy. It is tolerant. "Its yoke is easy." But the way of the creator of the future is hard. Its hardness pertains to one's own person as well as to others, for both are means in the realization of the future (448). The moving force in both loves is the ethical ideal—the idea of the human being as he ought to be. The task is to save the faith and high hopes of idealistic youth and to imbue them with the moral strength inherent in the ethos of maturity. The power of an ideal lies in the combination of intuited genuine values and the realistic conditions of their realization (451). The individual human being sees himself here embedded in a larger providence that sees beyond himself and yet is his own. The value of such an ideal reveals itself as a real and creative power in life. It has the form of a selection of values and, therefore, of the process in which the inertia of the value-consciousness is overcome. It is an anticipation of new values, a revolution of the consciousness of values, and the vision of a humanity that is in every respect more advanced and more complete than is the present. Within the limits of given possibilities, man ultimately becomes as he wills himself to be. Still, a person's conception of ideals always remains problematic; the pursuit of them remains hazardous. The moral quality of the intention, however, remains genuine and is valuable in a higher sense, reflecting the magnitude of the moral courage that is required even for taking on the task of pursuing the ideal (455). Only a profound and powerful faith animating the whole character of a person is adequate to it. Since the moral value lies here in the intention—as it does also in the case of love of one's fellowmen—it is impossible to impugn one of these loves for the sake of the other. Although their goals are vastly different, the values of the respective intentions are of approximately the same height.

But now the question arises, Does the life of the remote, when attained, culminate in the love of still another remote, and so ad infinitum? Even when we disregard the uncertainty of their realization, our ideals of the future cannot be ultimate. They must also contain absolute values of the present, for otherwise the future envisioned as an ideal is without value. There is no sense in seeing in moral tasks nothing but other moral tasks. Somewhere a concrete value of fulfillment must be involved. At every stage of development, humanity must have part of its value within itself. Otherwise the formation of an ethical ideal is unworthy of belief (457). But, in Hartmann's view, there are three types of values in which we find fulfillment of a special kind. The first of these is what Nietzsche called "*schenkende Tugend*" —bestowing virtue.

In the realm of spiritual goods a law of giving and taking prevails that is other than the law pertaining to material goods. No one can possess spiritual goods exclusively as one's own. They belong to everyone who can comprehend them. 'Possession' is here but a participation. One can, of course, withhold them from others as if they were private property; this would be spiritual avarice. But one can also freely offer these goods and make them available to others. To do so is the very essence of the life of spiritual richness and of bestowing virtue. But the bestowing of spiritual goods depends also on the capacity of others to receive them. The misfortune of the giver—of the spiritually superior, the poet, the artist, the thinker—is his loneliness if he finds nobody who understands him. "He is like the light that finds no world to illuminate" (458).

But he who bestows spiritual goods does not sacrifice anything. He merely obeys the basic law of spiritual Being and stands in its service. He lives in it. This bestowing virtue has no purpose beyond itself, as justness, charity, courage, and even love of the remote have. It is an ultimate among values: the limit of creation and of the ought, an ultimate meaning, an ethical being-in-and-for-itself.

He who bestows may well be also the creator—and perhaps the creator in the eminent meaning of that term. But his ethos is not that of the creator, for the true form of the continuing begetting of spiritual content is purposeless prodigality. The immeasurable richness and fertility inherent in the spiritual goods make the purposeless squandering the true form of the propagation of the spiritual content (461).

An individual can give meaning to a whole world of contemporaries insofar as that world is capable of participating in his achievements.

Even the love of the remote finds here a special justification, for the hope includes here a form of fulfillment. What can be envisioned only in an ideal finds here a form of realization. The bestowing virtue is thus the power of the ethos of the person of ideas.

In a sense every human being is by nature a personality. That is, he is a human being in his own unique way.[13] But in itself this existence is not the value-character of personality. That character is related to universal moral values, but its ought-to-be pertains exclusively to a single person. That person ought to be "so." In this sense we can speak here of a personality-value (*Persönlichkeitswert*). We must keep in mind, however, that we are here concerned with an inconceivable manifoldness of values, with an entirely new stratum of the realm of values and a new value-perspective; for the matter of the personality-value is different for every human being. It can be realized or missed in every conceivable degree. The moral value of an individual personality can thus be seen as the unique fulfillment of the intelligible character of the empirical person (*Ethik*, 466). Responsibility for that fulfillment coincides with responsibility for everything in general that lies in the power and freedom of human beings.

Strictly speaking, the personality-value is not an individual value, but only the value of an individual—the value of one unique and real person (469). This essential and real uniqueness of the value bearer constitutes the individuality of the personality-value. We encounter here a peculiar kind of connection between what is ideal and what is real, between a specific value and an empirically real person. No matter how little the real person may correspond to its specific personality-value, there always exists a relationship of approximation that has its own individual virtue and that would not be a virtue for anybody else. The individual ethos is here superimposed upon the common, and the deportment of the person ought to conform to both simultaneously.

In any given complex situation, many kinds of deportment are possible, depending on which of the involved values is taken to be decisive. Every human ethos includes a tendency of preference for specific value-directions and thus tends to neglect other values also involved in the given situation. Nobody can do justice to all tangential values at

---

13. *Ethik*, 463. For comments on Hartmann's interpretation of human being, see Sister Helen James, "Nicolai Hartmann's Study of Human Personality," in *New Scholasticism* 34 (1960): 204–33.

the same time. The richer and more individualized a personality is, the more it permeates the value realm with a many-sided order of preference. But this fact does not alter the order of rank of values, which is absolute (472). Within that order of rank every individual ethos has its own ought-to-be, an ought-to-be for which the mere order of rank is not sufficient. In a sense, the order of rank in general is related to all more specific value-differentations as justness is related to love. Even the type-values of whole groups of persons, of nations and of historical eras constitute a necessary positive supplement. The strictly individual personality-values are but the extremes of such differentiations. The strict meaning of the personality-value may be seen in the individuality and distinctness of that complex of values that in the ethos of a person constitutes the preferential direction of his inner attitude. Only with this directional attitude does the individual actually rise above the ought-to-be that is valid for all. The greatness of personality is purely an inner one, and is nothing other than the uniqueness of the value perspectives a person accepts for himself. He sees the world in the light of his preferential values, and lives accordingly.

But the height of the personality-values is stratified in two respects. First, the individuation of the ethos can itself be quite different in different persons. At the lower levels it sinks into the merely typical. Only at the highest levels do we find personality in the full sense. Related to this is, in the second place, the degree of approach of the real person to its ideal ethos (474). Only at a certain height of fulfillment and mutual interpenetration of both aspects do we encounter the ethical phenomenon of personality proper. As personality, the individual human being must will that, within the universal value structure, there is something unique in his deportment that no one else ought to do. If he renounces this, he sinks to the level of the masses and his existence as a person is meaningless. The meaning of the personality-value thus involves the tendency to want to be 'more' than merely one among many.

In Hartmann's view, this fact can be expressed in a reversal of Kant's categorical imperative: "Act so that the maxim of your will can never become altogether the principle of a universal law-giving" (476). Stated differently: Never act merely schematically in accordance with universal values only, but always according to the individual values essential to your personality. After all, the situations we face are always strictly individual; for situations are real, and everything real is unique. Even external situations that seem to be essentially alike are in reality unique for the experience of different individuals. And this means that they are ethically different. We forget this too readily because we are accustomed to thinking in terms of types.

In all morality the universal values have the character of a basis, and in this sense they have a priority. But above them can arise the highly differentiated realm of personal values. And this fact changes nothing in principle in the ought-character of the personality-values (479).

We have seen earlier that Hartmann distinguishes between love of one's fellowmen and love of the remote. He now argues that personal Being finds its completion in personal love, a love that is directed toward the personality-value of the loved one (484f.). It loves in the loved one what is inherent in his/her essence. Because the love is a mirror and fulfillment of the personal Being of the loved one, personal love creates a unique ethical situation—an intimate relation between person and person. It is a novel ethical situation that is not complete in either one of the persons involved but that may well grow beyond both in significance and strength and have a life of its own (486). But this love cannot be willed. It is a unique and primordial tendency. Yet there is also an aspect of volition in love. And this aspect is stronger the stronger the emotional value of the relationship is. It is manifest in the placing of one's own person in the service of the other. This altruism of personal love is essentially other than that of love for one's fellowmen. More closely related to it is the altruism inherent in the love of the remote; for it pertains, as does the latter, to the idea of being human. But it pertains to being human as this particular personality, not as mankind in general. No one who has experienced it can deny that a strong love has the power to make the loved one into that which it sees and loves in him/her (488).

When we see happiness as the value of love, we are mistaken in our interpretation; for happiness is always secondary. The unique eudaemonistic phenomenon in love lies in the fact that, from a certain emotional depth on, suffering and pleasure are indifferent to it. The specific emotional value of love lies beyond happiness and suffering. The inner elevation that is of the essence of genuine love rises above both (490).

And in love there is always a feeling-base understanding of the other. In a sense it is true that 'love is blind', for it does not see what is in plain view. But it would be more correct to say that love sees not what is obvious but what is not present as real. Love sees transparently. Its seeing is divinational. With respect to personality-values, the lover alone is one who sees. He who does not love is the blind one (493). The cognitive power of love cannot be universalized. It is always individual, as is its object: the ideal personality of the loved one. But within this limit, love is autonomous and may be regarded as undeceivable. Even when, in the end, the facts turn out to be otherwise, the lover remains ideally in the right, for experience pertains only to the real, not to the ideal, personality. The latter is seen *a priori* as beyond the former. Personal love sees the empirical person elevated into an ideal. But when the lover regards the real in itself as the ideal, he is obviously mistaken. Such a mistake can entail a great disappointment in life—just as a true understanding of the facts will entail fulfillment for both the lover and the beloved in the realization of their personality-values.

5. Laws of the Table of Values

The first thing that strikes us as we read Hartmann's analysis of the problems of ethics is the fact, as Hartmann himself admits, that "the unitary meaning of the morally good has been dissolved into a whole firmament of values" (*Ethik*, 495). There is not even a complete system of values. The most we can hope for is a kind of schematic arrangement of the values, and even then much will remain arbitrary. But the situation is not completely hopeless, for as Hartmann has pointed out, certain "regularities" stand out even in any incomplete 'table of values' and these regularities are "structural laws" of the table and therefore of the realm of values.

Hartmann has found six different types of laws of interrelation of the values, and these he has arranged in three groups (498):

1. Laws of Stratification	
2. Laws of Foundation	First Group
3. Laws of Opposition	
4. Laws of Complementation	Second Group
5. Laws of Value Height	
6. Laws of Value Strength	Third Group

A possible analogy of the relationships may be seen in the realm of categories that provides the universal system of principles of Being. Since ethical Being preserves those principles and merely adds its own, we can regard ethics as but an axiological supplement to ontological reality. But a mixture of categories and values remains metaphysically a speculative venture. What is important here is solely the strictness of the analogy in principle in the midst of a fundamental otherness. But when we keep this in mind, some aspects of a basic lawfulness may be fruitfully applied to the realm of values. Hartmann finds this to be the case when we deal with the basic character of the stratification of values. He specifically formulates four such laws:

1. The lower principles, or elements of them, recur as partial aspects of the higher strata. They remain structural elements.
2. In their recurrence the lower elements do not remain unaffected by the higher forms but are modified in many ways, depending on the role they play in the higher complexities. Only their basic meaning is retained.
3. The higher forms show a specific *novum* that is not contained in the elements. This *novum* determines the role the elements play at the higher stratum.
4. The stratification reveals a clearly discernible difference between the strata. Relative to the lower strata every higher stratum reveals a common *novum,* while the connection with them is formed by the recurrence of the modifiable elements. (503).

The recurrence of the elements thus forms a combination of divergent lines that connect the superposed strata. The law of recurrence remains generally in force; but the higher the strata are, the less compelling is that law. At the stratum of moral values, the recurrence seems to fail almost completely. The reason for this is that the laws of modification and of the *novum* come to dominate more and more. The modifications are greater, and the distance of the strata is larger (505). At the level of personal love, for example, the general value-elements—trust, faithfulness, altruism, solidarity, etc.—are elevated so far into being something new that, compared with the *novum* of personal devotion, they almost vanish.

This "loosening-up" (*Lockerung*) of the categorial laws in the realm of values does not mean that the categories are no longer determinative, but only that they are no longer the only determinative factors. The realm of values is simply more complex, as is manifested in the complex and specific mode of founding of the values of things and thing-relations (*Sachverhaltswerte*) and that of moral values. Values of intention have no semblance to intended values, and this fact is in principle other than the relationship of the various strata with respect to one another. According to Hartmann, three aspects of the relationships must be considered (507f.).

1. In the stratification of values, the lower value recurs as an element in the higher value. It is contained in the higher value in modified form but cannot be removed from its substance. In the foundational relation, on the other hand, the lower value does not recur in the higher. The moral value, for example, no longer contains anything of the character of the value of goods. The latter is but the axiological condition of the former. Furthermore, the moral value pertains to the person's intentions and actions; the foundational value of goods remains attached to things.

2. In the stratification of values, the realization of the higher value necessarily entails the realization of the constituent lower values. But if the lower value is only a foundation of the higher, the realization of the value for which it is the foundation does not necessarily entail the realization of the lower value of some object or situation intended. The realization of the moral value in the person does not depend upon the achievement of the intended goal; it depends only upon the intention itself.

3. In the stratification of values, not only is the 'matter' of the higher value determined, at least in part, by the 'matter' of the lower value, but the height of the higher value is also conditioned by the height of the lower value. This relationship, however, does not hold when the lower value is only the 'foundation' of the higher, for the "index value" and the 'value of the intention' stand in no discernible order of rank to each other. This type of independence reveals especially clearly the difference in principle between the two types of being valuable.

An analogous situation may be found in the foundational relation between aesthetic and moral values.[14]

In concrete situations we encounter conflicts among all values. It is true, however, that every value finds its true realization only in the

14. I shall deal with this in chap. 7.

synthesis with other values—and, in the ideal, in the synthesis with all values (526ff.). In this sense, ethics approaches the ancient Stoic idea of a "unity of virtue." For those of us who are speculatively inclined there is a great temptation here to follow through in this perspective. But, maintains Hartmann, this seductive ideal is practically and philosophically worthless. It is not particularly difficult to construct a dialectical synthesis; but values must be felt and, on the basis of that feeling, must be concretely intuited. There is no other way to assure oneself of their ideal in-itself-ness. The value-feeling, however, has its own law of progression, its own historical maturing into new perspectives. No speculative impatience can anticipate it. Here all bold dreams have their limits.

It is possible, however, to discern a categorial lawfulness that encompasses all real and ideal Being ontologically, and from here encompasses the realm of values also, thereby attaining a new meaning.[15] In this context Hartmann states three laws that define basic categorial relationships: the Law of Strength, the Law of Matter, and the Law of Freedom. Since the realm of values is, in effect, the axiological extension of the ontological realm of categories, the first two of these laws can at once be applied to the realm of values. In fact, we have already encountered them in earlier discussions. The third law, however, deserves special attention. Hartmann states it in this way:

> Every higher principle is, relative to the lower one, an entirely new form-giving principle. As such it has above the lower principles (the material and the stronger) an unlimited freedom. That is, despite its dependence upon them, the higher principle is free relative to the lower. (*Ethik*, 544)

It is this basic categorial law that assures man of his personal freedom to act in conformity with the demands of values encountered in concrete situations. And this is crucial; for morality does not consist in values as such, but in the realization of values in and through man's actions, insofar as these are the result of his own free choice.[16]

15. *Ethik*, 543. For a discussion of the crucial issue, see Meta Hübler, "Werthöhe und Wertstärke in der Ethik von Nicolai Hartmann," in *Philosophische Studien* 1 (1950): 117–25.

16. *Ethik*, 565. Hartmann discusses the problem of free will in detail in part 3 of his *Ethik* (565–746), which is vol. 3 of the Coit translation.

6. The Problem of Free Will

It is the uniqueness of moral values and disvalues that they are ascribed to persons who, as the originators of value-determined acts, are held morally responsible for those acts, and to whom merit or guilt is ascribed. But such ascription is justified only to the extent to which it was in the power of the individual to have acted otherwise—i.e., if he had the freedom of the will to act as he did.

However, the term 'freedom of the will' is generally taken in too narrow a sense, for the decision to act occurs prior to the act itself. This means that 'freedom of the will' is not freedom of the will alone but freedom of all inner attitudes and taking of positions, of giving direction to one's actions. The real problem of freedom lies, therefore, in the metaphysical aspect of the *ought*.[17] The whole meaning of morality would be annihilated if man's freedom should turn out to be an illusion (*Ethik*, 568). But this does not mean that without man's freedom there would be no justice, no truthfulness, no neighborly love, no moral values at all. All of the values exist as phenomena. But without man's freedom they would not be *moral* phenomena in the strict sense. The ontologically qualitative character of a person's action is obviously independent of whether or not that person could have acted otherwise. Only the *moral* character of the action is not independent of it. Without man's freedom his moral Being—even in its highest perfection—would turn into a morally indifferent Being.

We must note, however, that there exists no will that cannot be determined by the structure of a given situation. Real will always emerges from an actual situation and acts only within the range of possibilities inherent in that situation. In fact, what is given in the situation provides the positive and concrete possibilities for the will (583f.). Although human beings are creatively free in their decisions, their creativity can never lie outside what is actually present in the world.

And just as there is no freedom from the events in the world, there is also no freedom from internal occurrences within the individual. Connected with the external situation, there is always also an internal one

17. For Hartmann all 'metaphysical' problems are unsolvable problems; indeed, it is their unsolvability that makes them metaphysical problems.

of feelings and motivations; and the individual cannot separate himself from his moods and inclinations. And yet, if a person could never face an alternative of action in complete indifference, he or she would have in this state no free will. An individual's freedom can be real only if he or she has within himself or herself determining factors that he or she brings to bear upon situations out of himself or herself (387f.). The act of choice is itself clear evidence of a univocal determination, for it consists in the entering (*Eintreten*) of a decisive determinant.

This means that a "negative freedom of choice" is obviously not freedom of the will. The free will is not an undetermined will but a determined and determinately choosing will. The negative conception of free will is simply meaningless.

How, then, are we to understand the morally responsible free will?

Before Hartmann gives us his own conception of it, he develops critical reactions to the solutions of the problem proposed by others, especially those of Kant, Fichte, Schelling, and Leibniz (589–642).

After these critical evaluations Hartmann restates the problem as it must be seen critically and philosophically (643ff.).

1. How can there be freedom of the will in a world that onto-logically is causally determined throughout? If the axiological determination of the will were also part of that determination, there could be no free will. The antinomy of the ought-to-do implies that the independence of the moral principles (or values) is essential to moral freedom.

2. How can the will be free in relation to the principle to which, as moral will, it is to be subject? As free will it suspends precisely that which, nevertheless, is its condition.

3. If we assume that these difficulties have been resolved, there still remains a problem. Insofar as man's freedom is to be a moral freedom, its determinant must lie in an ethical principle or value. But if freedom is now to be asserted relative to ethical principles also, then the idea of such a principle as additional determining factor must be discarded; for if the will is to be able to decide in favor of or against such a principle, it cannot at the same time also be determined by that principle.

4. How can freedom be positive freedom vis-à-vis the principle? The so-called freedom-in-the-negative-sense is no freedom at

all, for it shows freedom only as indeterminate will; and free will, though indeterminate prior to a decision, is a determinate will after the decision.

5. How can positive freedom be individual freedom? If moral freedom were not the freedom of individual persons, how could any individual be held morally responsible for his actions? What, then, is that which is determinative in a morally responsible person? It must be something autonomous and positive without being the autonomy of a principle. The person must have his own individual autonomy along with the moral principle. This means that in the freedom of the will we encounter an antinomy of two autonomies—the autonomy of the principle, and that of the person. The question is, How can they exist together?

6. In view of the five problems just referred to, the question is, What forces us to the assumption of the individual freedom of a person vis-à-vis the principle? The answer is: solely the ethical phenomena. But phenomena as such prove nothing, for, ontologically speaking, they can be illusions. At best they give us only an 'apparent' freedom. The question is, How can we obtain from the phenomena a solid basis for the reality of moral freedom?

7. Self-determination

To be sure, consciousness of self-determination is a universal phenomenon. But does it warrant belief in *real* self-determination?

Insofar as our consciousness of self-determination has subjective certainty, it implies at least that in the determination of our will there is something that belongs to conscious will itself (*Ethik*, 655ff.) If our subjective certainty were also an objective certainty, freedom of the will would thereby be proven. The facts are, unfortunately, not that simple.

However, since our awareness of self-determination is real, it must also have a real basis. As a matter of fact, it is no easier to prove that self-determination is an illusion (*ein Schein*) than it is to prove that it is real. When we examine the thesis of the freedom of the will critically, we realize that it cannot be proven in terms of the phenomena; for our consciousness of self-determination is quite other than the moral judgment pertaining to freedom of a person.[18] In its moral reality the person takes responsibility for his actions; and this is not merely being conscious of something but is the very fact of moral existence itself. He who takes upon himself the responsibility for something must also carry the burden of it. That he is capable of doing so is an expression of his moral freedom—of the genuine individual freedom of the person (*Ethik*, 661f.). It is a freedom vis-à-vis the moral principle.

Responsibility always involves two realities: one that is responsible and one to which it is responsible. In the case of morality, the latter is the moral principle (as is every value). The former is the person in his ability to fulfill or not to fulfill the demand of the principle. If the person were completely determined by the principle, he would have no freedom, no personal autonomy. And if the person had no feeling for values, no feeling for their respective demands, he would have nothing relative to which to make a decision. In both cases the person would be without responsibility. That the person acts in a clear consciousness to bear the responsibility for his actions is evidence of his personal autonomy and the visible sign of his freedom.

Here we encounter an *a priori* basic relationship, one of intersubjective universal validity; for everybody sees the action of a person—his own and that of others—from the very beginning under the aspect of freedom. "He does not 'experience' this freedom, but presupposes it prior to all experience" (663ff.). And it is because of this fact that the action of a person is seen as a morally relevant fact for which the person can be held responsible.

Most revealing here is the fact that the person himself claims responsibility for his actions. The metaphysical meaning of this phenomenon lies in its relationship to real self-determination. The greater the capacity of a person to take on responsibility for his actions, the higher that person stands in the moral scale. Responsibility and accountability are unmistakably aspects of moral reality; so is the feeling of guilt (673ff.), which is uniquely related to self-determination—to the person as the originator of an action.

It obviously is beyond dispute that personal freedom is essential to moral accountability. Such freedom must therefore not only be possible but real as well. The question is, How is this freedom possible

18. *Ethik*, 659f. See also Michael Wittmann, "Zu Nicolai Hartmanns Lehre von der Willensfreiheit," *Jahrbuch der Görres-Gesellschaft* 55 (1942): 119–38.

in a world that is thoroughly determined? The determination of moral reality is not only one through laws of nature, but through the ought also. Neither of these modes of determination is rooted in the person, but the person is obviously subject to both. Personal will is that factor in the world in which both modes of determination collide (697f.).

These facts can be understood only if the persons include still a third mode of determination to which the freedom of the will pertains. Hartmann calls it the "principle of the person"—a "freedom above the law" (699f.). This "personal freedom" consists in man's ability to make specific values the determinants of his actions and thereby to transform 'what ought to be' into reality.

Man's will is not confronted by a determinism of values, but by their indeterminism—an indeterminism that gives him the choice of which values to pursue in his actions.

* * * * * * *

Hartmann's *Ethik* concludes with discussions of "unsolved" remaining problems (715–28) and of "apparent and real weaknesses of the theory" (728–35). But what gives new support to Hartmann's thesis of personal freedom is found in his analysis of the stratification of reality in the *Aufbau der realen Welt*, which was published more than twenty years after the *Ethik*.[19]

19. See chap. 2 above.

7

Aesthetics

AESTHETIC REFLECTION—the very essence of aesthetics—is always supplementary to an aesthetic experience proper,[1] and presupposes a "beautiful object." But it would be a mistake to regard aesthetic comprehension as a form of cognition. "Art is not a continuation of cognition," and aesthetics, though concerned with beauty, "is not a continuation of art" (*Aesthetik*, 4f.). And is beauty really the universal value of all aesthetic objects?

It is essential of all values that they have a negative counterpart—a corresponding disvalue. What is at issue in aesthetics is therefore the whole scale of value-dimension of which values and disvalues are the two poles. In considering the problems involved here one may start with the aesthetic object or with the experience for which it is the object. And as far as the object is concerned, one may inquire about its structure and mode of Being, or about its aesthetic value. And one may also be concerned either with the receptive act of aesthetic contemplation, or with the productive act of aesthetic contemplation, or with the productive act of the creator of an aesthetic object. Hartmann considers all of these alternatives.

Our everyday perceptual experience contains much that is not just a matter of pure sense data. "We enter a room and see the poverty or the

1. Nicolai Hartmann, *Aesthetik* (Berlin: Walter de Gruyter & Co., 1953), 3.

wealth, the slovenliness or the good taste of the inhabitants" (43ff.). Perception penetrates the visible forms and reveals the mental and the spiritual behind them. How is this possible? How can that which is not given in the sense data themselves be what is really essential in perception? We "see" the anger, the melancholy, the distrust in the expressions of faces. Even in things we see much that is not actually visible. Behind the mere sense data we clearly discern value-aspects. As Max Scheler put it, the field of perception is permeated by value-accents. Purely objectified perception is a late achievement of man's culture. It presupposes a certain degree of maturity not found in primitively natural consciousness of things. At this basic level the whole perceptual world is permeated with elements of emotions. Objective perception, as it is found in our sciences, is a late achievement of man's attempt to comprehend the world he lives in.

What is true in the case of perception in general is true in enhanced form in aesthetic perception. But here that which is also seen and felt is what actually is essential (50). Perception transcends itself and becomes "revelatory" (54ff.). That is, aesthetic perception is concerned neither with what is desired nor with reality or truth. Neither that which is important in itself nor that which is important for us is decisive here. The aesthetic perception moves on a different level. In the aesthetic experience the sensory and nonsensory content are both present and form an integrated whole. It is precisely this intertwining of these two elements that is the object proper of the aesthetic experience (58).

However, as a basic phenomenon, perception as such is not an aesthetic perception; for in the aesthetic experience the element of feeling, the *Gefühlston*, is what is essential (62f.). This means that the aesthetic object is not what is given to the senses but what is meaningful and significant. The aesthetic experience is thus a higher vision which itself may well be stratified, and it involves values.

We must note, however, that the values inherent in the feeling induced by the aesthetic object are by no means the aesthetic values. They are primarily values of the enhancement of life and moral values. Even values of goods in the broad sense may be involved. They may be presuppositions of the aesthetic value content but in themselves are not aesthetic values.

Quite distinct from the values referred to is the value of the feeling of pleasure involved in the aesthetic experience. This aesthetic pleasure is a feeling of satisfaction related to and derived from the object, and in this sense is itself 'objective'. We have no other value consciousness and therefore no other criterion of the value of the beautiful than this aesthetic pleasure (69).

1. The Aesthetic Experience

In the aesthetic experience two aspects are discernible: (1) The actual perception and the 'higher view' (*die höhere Schau*) of what is not actually perceived. (2) That which is perceivable is real and present; what is experienced in the 'higher view' is not real or need not be real. It is experienced in addition to the actually given, and involves an element of spontaneity on the part of the beholder of the aesthetic object (*Aesthetik*, 75). But the value of a work of art exists only for a subject who, in experiencing the object, enjoys it. "The aesthetic value-feeling is at the same time constitutive of value" (80f.). The aesthetic values do not exist prior to their being felt in the experience.

This means that aesthetic values are neither the values of what is real, as values of goods are; nor are they values of the merely ideal, as moral values are. They are values of something that is *only for us*— for a subject that experiences aesthetically. For this very reason these values are not objectively universal, as vital and moral values are, but are specific for each object.

A work of art is the objectification of a spiritual content in the realm of reality, a content that cannot exist without the supportive stratum of Being. But because of this objectification, the spiritual content of a work of art can survive not only the life of its creator but whole historical ages as well. Objectification thus is essentially a creating of something real that endures and in which the spiritual content can appear (85). As a work of art, the aesthetic object exists only relative to a receptive subject capable of appreciating it.

2. Beauty in Nature

A work of art is, of course, a product of human creativity. We can therefore readily understand that the artist intended to present something other than the merely external form. But what about beauty in nature? For nature works without an intention to disclose some spiritual content in what is real (*Aesthetik*, 132ff.).

It cannot be denied that we do take pleasure in seeing beautiful animals, and that we are impressed by their functionally integrated structure, their modes of behavior, and the suitableness of it all that is revealed in the organic existent. Our aesthetic pleasure in viewing an animal leads rather soon to a profound appreciation of the great metaphysical riddle that lies beyond the merely organic. We have the feeling that we stand here face to face with something miraculous.

A feeling of this kind is a genuine aesthetic pleasure in the perceiving. The depth of this pleasure varies with the objective depth of that which appears (143ff.).

But it is important to note that our admiration is by no means restricted to cases in which feeling of vitalistic sympathy is the initial experience. The same admiration extends to what is foreign to our own existence. The elegance in the leap of a squirrel high in the treetops also induces it, as does the flight of a swallow, the circling of a bird of prey, and the playful leap of a dolphin. Add to this also the butterflies and the world of microorganisms, which is full of "artforms of nature," and the world of flowering plants. Every growing thing in its fully developed form impresses us as a work of art. Everywhere in nature something of the mysterious purpose-like aspects of the living realities is revealed.

And something like this experience is found in connection with inorganic structures. At least some of them give us genuine aesthetic pleasure. This is especially true of landscapes that are experienced in pictorial aspects: the beautiful countryside, the mountain range. Here our own vital feeling turns into aesthetic pleasure. Man feels himself as being in the landscape, as surrounded by it as part of it. From this primitive feeling of oneness with nature arises the aesthetic objectification of the landscape (148f.). The view of a valley, framed by nearby trees, and of a village half-hidden in the distance—the whole is "just like a picture": not sought, not intended, perhaps a complete surprise. But the person who thus views it has an aesthetic experience. We may have such an experience when we see the play of sunlight upon the rippling waters of a spring half-hidden in a group of trees at the base of a rock formation. What makes it an aesthetic experience is the pleasurable absorption in what is objectively real.

It is quite true that the artistic view discovers the landscape and then makes it aesthetically accessible. But it is not true that artistic creation discovers it. In the artist it is not the creation that is first, but the seeing, the intuition—and, together with this, what counts is the aesthetic attitude toward the surrounding world (151).

In our aesthetic experience beautiful forms play an especially important role. We encounter them not only as spatial but also as tonal relations and as the interrelations of rhythms and of colors. It is not necessary that the principle determining the forms be known. The best example of this is the starry heaven, which since ancient times has been regarded as "the most beautiful and most perfect reality that can be seen by man" (153f.).

The justification of this valuation may well be questioned, but the valuation itself is a historical fact. Hartmann himself, whose hobby was astronomy, speaks with some feeling of the sublime aspect of the luminous groups of stars and constellations and their silent course across the night sky—something unknown to those who have never escaped our large metropolitan centers. What is essential here is the complete absence of regular forms, which means that we can value as aesthetically positive even irregularities in nature. Even the contrast of regularity and irregularity can affect us as an affirmative structural element of special charm. The "song" of birds is a beautiful example of this; for such a "song" is not based upon what, in the artistic sense, are musical principles. An object of nature makes no demand upon man. This is part of its indifference and unobtrusiveness. No spiritual content is recognizable in it. In this respect the beautiful object of nature is radically different from a work of art (*Aesthetik*, 156f.). But the object of nature entails a riddle which the contemplative viewer feels pressed to decipher. However, the riddle does not appear as a problem for the understanding, but more as a wonder for the feeling which, in losing himself in beholding the object, man devoutly accepts in order to enjoy it. But the object of nature remains silent. In the Metropolitan Museum in New York there is on display a large section of a giant redwood tree with two thousand yearly rings, and close to the center is a sign: "Birth of Christ"—as if the tree could tell a history of something "experienced." But the tree has experienced nothing. "It is marvelously silent." Just because they are silent and self-contained but not actively withdrawn, objects of nature have much to tell us not only about themselves but also about us and our relation to them.

In the natural object as aesthetically experienced we thus encounter a sensorially given foreground that, as an object of nature, is real; and we encounter here a background that is also real, if we mean by it a specific inner aspect of which the external form is an expression. This inner aspect, however, does not appear as consistency or adjustment but as an ideal form, as purposiveness and mysterious meaning. It is not real but merely an appearance (161f.). Its occurrence, however, is essential for the character of the aesthetic experience, for it is the charm of what is beautiful in nature.

In times past the view prevailed that, as creator, God stands directly behind the objects in nature, and that in his art man is God-like in creativity, although in but limited form. Today we are inclined to see this relation in reverse: The nonartistic aesthetic object is one in which unconscious nature approximates the inventive and creative spirit of man. In this form the paradox is clearer; for what is astonishing is the emergence of structures in which, for the human observer, there exists a transcendent phenomenal relationship even though the emergence of such a relationship could not have been anticipated.

3. Stratification in the Arts

Having thus encountered a stratification in aesthetically experienced objects of nature, we must now consider a similar stratification of the objects of art. But here an additional problem is involved. The problem is the aesthetic sense (*Aesthetik*, 164–200), and for its solution the simple stratification of foreground and background that we encounter in the case of beautiful objects in nature is not sufficient. In the work of art the foreground remains univocal; the background, however, is further stratified until it fades out into the depth of ideas.

Consider, for example, a portrait, such as Rembrandt's self-portrait. We can distinguish the following strata (167f.):

1. In the foreground is what alone is really given: the paint on the canvas in two-dimensional arrangement.
2. Through this foreground the first stratum of the background appears: the three-dimensional spatiality.
3. In the third place we discern the stratum of the facial expression.
4. Together with this there appears something else: the man in his inwardness, his character. This is perhaps the stratum that impresses us most in viewing the portrait. But it lies completely beyond mere sense impressions, lacking spatiality, paint, and

the nature of things—just as the living person is for us a reality beyond our sense impressions.

5. What is astonishing here is that this nonsensuously apparent stratum is transparent for something still other: our 'seeing' the moral character of the person in its uniqueness and ideality.

6. In addition to all this there is the humanly universal. Great works of art receive their greatness and lasting significance from this ultimate stratum.

What has been pointed out here has its validity for all works of art and for all art, although the sequence and the number of strata may change with the material involved. And its validity may change with the mode of beholding the art object.

In this stratified relationship only the first stratum is not one that "appears." It is necessarily real. Only the ultimate or innermost stratum is no longer a transparent one. It lets nothing further appear. All other strata of an object of art are both apparent and transparent.

The one example given of the art of painting is much too narrow to give us a proper understanding of the stratification characteristic of a work of art. Poetry and literature in general have the most inclusive range of material. Everything encountered in human existence —all happiness, conflicts, actions, and fates—belong to their subject matter. They have therefore quite often been regarded as the highest of all arts. But we must not overlook the fact that both are of the art that least depends on sense perception (174).

To illustrate the stratification in literature Hartmann quotes briefly from the poetry of Sappho: "The moon was setting, and so were the Pleiades; it was midnight; youth is going by and I lie here alone."[2]

It is a brief fragment, but contains everything. Directly it speaks only about a sleepless night, of the setting of the moon and of stars, and of lying alone. Nothing is said of the passionate longing for the loved one, but he who does not sense this cannot be helped as far as poetry is concerned. It is characteristic of all poetry that it does not explicitly state what is really essential. It presents it in the same way in which, in real life, fate, suffering, and loving are also given—in the external attitudes of human beings.

2. *Aesthetik*, 176. "Unter ging der Mond und die Plejaden, zur Mitte ist die Nacht, vorüber streicht die Jugend, ich aber liege hier allein. . . ."

Why does the poet choose this circuitous way of saying what he has to say? He does so because in this way he can really let us see what he wishes us to see. If he were to speak directly of hate and love, of jealousy, envy, fear, and hope, he would speak as a psychologist and not as a poet; and it is well known that all bad poets psychologize.

The view of the poet can perhaps be best described as an intuition of values (*Wertschau*)—"a genuine ethical intuition of values" (*Aesthetik*, 180). But this does not mean a confusion of ethics and aesthetics; for moral values are already the presupposition of our understanding of those human relationships, situations, and conflicts that provide the material for poetry. There is no reason to believe that individual personal values would be an exception. The contrary is the case; personal values, because they are especially concrete and manifold, are of special importance in the material of artistic objects.

Moreover, a literary work is concerned not only with the character and fate of individual persons but with the universally human as well. But dealing with the idea of personality requires a profound intuition, and not all literature reflects this. If the conception of personality becomes a construction, it affects us as an untruth, and the literary work is a failure.

Actually there are seven strata in the objects of a literary work (183ff.). But we find them only in literary works "in the grand style" —in an epic, a novel, a drama. And even these various strata are not always fully developed. Literary works of a lesser scope are very often much simpler. Lyric poetry, for example, develops no action, no conflicts. It moves at once from the sphere of what is external—such as given surroundings—to the stratum of feelings and moods. Beyond this, a poem may suggest something like fate (as in the Sappho fragment), or even something universally human; but it need not do so.

Because of this limitation, poetry quite often fulfills its task in the most perfect way. The *Gedicht* (poem) is a specific *Verdichtung* (condensation) of what can be said directly with what cannot be said but can be made to appear through what is being said. While recognizing the different strata that are characteristic of a literary work, we need not necessarily find all of them in each work. As far as a drama or a good novel are concerned, we may expect that all strata are involved. But their sequence may even then not be the same. 'Fate', for example, may appear directly in the mode of action (as in Schiller's dramas), or it may be revealed only in the subjectivity of our personal feeling.

Both elements may also be experienced together. In actual life they interpenetrate, but for literary art it makes a difference whether one or the other of them is predominant.

The middle strata are in actual life so closely related that it would be quite arbitrary if the literary artist were to exclude one of them completely and would yet try to depict life as actually lived. This is different, of course, in literary works of smaller scale that intend to transmit only moods, feelings, sorrow, and yearning—such as lyric poetry.

Stratification is highest in literature. No other art form approaches it. The plastic arts, however, are close to literature in one respect. They also let something *appear* in and through formed matter. Greek plastic art of the classical period shows as yet but little of it. Although it achieved an exalted presentation of the gods, it did not express their inner attitudes. Simpler in stratification, sculpture attained here the highest level possible with the means available.

What, precisely, are the strata present in classical Greek (186f.)? Hartmann recognizes four:

1. The foreground is the stratum of reality of the visible form.
2. This is followed by the ideal stratum of movement or rest in the bodily sense.
3. Beyond this there appears the vivacity which in its mediated dynamic distinguishes the presented object from a dead body.
4. There appears ultimately the superior calmness and sublimity, the power of the Divine.

But the last point changes when the struggling spirit—i.e., fright, suffering and the anticipation of death—finds expression in facial features—a development in the plastic arts culminating in the profoundly expressive works of Michelangelo: his fettered Slave, his meditating Madonna, his David.

In the plastic arts of our own times something humanly universal is brought to expression via the inner life of individuals—as in Rodin's *The Thinker* and many other works. The impossible has here been made possible. Although we do not know *what* he thinks, the fact *that* he thinks is made visible in the position and mien of the figure.

Plastic art and the art of painting have two things in common: *sensory* matter and access to the highest subjects available to man (188ff.).

The latter is evidenced by the fact that we have religious paintings and religious plastic art. But here there is also a fundamental difference; for, on the one hand, we have the pure form of space, and on the other hand, we have space reduced to two-dimensional projections, but with the whole scale of colors.

Both arts have their specific limitations. Plastic art is restricted to what is near, to what is living, and almost entirely to the human body. Painting can also be concerned with the human body; but it can also combine in a picture what is near with what is distant. This combination is not a compromise, for the spatial distance is not suppressed or camouflaged but actually represented in perspective.

And there are thematic aspects in paintings that are determined primarily by the interplay of colors. This fact is especially evident in the case of still-life paintings, but it is more important in landscape paintings. Here the interplay of colors and of light and shadow gives us perspectives that fade out into felt distances.

However, all of this pertains only to the external aspect, the foreground of a painting. But it is also the stratum through which movement and vivacity appear, and here we are face to face with the inner stratum of paintings. Paint on canvas moves as little as does marble in the plastic arts. From this radical inactivity only the narrow path of "letting it appear" leads to movements. It is the art of the painter that thus leads to the inwardness of human reality, as exemplified in a portrait—but not in a portrait only. Manifold themes, ranging from ordinary events in our daily life to religious miracles and mystery scenes, are encountered in the works of painters. Dutch painters, in particular, have shown how every harmless activity of men and women in their time—and much more of the human-all-too-human side of life —has its picturesque aspect. Although it may not have been originally intended, something of the joy of well-being is felt here and becomes the main content of the paintings. This occurs especially in paintings of historical and mythico-religious scenes, whether concerned with Christ or the Virgin Mary, or with God the Father and creator of the world —as in the ceiling of the Sistine Chapel (191).

Analysis will show that here we find again all the strata found in the case of a literary work, only now we find them in a modified mode of appearance. Hartmann characterizes the stratification in the objects of paintings in the following way (191f.):

1. The foreground is the real surface with the visible patches of paint.
2. Behind this there appear the three-dimensional spatiality, the things and the light in the picture.
3. Within this sphere of things there also appears movement—made visible in a special phase or pose of motion.
4. In this movement appears the vivacity of the forms—people or animals—strongly supported by "living" colors.
5. In the vivacity of movement there appears what is humanly innermost—the mental. There appear fragments of situations, of passions and dispositions, and of actions.
6. In rare cases there appears something of an individual idea (as in portrait heads of special depth).
7. Finally, there appears much of what are universal ideas. At times this aspect is consciously thematic (as in the case of religious scenes). At other times it is completely covered up. A special role is played here by one's knowledge of the meaning of the scene. But this knowledge is usually remarkably insignificant for an aesthetic viewing of a picture.

Compared with this stratification of paintings, the objects of the plastic arts show only four distinguishable strata. A literary work, on the other hand, has at least seven strata; but these are, at least in part, not the same as those we find in a painting. Also, in an object of literature the strata 2 to 5 of the objects of paintings are fused into one stratum. This is so because a literary work is concerned only with human beings and their situations and actions. The external world is but decoration or stage, whereas for paintings it is the strongest thematic aspect.

In the case of musical compositions, everyone believes to have contact at once with the "background" (197ff.): for it seems obvious that the sounds and segments of sounds are not produced for their own sake but for the psychical content that manifests itself through them. This content is the essential aspect of any composition, for it directly affects much of our emotional life, which cannot express itself otherwise.

In some respects, music is comparable to paintings. The wealth of sounds and sound sequences has its counterpart in the inexhaustible possibilities of color combinations. Pitch, stress of sounds, timbre, accord, modulation, rhythm, tempo and change of tempo—all these are expressive elements in musical compositions. And to hear the unity of musical phrases or of whole compositions is still another aspect. We can do justice to the manifold phenomena that are musical compositions only by viewing them as stratified units. Hartmann distinguishes four specific strata:

1. The closed musical phrase (four-quarter time, for example).
2. The broader themes and variations of them.
3. Musical phrases that in their strictest form are represented by a fugue.
4. The combination of phrases into a great opus of less strict form.

Other differentiations are, of course, possible. But the number of differentiations is not as important as are the modes of stratification. The variations in the strata are sufficiently large to bring forth a whole world in sounds only. The musically attentive listener is well aware of this fact.

We experience in music a mode of Being that shines through the mere tones and affects us emotionally in various ways. We can readily discern the solemn, the sublime, the 'dark depth', the luminous. But all such terms are feeble and too general. We have no adequate expression for what we experience in music.

Music is a general revelation of what cannot be expressed in any other language; and it is this because it awakens the mind of the listener to a participation, a becoming one with the community of listeners beyond all individual differences—a community otherwise hardly possible in life. No other art equals music in this respect. And this is true not just in the case of really great music, but also in the case of lower forms of music—such as music written especially for dancing, for marching, and for the merry little song. To be sure, the enjoyment is different in each case, and so is the level of the mind listening to it. But the music itself remains objective, and the question remains: How can tones and tone sequences express what is innermost in man's mind and is in itself inexpressive? Only a partial answer to this question is possible (203ff.).

The world of sound and that of the mind are not completely heterogeneous. Both are nonspatial and immaterial. Both are in flux, in transition, in movement; and both maintain themselves in agitation and quieting down, in tension and relaxing. Music enhances these emotional elements through melodic and harmonic development. The point is that even the 'matter' of music already contains the basis of all expressions of feelings. And only in the perceptible language of sounds is the mental content directly available. For our actual musical hearing, the context of musical compositions and mental life is self-evident. We experience it already in the gentle moving of a waltz, but it is characteristic of all music. Musical compositions of greater scope and profundity stir up the mind and reveal the depths of its reality. In rare cases they may bespeak even something like a contact with darkly felt, fate-like powers—something like Schopenhauer's "appearing of a world-will"; although this level is seldom attained. What is experienced here is not a dogmatic but a purely humanly-mental revelation— although it has a character of the metaphysical, the unknowable (206). Beethoven's symphonies illustrate the point, but so do Bach's preludes and fugues, which, as far as metaphysical content is concerned, are unique.

It is a particular aspect of music that it can be used as "second art" —as it is in songs, choral works, and operas. In all such cases the music can give a depth of expression and meaning that the literary work by itself cannot achieve (207–12).

It has often been said that "architecture is frozen music." Hartmann, however, maintains that architecture, although similar to music in that it is "free of the subject," is subject to practical purposes; and that this fact and the brittleness of its coarse materials seem to preclude a stratification. Yet even here we find a "playing with form," and we find also that it is precisely the resistance of the material that is the dynamically essential aspect (212ff.).

Seen as a whole, an architectural structure is a "composition" including many partial aspects. This compositional whole reflects something of the life and the worldview of the times in which it was created. This is obvious in such structures as temples, cathedrals, palaces, manor houses, and ordinary dwelling places. Man builds them in harmony with how they comprehend his life and ideals. Because of this fact, architectural structures, even their ruins, can reflect the cultural orientation of peoples and historical epochs.

The phenomena clearly reveal even here a stratification that, starting with given materials, includes the purpose-guided composition that determines proportions and space distributions, and culminates in mastery over the materials in dynamic composition.

The various architectural styles are essentially conditioned by human technical abilities. This fact shows clearly that the dynamic composition does indeed involve an aesthetic stratum of the architectural structures. What is important here is that the beauty of form lies not so much in the spatial proportions as such, but in the dynamic meaning of the forms. That is, it lies in the fact that the heaviness of the material and its overcoming in the construction is made intuitively evident in visual form. We sense and admire the achievement.

But it is not so evident that in architecture we also find "inner strata." The reason for this is the fact that the practical purposes of architectural creations are external to them and could be realized in nonartistic ways. The tenement houses of our large cities prove this. But it is already otherwise in the case of the framework houses in villages and small towns of the seventeenth century and of the houses of Upper Bavaria. But most convincing are old castles, palaces, and churches. Each architectural structure has its background strata which reveal something of the life and the mentality of the people who build it.

We can thus distinguish three inner strata of an architectural work:

1. The solution chosen for the practical task of construction. The decision here depends on the point of view adopted, and is largely a matter of the prevailing taste. Even at the first 'inner stratum' the architectural style and the style of life are thus closely related.

2. The total impression of the whole and its parts depends on the spatial components and their dynamic composition. Just as it is impossible to realize a practical result without following a specific constructive idea, so it is also impossible to create a spatial and dynamic whole without giving the created form a spatial expression. This is evident wherever really genuine compositions are encountered, and there are many of these. Specific form-types prevail with certain people and in historical periods. We speak of Pompeian villas, Byzantine churches, Chinese temples, etc.; and with each term we mean the inner character of the architectural structures, which is identical neither with the purpose alone nor with the spatial form and the dynamic construction. In and through all of this, something of the char-

acter and the common attitudes of the people who created it expresses itself in their architecture.

3. The purpose of monumental structures is not identical to the human idea that finds expression in them. We see this clearly in the case of grandiose temples and churches: They have been erected to the glory of specific deities and are always experienced as the expression of a will and grandeur that transcend the merely human. They reach into the realm of an ideality that is independent of all knowledge of dogmatic and cultural purposes. In this sense architecture is like religious music, religious painting, and religious sculpture. Only the themes are dogmatic. The artistic achievement is independent of dogma. It appeals even to the nonbeliever.

4. Falsification in Art

All art enjoys freedom in its intuition and creating, a freedom that human beings do not have in their other activities, not even in their ethos. The miracle of this freedom is the power to let the intuited idea itself appear in the artwork. The reverse side and the danger of it is arbitrariness and, because of this, to miss or to falsify the 'unity and wholeness' of form already achieved in nature (*Aesthetik*, 273). Three reasons may lead to such falsification:

1. Inability or lack of depth.
2. Idealism—man's imagination gives him the illusion of something 'more beautiful'.
3. Moral reasons, i.e., out of considerations other than aesthetic —pedagogical reasons, for example.

Actual arbitrariness of the artist is perhaps found only in cases 2 and 3; and even then such arbitrariness must not be confused with artistic freedom, which does involve a play with forms, a going beyond the empirical, a selection and omission. Freedom is here, as in all constructive activity, positive rather than negative freedom. It is not absence of determination, but a specific autonomous type of determination having its own laws. In other words, artistic creativity has its own principles of unity and wholeness that are not found anywhere else but that constitute the aesthetic freedom of creative spirit. The artist has the freedom to select whatever subject he pleases; but he can actually will only what has inner unity and necessity (35). When we accept this inner necessity as essential to artistic freedom, then it is easy to distinguish this freedom from arbitrariness; for the latter has no inner necessity, no principle of unity that determines the object.

The principle of inner unity and necessity prevails in all the arts, but is most evident in music, where relatively small phrases and passages form the constituent materials of large compositions in their wholeness and unity.

5. Aesthetic Values

Hartmann has devoted part 3 of his *Aesthetik* to a discussion of the "values and genera of the beautiful" (322–456). His main point is that aesthetic values are not values of acts but of objects—values as meanings of objects, not values of their usefulness. In fact, an aesthetic value is not simply the value of something real—as goods-values and even moral values are; it is rather the value of something that exists only in appearance for us. It has Being only for us (347–57). But it has Being in a great variety of forms: the pleasant, the charming, the idyllic, the delightful—all of which are obviously related experiences. The sublime, however, is of a different character. We find its purest expression in the realm of the mythical, the religious and, in general, in man's profoundest views of the world (365f.). Aesthetically, the sublime is encountered in nature and in morality. But it is encountered by persons—and historical periods—only to the extent of their aesthetic sensitivity.

In its purest form the sublime is in evidence where it may be least expected: in the nonrepresentative arts, in music and architecture.

The classical theory of the sublime we owe to Kant, but Kant stressed the quantitative aspect unduly.[3] Hartmann repudiates this, stressing instead the solemn, the profound, the overwhelming, the perfect, which in itself is complete (*Aesthetik*, 371). And he makes it clear that his opposition to Kant pertains only to Kant's stress on the quantitative aspect. By contrast, Hartmann contends that he feels himself

---

3. See Immanuel Kant, *Critique of Judgment*, trans. James Creed Meredith, 98: "The sublime is that, the mere capacity of thinking which evidences a faculty of mind transcending every standard sense."

inherently attracted by what is grand and superior; and this, Hartmann adds, is part of "the morally most beautiful traits of man." It is foundational to any appreciation of the aesthetic value of the sublime (375).

Hartmann does not neglect the comical or the humorous in art. He devotes forty-four pages to a discussion of it. I shall omit that discussion here.

The crucial question is, How does all of this—the analysis of aesthetic objects and aesthetic values—fit into Hartmann's *new ontology*?

The first point we must note is that all art—not only literature and painting, but music and architecture as well—remains closely related to human existence and therefore to Being. This is true not only of the comical and the sublime, but of all aesthetic experiences. And we have seen that all works of art are stratified. The question, therefore, is, How are the strata of aesthetic objects related to the universal ontic strata of the real world discussed in chapters 2, 3, and 5?

Hartmann's answer to this question is that they are essentially the same—sensory things, life, mind, and the world of the spirit. But in the arts these strata are further stratified in various ways. To the question, Why should the ontic strata of reality recur in the strata of the works of art? the answer is: Because all of the strata are realized in man himself and in his activities, they must recur in all representations of man in the arts.

In the background of all human existence and human activity we find the same moral-metaphysical reality. Art can and does penetrate into these depths and can let them appear. Really great art does just this. The sublime in particular is that mode of the beautiful in which the inner strata of reality dominate unconditionally. But works of art can be perfect only when they reveal the inner depths of reality intuitively and lifelike in adequate form even in the external strata.

The very essence of art, therefore, consists in this: that the creator of an artwork selects, "with somnambulant surety," adequate means and a proper form for expressing with intuitive certainty something of the profundity and depth of stratified reality (458ff.).

Bibliography

A. Works by Nicolai Hartmann

Platos Logik des Seins. Giessen: Töpelmann, 1909. Hardcover reprint. Berlin: Walter de Gruyter & Co., 1985. 512 pp.

"Des Proklus Diadochus philosophische Anfangsgründe der Mathematik." *Philosophische Arbeiten*, vol. 4. Giessen: Töpelmann, 1909.

"Zur Methode der Philosophiegeschichte." *Kant-Studien* 15 (1910): 459–85.

Philosophische Grundfragen der Biologie. Göttingen: Vanderhoek & Ruprecht, 1912.

"Systematische Methode." *Logos* 3 (1922): 121–63.

"Systembildung und Idealismus." In *Philosophische Abhandlungen der Preussischen Akademie der Wissenschaften* (Berlin, 1912): 1–23.

"Über die Erkennbarkeit des Apriorischen." *Logos* 5 (1914/15): 290–329.

"Logische und ontologische Wirklichkeit." *Kant-Studien* 20 (1915): 1–28.

"Die Frage der Beweisbarkeit des Kausalgesetzes." *Kant-Studien* 24 (1920): 261–90.

Grundzüge einer Metaphysik der Erkenntnis. 1921. 4th ed. Berlin: Walter de Gruyter & Co., 1949.

"Aristoteles und Hegel." *Beiträge zur Philosophie des Deutschen Idealismus* 3 (1923): 1–36.

Die Philosophie des Deutschen Idealismus, vol. 1: *Fichte, Schelling und die Romantik*, 1923; vol. 2: *Hegel.* Berlin: Walter de Gruyter & Co., 1929. 389 pp.

"Diesseits von Idealismus und Realismus." *Kant-Studien* 29 (1924): 160–206. Reprinted in *Kleinere Schriften*, 2: 278–322.

"Wie ist kritische Ontologie überhaupt möglich?" In *Festschrift für Paul Natorp*, 124–77. Berlin: Walter de Gruyter & Co., 1924.

"Kategoriale Gesetze." *Philosophischer Anzeiger* 1 (1925/26): 201–66.

Ethik. 1926. 3d ed. Berlin: Walter de Gruyter & Co., 1949. Translated by Stanton Coit under the title *Ethics.* 3 vols. London: Allen & Unwin, 1949.

"Zum Thema: Philosophie und Internationale Beziehungen." *Proceedings of the Sixth International Congress of Philosophy,* 318–89. Harvard University: 1926.

"Über die Stellung der ästhetischen Werte im Reich der Werte überhaupt." *Proceedings of the Sixth International Congress of Philosophy,* 428–36. New York, Columbia University, 1924.

"Kategorien der Geschichte." *Proceedings of the Seventh International Congress of Philosophy,* 24–30. Oxford University, 1931.

"Zum Problem der Realitätsgegebenheit." *Philosophische Vorträge der Kantgesellschaft,* vol. 32. Berlin, 1931.

Das Problem des geistigen Seins. 1933. 2d ed. Berlin: Walter de Gruyter & Co., 1949.

"Sinngebung und Sinnerfüllung." *Blätter für Deutsche Philosophie* 8 (1934): 1–38.

Zur Grundlegung der Ontologie 1935. 3d ed. Berlin: Walter de Gruyter & Co., 1948.

"Hegel und das Problem der Realdialektik." *Blätter für Deutsche Philosophie* 9 (1935): 1–27.

"Das Problem des Apriorismus in der Platonischen Philosophie." *Abhandlungen der Preussischen Akademie der Wissenschaften, Philosophisch-Historische Klasse* 15 (1935): 223–60.

"Der philosophische Gedanke und seine Geschichte." *Abhandlungen der Preussischen Akademie der Wissenschaften, Philosophisch-Historische Klasse* 5 (1936): 1–47.

"Der Megarische und der Aristotelische Möglichkeitsbegriff." *Abhandlungen der Preussischen Akademie der Wissenschaften, Philosophisch-Historische Klasse* 10 (1937): 1–17.

Möglichkeit und Wirklichkeit. Berlin: Walter de Gruyter & Co., 1938. 481 pp.

"Aristoteles und das Problem des Begriffs." *Abhandlungen der Preussischen Akademie* 13 (1939): 1–32.

"Zeitlichkeit und Wirklichkeit." *Blätter für Deutsche Philosophie* 12 (1938/39): 1–38.

"Zur Lehre vom Eidos by Platon und Aristoteles." *Abhandlungen der Preussischen Akademie* (1941): 1–38.

"Die Anfänge des Schichtungsgedankens in der alten Philosophie." *Abhandlungen der Preussischen Akademie* 3 (1943): 1–31.

Neue Wege der Ontologie. 1943. 3d ed. Stuttgart: W. Kohlhammer Verlag, 1949. Translated by Reinhard C. Kuhn under the title *New Ways of Ontology.* Chicago: Henry Regnery Co., 1952.

"Die Wertdimensionen der Nikomachischen Ethik." *Abhandlungen der Preussischen Akademie* 5 (1944): 1–27.

Der Aufbau der realen Welt. Berlin: Walter de Gruyter & Co., 1940.

"Ziele und Wege der Kategorialanalyse." *Zeitschrift für Philosophische Forschung* 2 (1948): 499–536.

Philosophie der Natur. Berlin: Walter de Gruyter & Co., 1950.

Teleologisches Denken. Berlin: Walter de Gruyter & Co., 1951.

Aesthetik. Berlin: Walter de Gruyter & Co., 1953.

Kleinere Schriften. 3 vol. Berlin: Walter de Gruyter & Co., 1955, 1957, 1958. These volumes, edited by Mrs. Hartmann, contain most of the shorter works listed above.

B. Works About Hartmann
(in alphabetical order by author)

Arago, Mitjans Joaquin. "Die antimetaphysische Seinslehre Nicolai Hartmanns." *Philosophisches Jahrbuch der Görres-Gesellschaft* 67 (1959): 179–204.

Ballauff, Theodor. "Nicolai Hartmanns Philosophie der Natur. Zu ihren Voraussetzungen und Grenzen." *Philosophia Naturalis* 2 (1952/53): 117–30.

Baumann, Willibald. "Das Problem der Finalität im Organischen bei Nicolai Hartmann." *Monographien zur Philosophischen Forschung* 6 (1955).

Becker, Oskar. "Das formale System der ontologischen Modalitäten (Betrachtungen zu Hartmanns Werk *Möglichkeit und Wirklichkeit*)." *Blätter für Deutsche Philosophie* 16 (1934): 387–422.

Belage, Manfred. "Die Schichtenlehre Nicolai Hartmanns." *Studium Generale* 9 (1956): 297–306.

Breton, Stanislas. "Ontology and Ontologies: The Contemporary Situation." *International Philosophical Quarterly* 3 (1963): 339–69.

Blumenthal, Walter. "Die Grundlagen der Ethik Nicolai Hartmanns." *Kant-Studien* 53 (1961/62): 3–28.

Cadwallader, Eva Hauel. *Searchlight on Values: Nicolai Hartmann's Twentieth-Century Value Platonism.* Washington, D.C.: University Press of America, 1984.

Collins, James. "The Neo-Scholastic Critique of Nicolai Hartmann." *Philosophy and Phenomenological Research* 6 (1945/46): 109–32.

Del Negro, Walter. "Erkennen und Sein: Zum Verhältnis von Erkenntnistheorie und Ontologie." *Zeitschrift für Philosophische Forschung* 15 (1961): 399–415.

Geyser, Joseph. "Zur Grundlegung der Ontologie. Ausführungen zu dem jüngsten Buche von Nicolai Hartmann." *Philosophisches Jahrbuch der Görres-Gesellschaft* 49 (1936): 3–29; 289–338; 425–65; 50 (1937): 9–67.

Heimsoeth, Heinz, and Robert Heiss, eds. *Nicolai Hartmann, Der Denker und sein Werk.* Göttingen: Vanderhoek & Ruprecht, 1952.

Hein, R. "Nicolai Hartmann, A Personal Sketch." *The Personalist* 42 (1961): 469–86.

Herrigel, Hermann. "Der philosophische Gedanke Nicolai Hartmanns." *Kant-Studien* 51 (1959/60): 34–66.

Hoefert, Hans-Joachim. "Nicolai Hartmanns Ontologie und die Naturphilosophie." *Philosophia Naturalis* 1 (1950/51): 36–55.

Hossfeld, Paul. "Nicolai Hartmanns Kategorien des Naturprozesses." *Philosophia Naturalis* 6 (1960/61): 377–90.

———. "Die Voraussetzungen zu Nicolai Hartmanns Begriff der Realmöglichkeit." *Philosophisches Jahrbuch der Görres-Gesellschaft* 67 (1958/59): 205–21.

James, Helen. "Nicolai Hartmann's Study of Human Personality." *The New Scholasticism* 34 (1960): 204–33.

Kanthack, Katharina. *Nicolai Hartmann und das Ende der Ontologie.* Berlin: Walter de Gruyter & Co., 1962.

Klöster, Joseph. "N. Hartmanns Kritische Ontologie." *Philosophisches Jahrbuch der Görres-Gesellschaft* 41 (1928): 405–31; 42 (1929): 25–41.

Knittenmeyer, Heinrich. "Zur Metaphysik der Erkenntnis. Zu Nicolai Hartmanns *Grundzüge einer Metaphysik der Erkenntnis.*" *Kant-Studien* 30 (1925): 494–514.

Kuhn, Helmut. "Nicolai Hartmann's Ontology." *Philosophical Quarterly* 1 (1950/51): 289–318.

———. "New Ways of Ontology." *Journal of Philosophy* 51 (1954): 108–12.

Landmann, Michael. "Nicolai Hartmann and Phenomenology." *Philosophy and Phenomenological Research* 3 (1942/43): 393–423.

Mayer, Emmanuel. *Die Objektivität der Werterkenntnis bei Nicolai Hartmann.* Meisenheim/Glen: Westkulturverlag Anton Hain, 1952.

———. "Die organische Zweckmässigkeit im Blickfeld der Teleologie bei Nicolai Hartmann." *Wissenschaft und Weisheit* 21 (1958): 30–50, 117–33.

Mohanty, J. N. "An Inquiry into the Problem of Ideal Being in the Philosophy of Nicolai Hartmann and Alfred North Whitehead." Ph.D. diss., Göttingen, 1954.

———. "Nicolai Hartmann und die Phänomenologie." In *Symposium zum Gedenken an Nicolai Hartmann.* Göttingen: Vandenhock und Ruprecht, 1952.

———. "Remarks on Nicolai Hartmann's Modal Doctrine." *Kant-Studien* 54 (1963): 181–88.

———. *Nicolai Hartmann and Alfred North Whitehead.* Calcutta: Progressive Publications, 1957.

Molitor, Arnulf. "Bemerkungen zum Realismusproblem bei Nicolai Hartmann." *Zeitschrift für Philosophische Forschung* 15 (1961): 591–611.

Münzhuber, Joseph. "Nicolai Hartmanns Ontologie und die philosophische Systematik." *Blätter für Deutsche Philosophie* 13 (1939): 173–84.

———. "Nicolai Hartmanns Kategorienlehre." *Zeitschrift für Deutsche Philosophie* 9 (1943): 187–216.

Oakeley, Hilda D. "Professor Nicolai Hartmann's Concept of Objective Spirit." *Mind* 44 (1935): 39–57.

Patzig, Günther, ed. *Symposium zum Gedenken an Nicolai Hartmann.* Göttingen: Vanderhoeck & Ruprecht, 1982.

Schilling, Kurt. "Bemerkungen zu Nicolai Hartmanns Ontologie." *Archiv für Rechts- und Sozialphilosophie* 39 (1951): 533–55.

Smith, John E. "Hartmann's New Ontology." *Review of Metaphysics* 7 (1954): 583–601.

Wein, Hermann. "Der Streit um die Ordnung und Einheit der Realwelt. Für und Wider Nicolai Hartmann." *Philosophia Naturalis* 5 (1958/59): 174–220.

Wirth, Ingeborg. *Realismus und Apriorismus in Nicolai Hartmanns Erkenntnistheorie.* Berlin: Walter de Gruyter & Co., 1965.

Wolandt, Gerd. "Hartmanns Weg zur Ontologie." *Kant-Studien* 54 (1963): 304–16.

Index

Accidental: may in itself be necessary, 70

Action: reciprocal, 46

Acts: of comprehension, 3; mental acts not merely mental, 43; transcendental, 32

Aesthetic experience, 224f.; and aesthetic objectivity, 82; and aesthetic pleasure, 226; and aesthetic values (pleasant, charming, idyllic, delightful), 238; of a beautiful form, 227; as containing an element of feeling, 228; as an enhanced form of perception in general (Gefühlston), 224; as the 'higher view' (die höhere Achau), 225; pleasurable absorption in the objectively real, 226; and the sublime, 239

Angst and Sorge: their role in Heidegger's philosophy, 8f.

Anselm of Canterbury: argument for the existence of God, xi

Ansichseiendes: as what is extant, 3

Anticipatory insight, 168

A priori: a priori insights as involving each other, 30f.; basic principle of the a priori as entailing a position between realism and idealism, 37; as comprehension of an 'essential prius' or universal essence, 12; concerned with ideal Being, 24; cognition and mathematics, 13; as a higher form of intuition, 14; intersubjective universality of, 25; as objectively valid when intertwined with what is given in perception, 19; as pertaining in principle only to what is universal and necessary, 16

Arago, Joaquin: on Nicolai Hartmann's realism, 5

Architecture: as 'playing with form', 237; as reflecting something of the times, 237; as revelatory of the mentality of the builders, 138

Aristippus: theory of ethics, 195

Aristotle: aporetic as a method, 1; conception of matter, 113; definition of metaphysics, xi; problem of the rank of values, 198; purpose behind cause-effect relation, 122

Art: Dutch painters, 232; falsification in, 237f.

Bach, Johann Sebastian: preludes and fugues, 235

Baumgarten, Alexander Gottlieb: ontology as a doctrine of Being, xii

Becoming: as universal mode of Being, 48

Beethoven, Ludwig van: spirit of, 119; symphonies of, 235

Being: as the basic structure within reality, 26; 'being in itself' as meaning total independence of the subject, 33; ideal Being

Hume, David: on 'association' as containing *a priori* elements, 38; on causality
as a schema of understanding, 72; as
correct in maintaining that we cannot
know directly that a cause is a cause,
155; as erroneously inferring contingency
of the law of causality from contingency
of our determination of the law, 125;
and the question of the validity of causal
efficacy, 122
Husserl, Edmund: bracketing of 'essences',
xvi; Heidegger's modification of Husserl's
position, xiv; phenomenological reduction, xiii; pioneer in analyzing
essences, 27

Ideal Being: in the basic structure of everything real, 26, 28; best known in mathematics, 25; and the realm of essences,
83f.; relative independence of, 26
Individual: link in a chain of ancestors and
descendants, 141
Induction, 73; as presupposing universality
in major premise, 127
Irrational: awareness of, 31

James, William: no transempirical connections as unnecessary for the directly
apprehended universe, 10
Judgment: about reality, 16

Kant, Immanuel: on alteration, 109;
and the categorical imperative, 209; on
categories as not derivable from the
understanding, 37; on categories as determinants of Being, 33; on categories
as principles of Being, 33, 117; that the
concept of cause contains the concept of
necessity, 125; on conditions of sensibility as the universal conditions for the
application of categories, 16; on cosmological categories, 109; on the definition
of reality, 16; and the first *Critique* as a
treatise on method, vii; and the idea that
an organism develops 'as if' purposive
determination were involved, 150f.; and
the idea that any reference to Being is
but the positing of a thing, xii; on intuitive space, 97; on matter, 107; and the
mechanism-vitalism controversy, 136;
on nature as dynamic whole, 132; on
organized natural products, 149; on per-

ception as the sole character of reality,
xiii; on the permanent in time, 114; on
the problem of the First Cause, 122; on
pure forms, 36; on the purposiveness of
nature, 136; as rejecting a teleological
interpretation of nature, 143; on space
and time as forms of 'presentation', 91;
on space as form of outer sense, 97; on
spatiotemporal aspects of experience,
16f.; on the sublime, 238; on substance
and accidents, 106; on substance and
causality as central, 105; on substance
as substrata of all processes, 114; on
synthetic judgments *a priori,* 12; on time
as a real category, 91; on transcendental
purposiveness, 150
Kanthack, Katharina: as mistaken in her
interpretation of Hartmann, 8

Labor: as always labor 'on something', 9
Law: of entropy, 111; of freedom, 66; of
matter, 66; of modification, 60; of the
objective spirit, 190; of over-forming
(*Überformung*), 43; of uniform succession in time as basic to all real Being, 103
Laws: basic, of modality, 71f.; as basis of
reality, 77; of connectedness (categorial interconnection, unity of a stratum,
wholeness of strata implication), 53; as
determinant in two directions: that of
thinking and that of real Being, 103; as
entailing necessity, 128; of the equivalence of the modalities, 75; of exclusion,
74f.; intermodal laws, or reality, 75f.; of
logic, 38; as mathematical in structure,
129; of mathematics as indirectly laws of
reality, 26; of nature as similar to categories, 127; statistical, 130; as valid in
the world we live in, 27
Leibniz, Gottfried Wilhelm: on the problem
of free will, 219; on the purpose behind
the relation of cause and effect, 122
Levels: of reality, 38
Life: as a deep riddle, 48; as maintaining
itself through assimilation and reproduction, 119; and purposiveness in all
living things, 142; as self-activity, 139;
as a special form of process, 138; sphere
of, 139; and suitableness and the *nexus
organicus,* 152f.; and transcendental
concept of purposiveness, 150; and
wholeness-determination, 147